PRAISE FOR

Once a Girl, Always a Boy

"This is a story of how acceptance happens. It is a universal one about how good people can struggle to find the right path when challenged by the unfamiliar. This optimistic book is an excellent read for anyone nervous about sharing their private lives and thoughts with their loved ones, and for those who are unsure about how to respond. *Once a Girl, Always a Boy* guides us through the key decision points Jeremy and his family got to and got through as parents, siblings, and Jeremy himself all moved toward acceptance—at different speeds, but ultimately, together."
—MARA KEISLING, founder and executive director of the National Center for Transgender Equality (NCTE)

"Familial support is so crucial to reducing misconceptions and stigma surrounding the trans community. It is often the difference between success and support vs. crisis and instability. This beautifully written and vulnerable narrative does a phenomenal job of telling the story of the Ivester family's journey as their son and brother came to embrace his truth and live in it. The insight and perspective Jo so skillfully shares while keeping the reader engaged throughout the story makes this a must-read."
—EMMETT SCHELLING, executive director of the Transgender Education Network of Texas (TENT)

"When I read Ivester's book, I had to put it down and come back several times because it addresses so honestly the difficult issues I personally faced growing up as a transgender man. In my professional life, I work with families like the Ivesters every day and see firsthand how they want to be supportive but sometimes don't know how. *Once a Girl, Always a Boy* is a testament to a family who tried and succeeded and grew closer to one another on the journey. I cannot wait to share it with the families I seek to help through Trans-Cendence International."
—FINNIGAN JONES, executive director of Trans-Cendence International

"The author of *The Outskirts of Hope* tells another real-life tale that we all need to hear, especially the large number of us with no experience of a subject rightly seeking its place on the national stage. The more people read this enlightening family story, the easier the journey will be for those still subject to the discriminations of ignorance and prejudice."

—MURRAY BIGGS, adjunct associate professor,
Yale University

"This book will save lives. It is a testament that love and kindness can and do win out. A moving, powerful, and life-changing story not just about how a family cares for one another but also of how they've used the lessons of their transgender journey to pave the way for others. I've spent a lifetime searching to find myself reflected in the world around me. And now, it's as if someone found the movie reels of my childhood and told my story, only in a different family, in a different town, and with more of a fairy-tale ending. This is the book I wish I could have read when I was on my own journey of self-discovery."

—SAM SLATE, member of the National Board
of Directors of the Human Rights Campaign

"This heartfelt book shines the light on how important unconditional love is when someone is transitioning to become their authentic self. The way Jo and Jeremy Ivester track this journey in *Once a Girl, Always a Boy* gives people insight into what it really means to be transgender. The Ivesters are amazing allies in the fight for equal rights and dignity and respect for the LGBTQ community."

—ANGELA HALE,
acting chief executive officer for Equality Texas

"Raw, insightful, and told from multiple perspectives, *Once a Girl, Always a Boy* is a poignant reminder that transgender people are our family, our friends, and our neighbors. A book that is both painful and inspiring to read, this memoir is a deeply emotional journey, one that will resonate for everyone. Whether you're learning about transgender people for the first time or seeking inspiration and community, Ivester's book is a must read."

—KASEY SUFFREDINI,
chief executive officer of Freedom for All Americans (FFAA)

"Being transgender is a foreign concept to most people. For the Ivester family, it crashed into their lives when the child they thought was their daughter started to seek his true identity. Jo and Jon Ivester scrambled to support this quest with sensitivity and compassion. *Once a Girl, Always a Boy* is not just the story of a transgender journey but also of a family's acceptance of one of its own. Told in frank and warm-hearted terms with a touch of humor, this gripping tale will stay with its readers for years to come."

—FORREST PREECE, columnist, *West Austin News*

"Unconditional love and support—the very fabric that weaves a family together—is profoundly illustrated in this real-life story of one young man's journey to become the person he was born to be. Courageously sharing their personal experiences, Jeremy and his family provide honest insight into how they navigated the challenges and triumphs of being transgender and having a transgender son. The Ivesters will undoubtedly touch their readers' hearts as they share theirs with us."

—GREGORY ABBINK, senior police officer,
Austin Police Department,
Austin's first openly transgender police officer

"A unique addition to transgender memoirs, *Once a Girl, Always a Boy* centers author Jo Ivester's and her family's voices alongside that of her transgender son, Jeremy. Ivester elevates the questions, worries, and support of the entire family along Jeremy's journey. *Once a Girl, Always a Boy* reveals the not-so-linear process of transition, love, and acceptance."

—SETH M. MARNIN, board chair of Keshet and former VP for
Civil Rights at the Anti-Defamation League

"I wish all transgender people could experience the love, compassion, and acceptance demonstrated in *Once a Girl, Always a Boy*. Ivester's book is a poignant reminder that all of us—transgender or not—are on a journey toward understanding and self-acceptance."

—MASEN DAVIS, co-chair of the International Trans Fund
Steering Committee, former executive director of Transgender
Law Center, and former CEO of FFAA

"While discovering and exploring one's gender identity is a profoundly personal and internal process—no one transitions 'at' anyone—the open honesty of Jo, Jon, and their transgender son, Jeremy, highlights how the ripples cast by one's identity wash over the people in our lives. Fortunately, in *Once a Girl, Always a Boy*, Jo Ivester authentically portrays meeting the unexpected with love, openness, and compassion."

—REBECCA KLING, transgender educator and advocate, inaugural member of The Trans 100, and former education program director of the NCTE

"*Once a Girl, Always a Boy* is a heartwarming affirmation of one family's journey to navigate a just path and to realize and celebrate the remarkable potential unleashed when they embrace a transgender son and brother. While some in our society would exclude and marginalize those who are different, the Ivesters welcomed their son Jeremy as his authentic self. The family's learned experience has led them to be vocal advocates for everyone on the LGBTQIA++ spectrum. By bravely sharing her family's personal story, Jo Ivester invites her readers to be more accepting and to recognize that transgender individuals are due the same love, dignity and respect we all should enjoy."

—STEVE ADLER, mayor of Austin, Texas

". . . a heartwarming story that anyone with a complicated life and identity can relate to. A multifaceted, rich, and moving exploration of the trans experience."

—*KIRKUS REVIEWS* (starred review)

"A story that shines the light on a family's journey to acceptance. Centered on unconditional love, this is a story that will not only motivate readers to become advocates, but will also provide a path for doing just that. LGBTQIA+ individuals and their allies will find themselves moved to action."

—RICARDO MARTÍNEZ, chief executive officer of Equality Texas

once a girl,
always a boy

once a girl, always a boy

a family memoir of a transgender journey

———

Jo Ivester

SHE WRITES PRESS

Published 2020
Printed in the United States of America
ISBN: 978-1-63152-886-6 pbk
ISBN: 978-1-63152-887-3 ebk
Library of Congress Control Number: 2019916863

For information, address:
She Writes Press
1569 Solano Ave #546
Berkeley, CA 94707

She Writes Press is a division of SparkPoint Studio, LLC.

I Hope You Dance
Words and Music by Tia Sillers and Mark D. Sanders
Copyright (c) 2000 Sony/ATV Music Publishing LLC, Choice Is Tragic Music, Universal Music Corp. and Soda Creek Songs
All Rights on behalf of Sony/ATV Music Publishing ILC and Choice Is Tragic Music Administered by Sony/ATV Music Publishing LLC, 424 Church Street, Suite 1200, Nashville, TN 37219
All Rights on behalf of Soda Creek Songs Controlled and Administered by Universal Music Corp. International Copyright Secured
All Rights Reserved
Reprinted by Permission of Hal Leonard LLC

Book design by Stacey Aaronson

All company and/or product names may be trade names, logos, trademarks, and/or registered trademarks and are the property of their respective owners.

Names and identifying characteristics have been changed to protect the privacy of certain individuals.

Based on the video journals

of

Jeremy Ivester

—·—

Including writings

from

Jon Ivester, Elizabeth Norman,

Ben & Jenn Ivester, and Sammy Ivester

For transgender, nonbinary, and nonconforming people everywhere, along with their families, friends, and allies

TABLE OF CONTENTS

Photographs   *i*

Preface   *1*

1   The Dress   3
2   The Haircut   10
3   The Tomboy   19
4   Puberty   34
5   The "Swoose"   43
6   Are You Gay?   56
7   The Old College Try   72
8   "Is That Even Possible?"   84
9   I'm Not Broken   96
10   Introducing "Em"   104
11   I'm Not Ready *to* Grow Up   113
12   Once *a* Girl, Always *a* Boy   121
13   Maid *of* Honor   129
14   Flying High   150
15   It's Almost Time   158
16   What's *in a* Name?   170
17   I'm Awesome *at* Denial   183
18   Honorary Bro   190
19   More Baby Steps   198
20   Terrified   207
21   Call Me Jeremy   213
22   Mom's Story   221
23   A New Start   233
24   Jeremy's Day *in* Court   245
25   A Book? Really?   251

26   I Just Am   259
27   Making *a* Difference   270
28   My Growing Advocacy   285
29   Changing Hearts and Minds   293
30   An Update   304

Epilogue   313

Acknowledgments   *315*
Advice to Parents and Friends
    of Transgender Individuals   *319*
Glossary   *323*
Book Club Discussion Guide   *327*
About the Author   *329*
About Jeremy Ivester   *330*

PHOTOGRAPHS

*All photographs are from Ivester family photo albums and
cell phones unless otherwise specified.*

cover photo

Jeremy Ivester (29). Taken by KerryLDphotography.

chapter two

Jeremy in a dress at six years old.

Jeremy in boys' clothes at six years old.

chapter four

Jeremy (11) with hair in a ponytail.
Taken by Hill Country Middle School.

Ivester family in 1996. L to R: Jeremy in a baseball uniform (6);
Elizabeth in a soccer uniform (11); Jon dressed for golf (31); Ben
with a basketball and soccer cleats (9); Jo ready for tennis (29);
Sammy (2). Taken by Don Rogers Photography.

Ivester family in 1998. L to R: Elizabeth (13); Ben (11); Jon (33);
Sammy (4); Jeremy in a dress (8); Jo (31); Grandma Aura (76). Taken
by Don Rogers Photography.

chapter five

Jeremy playing football in seventh grade (12).
Taken by The Photo Guy.

chapter seven

Jeremy (18) during senior year of high school.
Taken by Gray Hawn.

Self-portrait. Sketched by Jeremy Ivester.

chapter eleven

Jeremy (21) practicing at keyboard.

chapter thirteen

Jeremy (23) with Elizabeth's (28) bridal party.
Taken *by* Cory Ryan.

Ben (26) and Jeremy (23) at Ben's wedding.
Taken *by* Liz and Ryan Photography.

chapter fourteen

Jeremy (23) at the airport following surgery.

chapter twenty-two

Jo at twelve years old.

chapter twenty-four

Jeremy (25) in court with Judge Stavely.

chapter twenty-five

Jeremy (25), Jo, Connie, and Philip at the Texas State Capitol.

chapter twenty-seven

Jeremy (26) with niece Ellie.

chapter twenty-eight

Jo, Jeremy (27), and Jon protesting Texas Senate Bill 6.
Taken *by* Susan Risdon, Equality Texas.

chapter thirty

Jeremy (30) as his authentic self.
Taken *by* Susan Risdon, Equality Texas.

about the author

Jo Ivester. Taken by KerryLDPhotography.

about Jeremy Ivester

Publicity photo of Jeremy Ivester.
Taken *by* KerryLDPhotography.

preface

—·—

My transgender son, Jeremy, was identified as female at birth. At twenty-three years old, although still presenting as *Emily*, he had what is called top surgery, removing his breasts and sculpting his chest to a more masculine shape. A year later, he changed both his name and his use of pronouns. He also began taking hormones.

I faced a major decision in writing his story. Should I refer to him as *Emily* and *she* when writing about him as a child and a young adult? That's how we thought of him at the time. Would doing so help readers experience Jeremy's journey with him, instead of jumping ahead to when he'd figured out who he really is? It feels uncomfortable for me to write *Emily* and *she*, and I worry whether it's disrespectful to the transgender community, given that so many who have transitioned wince at the use of their former names and pronouns.

Should I instead call my son *Jeremy* throughout the book? Is that revisionist writing? Will it confuse readers? Is it okay for them to be confused? After much deliberation, I found a compromise. I refer to Jeremy as *she* and *Emily* until the moment he transitioned. From that point forward, I refer to him as *he* and *Jeremy*. This may feel awkward. But that's okay. Jeremy felt awkward for years.

Finally, is it okay to use the phrase *Once a Girl* in the

book's title? When we welcomed Jeremy into the world thirty years ago, we thought he was our daughter. Today, I think of Jeremy as male, even when I picture him as a four-year-old. Even when I picture him wearing a dress. He was never a girl.

Jeremy created a video journal to document his transition. That journal is the basis for his voice in the true story you are about to read. Beyond that, this book is based on numerous interviews of family and friends, research, and my own memories. At times, I have changed the names of individuals to protect their privacy.

one

THE DRESS

——

Winter 2013 — Boulder, CO
Emily (23 years old)

T he box had plagued me for weeks. I was over-whelmed by its very presence. Not by its size, which was actually quite ordinary. What terrified me was what was inside, boldly hinted at by the return address, by the pink store label that included the word *bridesmaid*.

Leaning against the wall in a corner of my room, barely visible under the many jeans and T-shirts I'd tossed in its general direction, it accused me, though of what I'm not quite sure. Usually, I'm pretty good about keeping my place neat. I pride myself on it looking nicer than the typical student apartment. Instead of posters covering the walls, I have framed pictures my mother stitched for me and pen-and-ink drawings I made in my studio art class. Although only a few minutes from the University of Colorado campus where I'm a math major, my home with its large rooms and fresh coat of paint is a clear step up from most student housing.

These last few weeks, however, I'd let the mess take

over. Dishes were piled up in the kitchen sink. Dirty laundry was scattered about my bedroom. I couldn't focus, couldn't study for my calculus midterm, couldn't think of anything but that wretched box.

I'd dreaded its arrival for months. When it came, I'd left it unopened, not wanting to deal with what it contained. I'd tried to push it out of my mind, tried to ignore how it made my stomach clench with anxiety. I didn't even want to think about the dress inside, let alone look at it.

Why had I said "yes" when my big sister, Liz, asked me to be her maid of honor? I'd known right away that it felt wrong. I hadn't listened to the voice inside me crying out that I'd be miserable, that I would detest walking down the aisle in some frilly gown, on display for all to see. I'd ignored it because I was thrilled that Liz wanted me by her side. I'd ignored it because I couldn't say "no" to my sister, could I?

The thought of disappointing Liz kept me awake at night, tugging at me as I tried to sleep. It was distressing, a rock in the pit of my stomach. Picturing myself wearing the bridesmaid dress, however, was even worse. I was distraught. So much so that my best friend and roommate, Colin, said, "Maybe you should just send it back."

I'd met Colin through some mutual friends at the university, and we hit it off right from the start. He was really smart but also laid-back. He was as comfortable in the physics lab as he was writing computer programs, working two jobs while carrying a full course load. He had time because he and his girlfriend, Meg, who he'd been with since high school, were doing the long-distance thing while she was away at the University of Washington.

Colin had accepted me despite my boyish appearance

and my desire to be treated like one of the guys. I like to think I look a little like Colin, with his slight frame and eclectic taste in clothes. I recently bought a newsboy cap like his, and sometimes I wear my jeans rolled up like he does when he's riding his bike, even though I don't ride.

Each time I considered backing out of being in Liz's wedding party, the way Colin suggested, I'd picture a confused look on her face and hear her saying, "Why, Emily? Why did you wait so long to tell me? Everything's planned."

The longer I waited, the worse I felt. So on a February morning, six weeks before the wedding, I used a kitchen knife to cut the tape holding everything together and opened the box, determined to look at what lay inside. I stared at the crinkly tissue protecting the delicate contents and then froze for a moment, unable to go any further.

Finally, inhaling deeply and gritting my teeth, I slowly reached in for the blue chiffon gown, pausing for a moment as I felt its smooth texture on my fingertips. I pulled it from its packaging and spread it on my bed. All I had to do was try it on. I could do that, I told myself, wincing at the thought. I *should* do that. But not yet. When I got home from school.

All day long, with every word of every lecture, my mind drifted back to my bedroom, to the dress waiting for me. Why was this so hard? It was only a few years ago that I put on a lacy, formfitting dress to go dancing with Liz, my big brother, Ben, and Ben's girlfriend, Jenn, when we celebrated my high school graduation with a vacation on a cruise ship in Italy. I hadn't liked it and would've preferred to be in the same slacks and button-down shirt that Ben wore, but I managed. I was even okay with it when people told me I looked pretty. It was all right because I cared about pleasing my big brother and sister.

I tried to convince myself that I could dress that way again, one more time.

After arriving home from class, I walked slowly into my bedroom. My pulse racing, I stripped down and slipped the dress over my head. The fabric was cool to the touch. In other circumstances, I would have liked how it felt, the silky luxury of it. On somebody else, I would have thought it beautiful, no question.

But not on me. I cringed at the thought of wearing it in front of everybody. Our whole family would be at Liz's wedding, as would her close friends whom I'd known for as long as I could remember, their parents, and their little brothers who'd played with me when we were kids, back when they didn't care that I was a girl.

I cringed because that flowing dress was so totally and completely inappropriate for me, a prison uniform instead of a beautiful gown. It was the exact opposite of what I like, of who I am. I'm not feminine, and I don't want to look that way. My throat tightened as I felt my eyes tear up in frustration. I tried to control my breathing, sucking in air and pacing back and forth as if that could somehow make the dress go away. With each breath, it grew more difficult.

Deciding to face my angst head-on, I stood in front of my mirror and looked at the person staring back. I shuddered at my reflection, at the tightly fitting bodice that pushed up and magnified my breasts, accentuating every curve. I hunched my shoulders forward, trying to make my shape less noticeable, but it didn't work.

Were it not for the dress and my chest, I could have been mistaken for a fourteen-year-old boy, with my short pixie haircut, my unplucked eyebrows, my hairy legs, and my Harry Potter–style glasses. My reflection smiled back at the thought, but it was a sad smile.

Leaving the safety of my room, I walked over to Colin, sitting in his usual spot at his desk in our living room, gaming with some friends as a break from his endless hours of homework. I raised my arms and spun around, allowing him to take it all in. He stared at me, his lips held tightly together and his brow furrowed as he tried to figure out what to say. Seeing the devastation on my face, he finally spoke. "You have to tell her. You're tearing yourself apart."

He was right. I couldn't think of anything else. The very idea of the dress was a constant reminder of how much I hate my body. I have ever since puberty, when there was no avoiding the fact that I was turning into a woman. I'm not supposed to have curvy hips and breasts. I'm supposed to be flat. I know that. I just have no idea what to say to my big sister.

I've looked up to her ever since I was a little kid. Five years older than me, she excels at everything she does. Her high school grades were good enough to get her into the University of Pennsylvania, where she played on the women's soccer team. Always surrounded by a small group of close friends, she seems confident and sure of herself, even more so since Dustin proposed.

Liz and her fiancé had met on a coed soccer team a few years ago, when he was the men's soccer coach at a small university in Houston and she worked for Hewlett-Packard in human relations. She still works for HP, telecommuting from their new home in Oregon, but he's moved on to a much bigger program at Oregon State University in Corvallis.

Liz had texted me several times in recent weeks, asking me what I thought of the dress, how it fit. I'd kept putting her off, replying that I hadn't had a chance to try it on yet. Eventually, though, I knew we had to talk. We scheduled a time when we could do so via Skype, when Liz was in California visiting a grad school friend who was in the wedding party. It was a perfect opportunity.

I planned out what I was going to say, not wanting to present her with a problem without having a solution. Despite that, I was nervous. Twice I tried to connect on Skype but hung up before the call went through. On the third try, though, I stayed on the line until she picked up. She looked relaxed and happy, her long brown hair pulled back in a ponytail. She wore a light gray top that showed off her well-defined shoulders and arms, the product of hours spent in a yoga studio.

"Hey, Liz," I said. "How's it going?"

I couldn't concentrate as she described all the pre-wedding activities. I focused real fast, though, when she said, "Does your dress fit? Do you need to get it altered?"

I didn't answer.

"You did say that it got there, right?"

"Ummm, yeah," I managed to stammer out. "A few weeks ago."

"Did you try it on yet?"

"I did."

Liz waited for me to say more. When I didn't, she prompted me. "How'd it look? Can you put it on now so I can see?"

"It's pretty," I said, sounding unconvinced, my words more of a question than a statement.

"There's a 'but' in there. What is it?"

Swallowing hard, I decided to just say it. "I can't wear it, Liz."

"What do you mean? Why not?" she asked slowly, her head tilted and her forehead wrinkled as she let my words sink in. "Tell me what's going on."

"It's beautiful, Liz. Really. It's just—"

"What?" Liz asked again, her impatience mixed with concern.

"I dunno. I . . . I can't really explain," I stuttered.

"Can you try?" she asked gently.

How could I tell her that asking me to wear a gown was the same as if she'd expected Sammy or Ben to do so? I didn't understand myself why I felt that way, so how could I explain it to Liz? I desperately wanted her to understand, to figure out what I was trying to say without me having to actually say it. Maybe then I wouldn't have to say it to myself.

two

THE HAIRCUT

━━

August 1995 — Austin, TX
Jo (Mom; eighteen years earlier)

Emily was a happy child. The third of four, she worshipped her big brother, Ben, wanting to be like him in every way possible. She loved her big sister, Elizabeth, too, even though she had no interest in wearing Elizabeth's hand-me-down clothes; she much preferred Ben's. Then there was baby Sammy. Playing with him was much better than having a doll. Dolls were for girls, but it was fun having a real live baby brother. Emily read to him and showed him pictures and waved toys in front of his face.

At five years old and ready to start kindergarten, Emily was short for her age. She made up for that in boundless energy; she didn't know she was short. Instead, she knew she could accomplish whatever she desired. Catch a football thrown halfway across the yard by Ben? Check. Rollerblade with the neighborhood kids? Of course. She was one of the gang, totally accepted by the cadre of little boys from all the nearby homes.

There were almost twenty children in the two cul-de-sacs that made up our neighborhood in West Lake Hills, a wooded suburb of Austin that sometimes felt as if its twenty-five hundred residents were far out in the country rather than ten minutes from a big city. The houses, built from Texas limestone or brick, were more than spacious enough for the large families inside. Most gave off a sense of elegance with their intricate architectural design and manicured lawns. Ours was designed to feel like a welcoming country home instead, complete with a wraparound porch that invited folks to come and sit awhile.

Growing up in Massachusetts, I never thought I'd end up in deeply conservative Texas, where I was sometimes told not to "worry my pretty little head" about manly topics like construction, and people found it hard to believe I'd once run a factory for a high-tech company. Texas was a religious state, with football teams praying before games, students spending Wednesday nights with church youth groups, and the wall between church and state far from impervious.

Austin, however, was a liberal bastion in a conservative state, and West Lake Hills, with its top-notch school district and highly educated community of professionals, was even more so. We'd moved there from the San Francisco Bay Area, where my husband, Jon, and I worked as manufacturing directors for Applied Materials, a company that built equipment used to make computer chips. It was Jon's job that had brought us to Austin. He'd been asked to transfer to start up a new factory.

My mother, Aura Kruger, who'd lived with us ever since she retired from teaching the year after Ben was born, encouraged us to accept the job offer. Less than five

11

feet tall with short, curly salt-and-pepper hair and a bird-like delicacy, she was vibrant and willing to tackle whatever came her way. When Jon and I couldn't decide between continuing our lives in California or uprooting the family to take advantage of new opportunities in Texas, she said we should go. "Every time you move, you encounter new situations," she told us. "That makes you grow. If you're truly indifferent between the two options, then make the move."

I wasn't indifferent; I wanted to go. I'd known for a while that I was ready to walk away from my job, take myself off the fast track, have a fourth child, and be a stay-at-home mom, at least for a while. As long as we remained in California, I would keep delaying so I could finish one more project, wait for one more promotion. Moving to Texas had provided the impetus I needed to break away from all that.

I shared my thoughts with Jon, as I always did. We were able to talk about everything and had pretty much done so from when we first got together. I was nineteen when I picked him out of all the other MIT men as the most responsible, the most considerate, the most fun. And it didn't hurt that he was also the most handsome.

We met through the Shakespeare Ensemble at MIT, a repertory theater company made up primarily of MIT undergraduates. It was a perfect setting for me to find someone who shared not only my love of math, science, and engineering but also my passion for theater and literature. The fall of our senior year, Jon and I were cast in *The Taming of the Shrew* together, I as Kate and Jon as Petruchio's best friend, and we saw each other often at rehearsals.

It was at a cast party, however, that we grew to know each other as more than friends. Listening to music that night, sitting next to each other on the couch, we held hands without saying a word. The following week, we went to the movies for our first date. By the end of our senior year, we were a firmly established couple. By the time we were contemplating the move to Texas, we'd been married for twelve years and had three children, Elizabeth, Ben, and Emily.

Jon pointed out that I could do exactly as I liked even if we stayed in California, that we didn't have to move for me to quit work. Nevertheless, feeling constrained by my responsibilities, I was eager to get away. We considered our alternatives one last time and decided to go for it.

Once we settled in Austin, I didn't miss work in the least. I loved staying home with our fourth child, Sammy. Meanwhile, our older three children wasted no time adjusting to their new lives. They played sports and made friends, thriving at school and in the neighborhood.

Jon and I made new friends as well. Although many were somewhat conservative, nobody seemed bothered by our younger daughter's tomboyishness. Their sons never thought twice about it, either, accepting Emily as one of them despite her long, curly hair that was always a mess because she couldn't be bothered with brushing it out. They knew she had to wear a dress on special occasions, but they loved that she played hard and was good at every sport.

Emily never stood still, always bouncing back and forth from one foot to the other. She ran and climbed trees, built forts and played ball every chance she got. Almost any kind of ball—football, baseball, basketball—but not softball.

Softball was for girls, and Emily didn't like being a girl. Years later, she told us that every night as she lay in bed, she hoped for some magic that would transform her into a boy while she slept.

She knew she was different from her guy friends, and it bothered her. She never referred to herself as a girl. She said instead that she was a tomboy, viewing that as a special kind of boy. Jon and I thought we knew what she meant by the term, but we didn't. We saw in Emily not a boy but a girl who was more comfortable with traditionally male clothing, activities, and friendships. A girl whose behavior was similar to my own at that age.

Like Emily, I had a brother three years older. I adored Philip and wanted to be just like him. He had a paper route; I wanted a paper route. When he got bored with his when he was ten years old and I was seven, I took it over, thus becoming the first girl to deliver newspapers for the *Boston Globe*. Back in 1964, that was pretty unusual.

Philip sang with a band; I wanted to sing too. He wore pants to school and pitched with the Little League; I would have given anything to be allowed to do the same. He and my other brother, Charles, one year older than me, swam in nothing but bathing trunks; so did I, my bare chest exposed for all to see. At least, I did until a teenage neighbor began leering at me. After that, I wore baggy shirts, hiding my developing body.

I felt lucky that my parents had given me the name *Jo* because sometimes people hearing it for the first time assumed I was a boy, and I liked that. No fairy princesses and ballerinas for me. I refused to go to gymnastics classes because my mom wouldn't let me wear the black tights and white T-shirts the boys wore.

My big sister, Connie, nine years older, didn't like girly clothes either. She wore dresses because it was required, not because she liked them.

At Halloween, I chose costumes that concealed my femininity. In second grade, I hid behind a Frankenstein mask, avoiding conversation so my classmates wouldn't recognize my voice and would think it was a little boy underneath. I read the *Hardy Boys* books and rejected the *Nancy Drew* series, preferring the former because the latter were written for girls.

Times were different when Emily was growing up in the 1990s. We never made her wear skirts and dresses, except when we attended big family events like weddings and bat mitzvahs. We encouraged her to play sports and be physically active. We offered her blocks and trucks right along with what society thought of as little girl toys. We just wanted her to be happy and had no problem with her choices.

When she was five years old, Emily asked to be taken to Sport Clips, where all the little boys got their hair cut. The stylist said she was fine cutting girls' hair, too, but that turned out not to be the case. The results were uneven, the curls trimmed at exactly the wrong place so that several clumps stuck straight out.

Although Emily didn't complain, I could tell from the faces she made in the mirror that she didn't like the haircut. She kept pulling the hair on one side, as if trying to make it as long as the other. After watching the stylist try several times to even things out, I finally said, "Let's just finish up." Then, turning to Emily, I added, "Don't worry, sweetie. I'll fix it when we get home."

Emily trusted me. She stopped squirming in her seat,

smiled at the hairdresser, and settled in to wait. The moment she was done, she jumped up and ran to the car, saying, "Mommy, it's okay. You'll make it look better."

I didn't know until an hour later just how prophetic her words had been.

The moment we got home, we headed straight for the bathroom. I dragged my desk chair in from my study and placed it facing the mirror. Emily climbed up, eager to see how I was going to change her bedraggled appearance. "Have you ever done this before?" she asked.

"Sure," I answered, with more confidence than I felt. "I used to trim Ben's hair all the time."

"What are you going to do? How do you know where to cut? Will I look like Ben when you're done?"

Her questions tumbled out, faster than I could answer. Instead of trying, I just went to work. The stylist had done such an uneven job that I had to trim the hair really short before I could get it to look right. I don't know whether it was my inexperience with the scissors or the growing grin on Emily's face, but for some reason, I kept on cutting. And the more I cut, the more Emily beamed.

By the time I was done, she looked exactly like Ben had three years earlier, when he was five years old. She had a traditional boy's haircut, parted at the side and clipped neatly around the ears, long enough to need a comb but not so long as to require brushing. The short hair made her brown eyes stand out and her deep dimples more evident.

I didn't have the words to explain why Emily was ecstatic, but for the first time since becoming aware of how she looked, I could tell that she liked what she saw. Despite not understanding completely, I shared her joy. It didn't matter to me that her pleasure in looking like a boy was unusual. I even kind of got it, remembering how I'd felt much the same way back when I was a child. All I cared about as a mother was that somehow, in some way, I'd made my child happy.

Jeremy in a dress at six years old

Jeremy in boys' clothes at six years old

three

THE TOMBOY

==

August 1996 — Austin, TX

Jon (Dad)

As we walked into the Sears department store on the last Saturday afternoon of the summer, I grabbed six-year-old Emily around the waist and launched her up onto my shoulders, all forty-three pounds of her. She laughed and reached her arms around my head, patting my ears and knocking my baseball cap away. Although I couldn't see her face, I knew she was enjoying the view from six feet in the air.

Suddenly, I found it difficult to hold on because Emily was squirming about, squealing, "Put me down! Put me down!" We were passing through the boys' part of the store, and she had noticed a table with a pile of polo shirts under a sign that read, *First Day of School*.

Within moments of her feet touching the floor, Emily found what she wanted. "I like this one," she said, rubbing her fingers over a striped blue shirt that looked just her size.

Knowing that almost the exact same shirt was available

in the girls' department, I lifted Emily back up onto my shoulders and said, "Let's go over there." Carefully avoiding any mention of the word *girl*, I added, "Looks like they've got a lot of cool stuff and more colors to pick from."

I tried to sound excited, but what I was thinking was, *Why is Emily so stubborn about this? Why does she insist on shopping in the boys' section?* I found it strange that she always wanted to dress like a boy and I worried about her, partly because she was so different from her big sister, Elizabeth, who had almost always picked feminine clothing as soon as she was old enough to know the difference. A big, floppy Easter bonnet with pink tights and strappy shoes to match. Grandma Aura's elegant purse on her shoulder. Walking about in Jo's high heels, her legs shaking as she struggled to stay upright.

Elizabeth had also gravitated toward toys that were considered girlish. This surprised Jo and me, for we believed that the labeling of toys or activities as *male* or *female* was a cultural construct, and I tried as a father not to push our children in any one direction, believing it better to make all options available. Despite my best efforts to avoid stereotyping, however, Elizabeth loved things "little girl." Then Ben came along and loved the traditionally "little boy" stuff. It made me wonder if femininity was more hardwired than I'd initially thought.

When Emily came along, however, she was the exact opposite of Elizabeth, preferring Ben's hand-me-down clothes and toys. I worried sometimes that she was unhappy with being a girl, concerned that maybe she wanted to be more like Ben because I had done something to make her think I loved my son more than I loved my daughters. Did Emily think that girls weren't as good as boys? Jo believed that society viewed being a boy as better than being a girl. Had we unintentionally perpetuated that message to Emily?

My thoughts were interrupted by Emily yelping, "No, no, no!" and wiggling about as she reached again for the boys' shirts that drew her like a magnet. I changed and spoke more directly. "Don't you want to look at the girl clothes?"

"Silly Daddy," she answered. "I'm a tomboy."

It was incredibly sweet and cute, and I didn't have an answer to that confident statement, so I smiled and hugged her, placed her back on the floor, and agreed that she was indeed a tomboy. Then we picked out a couple of shirts and some shorts from the boys' section for her to wear on the first day of school.

I was happy to have a tomboy for a daughter. In some ways it seemed more natural to me than Elizabeth's overt femininity. After all, my mother preferred her boyish nickname, Ted, to her given name, Winifred. She was happier riding a horse or a tractor than taking care of a house. As a girl on a farm, she had played the role of a son, taking on the outdoor chores of milking cows and feeding the animals, while her older sisters handled the house. As a child, she preferred a boyish appearance and liked the simplicity of short hair and blue jeans.

Jo did as well, even as an adult. She complained that women's business attire was less comfortable than men's and regarded any skirt or dress, no matter how casual, as too restrictive. My mother-in-law, Aura, was different. She loved to dress up. But even she sometimes acted in a traditionally male manner, having been trained by her father to help with his chores because he didn't have a son to work by his side.

My wife was a civil engineering major at a time when few women were attracted to the field. I was proud of her and of Emily's grandmothers and was happy to have Emily emulate them, albeit unknowingly. She was a lot like them in many ways, choosing boyish activities and an androgynous appearance. Despite that preference, though, she hadn't protested about shopping for girls' outfits until halfway through kindergarten. That's when she decided that clothes designed for girls were no longer okay. Instead, she wanted to shop in the boys' sections. It had nothing to do with comfort or utility, the way it did for Jo and my mother. For Emily, the attraction to boys' clothing was simply that they were supposed to be for boys.

The more intense Emily grew in her opposition to girls' clothing, the more concerned I became, worrying that something else was going on, something we didn't understand. Toward the end of the school year, I tried sharing my thoughts with Jo. "Do you think, um . . . ?" I asked, my voice trailing away as I couldn't quite find the words to express my fears.

"What?" Jo prompted, tilting her head a bit to the side, the way she did when paying close attention to something.

After hesitating again, I finally just blurted it out. "Is something wrong with Emily?"

"What do you mean?" Jo asked. "In what way?"

"She doesn't seem to like herself, physically. She doesn't notice when she's grimy, and she doesn't take care of herself. Then there's this not wanting to dress like a girl. She's getting extreme about it." I didn't want to make it a bigger deal than it was, but I had started to think Emily might have a problem.

"She's fine," said Jo. When I didn't respond, she added, "I was the same way."

I waited, torn between wanting to trust in Jo's judgment, which was very good when it came to understanding our children, and feeling a responsibility to help Emily if she needed our help.

"If I'd been allowed to wear pants to school," Jo said, "I never would've worn a dress. It was awkward if I wanted to climb a tree or hang from the jungle gym, or swing, or just run around. I couldn't wait to get home and change into my playclothes."

"But maybe it's more than that with Emily," I prodded as gently as I could, not wanting Jo to interpret my misgivings about our daughter as a criticism of *her*. I felt a need to make it obvious that I saw my wife as beautiful in whatever she wore, that I was fine with her rejection of femininity, and viewed it as in line with the women's liberation movement that was so important to our generation.

That wasn't the issue for Emily. She was different. Both she and Jo were stubborn about their personal preferences, and both favored short hair and pants over long hair and skirts, but for Jo it had the feeling of pushing boundaries, whereas with Emily it seemed as if she wanted to be on the other side of the boundary.

"She'll outgrow it like I did," said Jo. "Remember, I hated girls' clothes until I was thirteen."

"That's when—"

"Yeah. A guy kissed me, and all of a sudden I wanted to look as feminine as I could. It all changed pretty quickly. Tight shirts and push-up bras. Makeup. You'll see. That's what'll happen with Emily. She's just like I was."

October 1998
Jon (two years later)

IT WAS A PERFECT DAY FOR FLAG FOOTBALL WITH the
West Austin Youth Association. A blue October sky, a
slight breeze, the sun not yet so hot as to melt the players
and parents alike. It was late in the season, and the brutal
Texas summer days of over one hundred degrees were
over. The community field down by Town Lake didn't look
quite as healthy as it had a couple of months earlier, the
grass worn thin in the center and the yard markings half
rubbed away. It had been a while since the other dads and
I had come to the field after work to repaint the lines.

Eight-year-old Emily loved football, and I was proud of
her willingness to be the only girl on the team and of her
ability to compete with the boys on their own terms. She
was as passionate about the sport as any of them and could
play better than most. I enjoyed it when other dads came
up to me to praise my little girl's athletic prowess. The
moms were more likely to talk about how important her
participation was for women's rights. But when they expressed that sentiment to Emily, my daughter's response
was to shrug and answer, "I just like to play."

She was like Elizabeth when it came to sports, a fierce
competitor no matter what the game, though Elizabeth
preferred soccer. She'd made the West Lake High varsity
team when she was only a freshman, an impressive feat at
a school with more than twenty-five hundred students,
many of whom had been playing soccer since kindergarten.

In seventh and eighth grade, Elizabeth had competed
on the Hill Country Middle School's coed soccer team and

never thought twice about having teammates who were boys. A few years earlier, Jo had registered her for a baseball camp that promoted itself as coed. When they showed up for the first day, they discovered that Elizabeth was the only girl. Jo told her she didn't have to attend, but Elizabeth was determined to stick it out. So determined, in fact, that by the end of the week, the camp organizers had to modify their highly coveted *Mr. Hustle* award to read *Ms. Hustle.*

Emily, in third grade, was accepted by the boys in the same way that Elizabeth had been. They didn't think twice about whether Emily belonged on their football team. Their voices were still high, and their female classmates still had flat chests. The only way you could tell who was a boy and who was a girl was by how they dressed and wore their hair.

Most of the girls Emily's age kept their hair long, and she was no exception. She'd loved the short haircut Jo had given her a few years earlier, but toward the end of second grade, she'd decided she didn't want to be different from everyone else. So even though we'd assured her that she could keep her hair short if she wanted, she chose to wear it shoulder-length. Not the middle-of-the-back style that so many of the Texas girls liked, but longer than any but the most rebellious of the boys.

The other football parents weren't bothered by Emily's boyish attire. They accepted her as a tomboy, the girl who hung out with their sons and played sports as well as any of them. Those parents on the sidelines were some of our closest friends, like John and Joy Cox, who were there watching their son, James. He was tall and lanky with a shy smile and a shrug for everything. He was also Emily's best friend, and they'd played together practically every day since they were three years old.

One summer, the two children decided to see how many nights in a row they could sleep over at each other's homes. James was often at our breakfast table and Emily at his. They tossed a football around in the early-morning light and played flashlight tag once the sun went down. They explored every inch of both our yards, hiding out in the woods as they pretended to be pioneers, building forts and tree houses with whatever stray material they could find. James never cared that Emily was a girl. She was just his best friend. His dad thought the two would marry one day and said so frequently, much to the embarrassment of the two kids.

Sometimes Emily and James were joined by their friend Clay Wimberly, a slight kid no bigger than Emily but with an impressive throwing arm. He often threw to Emily, for her quick hands and sure-footed running made his passes look even better. Emily had her big brother, Ben, to thank for her practiced skill on the football field. He was an eleven-year-old middle schooler with a quick smile and an easy way about him. But when he competed at sports, his grin changed to a focused look of determination.

Shy when it came to interacting with adults, Ben was outgoing and fun-loving with his circle of friends. One of the littler guys, he played beyond his size, happy to wrestle with friends who outweighed him by thirty pounds and were a whole head taller. He wore his light brown hair in a buzz cut during the heat of the summer but loved to grow his long, tight curls out as the weather cooled.

Most of the time, Ben didn't mind when Emily hung

out with him and his friends. He was glad to have someone with whom he could train, and he had his little sister constantly running plays in our front yard. She worked hard to catch every pass he threw, craving his praise when she held on to the ball. She knew how to run a post play before she could read, running toward the tree that served as our goalpost as fast as she could, looking back over her shoulder with her hands up in the air, ready to receive Ben's pass.

During Emily's third-grade flag football season, Ben helped her learn the maneuver that would become known as the "Emily play." It was late October, less than a month before Emily's ninth birthday, when the coach decided the team was ready. The offense had perfected the trick play and was impatient to try it out, confident that they'd kept it secret from the other teams.

Emily was a wide receiver, but she occasionally lined up near quarterback Clay, ready for a handoff, hunched forward with her knees bent just the right amount. If it weren't for her long hair, she would've looked exactly like the little boys, though a bit smaller than most. On this day, as soon as the ball was snapped, Emily stepped toward Clay and he faked a handoff to her. Then she ran toward the far side of the field drawing all the defenders away.

She dodged and twisted to avoid the hands reaching out to grab a flag from the belt wrapped around her waist. Her arms were positioned perfectly, looking as if she were holding the ball, her right arm cradled around the imaginary pigskin, the left one held stiffly to the side to keep defenders at bay. Everyone—the parents, the players on the other team, even the other coaches—believed she really had the ball. Our fans began shouting, "Go, Emily! Go!

Go!" eager for what could be the game-winning touch-down. I hollered along with the rest of the parents.

In the meantime, Clay jogged slowly toward the goal line, nobody noticing that he still had the ball. Only when he was on the twenty-yard line, with all the defensive players still focused on Emily, did he take off running.

At first, nobody detected his sudden movement. Not until Emily stopped running and, dropping all pretenses, started yelling, "Go, Clay!" did everyone understand what was happening. Within seconds, he'd run the few remaining yards and scored.

The other team stood around, their mouths gaping open. The parents cheered, alternating between congratulating Clay and praising Emily.

These are the plays that children remember their whole lives. These are the plays that get parents choked up with pride. And in my case, this was the play that solidified for me just how completely Emily had been accepted as a valued member of her team. More than that, watching my daughter play that afternoon, I realized how much I delighted in her strength and determination, in her willingness to play the sport she wanted to play, even though doing so meant that she was one of only two girls in the league.

May 1999

Jo

IT WAS ALMOST THREE THIRTY ON A FRIDAY afternoon, that quiet moment before the school bus arrived, after which I would focus all my energy and attention on my children. Sitting at my desk in the study just off our bedroom, surrounded by my books and files and piles of paper, I gazed out the window at the red-tipped photinia shrubs we'd planted six years earlier, now grown into trees tall enough to create a shady, private backyard.

The phone rang. It was Megan, one of the football team moms, calling to work out the logistics for the evening's sleepover at her home. Her son, Peter, and half a dozen of the other boys and Emily were going to practice in her yard and then watch *Rudy*, one of their favorite football movies. Emily's overnight bag was already packed and waiting in the back hall.

"This is a bit . . . umm . . . awkward," Megan started.

"What is?" I asked.

"About tonight. Can you pick up Emily around eleven?"

"Sure. But what's up? I thought the kids were staying over. We can move it to our house if there's—"

"No, that's not it. It's just that Emily . . ."

I waited several seconds, curious to see where the conversation was headed.

"What about Emily?" I finally asked.

"It's not okay for her to sleep with the boys," Megan answered.

"Oh," I said, my thoughts racing ahead to how I would tell Emily, knowing she'd be crestfallen at being sent home when everyone else got to stay.

Then Megan started to talk quickly, her words a rapid staccato, as if she had to get them out before stopping to think of their effect. "She can stay for the movie and hang out afterwards, but she has to leave before bedtime."

Ouch. I let my breath out slowly as what she said hit

me like an unexpected ocean wave. With one phrase by one concerned mother, Emily had been excluded from the fellowship of all the little boys she'd been playing with for years. It was too soon. Perhaps it was inevitable, but the children were only in third grade. It was only a few months earlier that we'd hosted Emily's ninth birthday, and every single friend she'd invited had been a boy.

I alternated between being furious at my friend and trying to squelch my reaction because, in reality, I got why she no longer thought it appropriate for a girl to be at a sleepover with the boys. I thought she was wrong, that we had more time, but I did understand.

But Emily wouldn't. She loved the conversations after lights out, when everyone relaxed and made inappropriate jokes and told stories they hesitated to share in the light of day. She was living in a dream in which there would never be any difference between her and her guy friends, in which she would always be accepted as one of them. Maybe I should have prepared her better, let her know that her friendships were unusual and unlikely to last through puberty. Perhaps if it hadn't happened so soon, I would have done so.

I should have known better, because I remembered going through the same thing when my brother Charles and I played together with his best friend, Gerry. The three of us were inseparable throughout elementary school as we pretended to be superheroes or wrestlers or walked to the drugstore to look at comic books or just hung out in the yard, climbing trees and staring at the clouds. I was devastated when one afternoon they told me to go away, Charles saying bluntly, "We don't want a girl around."

My mother consoled me at the time with, "Don't worry,

Jo. Someday, boys will want to play with you again, only then they'll be happy you're a girl because they'll want you to be their sweetheart."

She thought that would make me feel better, but it didn't. The idea of being someone's girlfriend didn't appeal in the least. At nine years old, I only wanted to be buddies, to play together. When I explained that to my mom, she laughed and said, "You'll feel differently when the time comes." She was right, but on that day when I was still in the fourth grade, her response just made me mad. I went up to my room and watched out the window for the boys to come back inside, not knowing whether I wanted them to return quickly or stay outside forever.

It wasn't just that I wanted to play with Charles and Gerry. I tried to look like them as well, wearing Charles's clothes even though they were way too big for me. I even borrowed his underwear one time just to see what it was like to wear boys' underpants. That was about the same time that I cut my hair short and didn't correct people if they assumed I was a guy.

When my family moved to an all-black town in the Mississippi Delta when I was ten, I got mistaken for a boy fairly often, probably since the boys there weren't used to seeing white kids. My father moved us there so he could start a clinic. Behind the stands at our first high school football game, some high school boys pinned me down and tried to pull my pants off, teasing, "Are you a boy or a girl?" I'm pretty sure they thought I was a boy, or they wouldn't have done that.

That bullying behavior grew worse a couple of years later when I was molested and beaten, ending up with a concussion and two broken ribs. After that traumatic experience, we left town and moved to South Florida. I retreated into my tomboyishness and dressed even more like a boy. At eleven years old, I not only wore boys' clothing, I also wore a jacket at all times, despite the heat of a Miami summer. I was trying to hide the fact that I'd hit puberty and was developing.

Lost in my childhood memories, I barely heard Megan on the phone as she spoke about the evening's logistics. After hanging up, I went downstairs, retrieved Emily's overnight bag from the back hall, brought it up to her bedroom, and slowly emptied it out, placing each item carefully in her bureau. By the time I got to the sneakers at the bottom of the bag, I'd let my emotions take over, and I threw them as hard as I could into the corner of her closet.

As if on cue, I heard Emily and Sammy burst through the front door, laughing, and head straight for the kitchen where they knew I'd have a snack waiting for them. I let out a sigh as I planned how to tell Emily about the phone call. Before heading down the stairs, I picked up her sneakers and carefully arranged them in their usual spot.

Sitting at the table a few minutes later, Emily looked confused. "Why is this happening?" she asked. "Seriously?"

I wanted to make it right for her, to call Megan back and convince her that it was okay for Emily to spend the night, but I didn't. Instead, I tried to explain. "I know it shouldn't matter that you're a girl—"

"No, it shouldn't," Emily interrupted. "It matters that I'm fast and funny. I'm good at football. Even better than some of the guys. Nobody cares that I'm a girl."

"You're right, babydoll."

"It's the parents. Why do they have to muck it all up?"

Five-year-old Sammy nodded as if he knew what was

going on, but of course, still in pre-kindergarten, he couldn't really understand.

"It's not fair!" Emily exclaimed. "Now I'm gonna miss everything."

"You'll still be able to go until bedtime. You can still be a part of it all."

"It's not the same," Emily grumbled.

"I know, sweetie, I know."

"I just wish it were different. They wouldn't kick me out if I were a boy."

four

PUBERTY

—·—

Fall 2001 — Austin, TX
Emily (11 years old)

So, sixth grade. Everything about it is frustrating. I know that's the case for pretty much everybody, but we're talking about me. The last couple of years of elementary school were rough, especially as one by one, families stopped letting me come to sleepovers. Now suddenly it's middle school, and it's even harder. The guys are ignoring me, even during the day. It's like they've forgotten how to talk to me, and they don't treat me the way they did before. Instead of liking that I'm a tomboy and saying, "Oh, cool, a girl we understand," they've started thinking, "Eww, tomboys are gross. We're more interested in girly girls."

The other day, I sat down in the cafeteria with Clay and some of the other guys, and they were talking about getting together at James's house before football practice to throw the ball around. They changed the subject right after I joined them, but I didn't really pay attention and assumed I was included in the afternoon plans. As soon as I got home from school, I dropped off my backpack in the front hall and raced down the hill without even stopping for a snack.

I opened the front door and walked in, expecting to find James and the others there. "Hey, anybody home?" I called out, standing in the kitchen.

At first nobody answered. Then James's big brother Joey walked in from the family room and said, "Hey, Emily. What's up?"

"Where's James?" I asked. "We were gonna meet up."

"He just left," Joey said.

"Where'd he go?"

"Clay's mom picked him up, and they went over there."

Why hadn't they waited for me or come up to my house to get me too? Confused and hurt, I knew the answer. I just didn't want to admit it. They didn't really want me around. That's why they'd stopped talking about it at lunchtime after I sat down with them. This had happened once before, but then I thought it was a misunderstanding and I'd messed up somehow. This time it was obvious. They'd ditched me.

It's because we've gone from being little kids playing together to instead copying the teenagers who only care about pairing up. I've gone from being one of the popular kids to being weird, and the guys don't like that.

The girls aren't really any better. They like having me on their teams in phys ed because I score points. But when I try to sit with them in the cafeteria, they sometimes say, "Go away." Literally.

That happened a couple of weeks ago with my friend Lily. She used to be a tomboy like me, with dirty blond hair even shorter than mine and coveralls that hid her body the way my baggy shirts hide mine. I could walk through backyards and get to her house in about ten minutes and only had to cross one quiet street to do it, so my parents let me go on my own, even when I was little.

We spent hours in the tree house in her neighbor's yard, helping each other to climb up to it because neither of us was very tall. We tried to fish in a creek that had barely enough water to get your toes wet. We didn't talk a lot, but when we did, it was about the adventures we were gonna have, never about boys and dating. Then she started wearing dresses and makeup and didn't want to climb trees anymore.

Around the time Lily changed, I was wandering the cafeteria to figure out where to sit. I'd tried to get eye contact with my football buddies so that they'd all smoosh together and make room for me, but they didn't notice me. So I walked to where some girls from my recreational basketball team were sitting. Their table was right in front of the one where the coaches sat, keeping order in the lunchroom. The coaches knew all the students and would call them out by name if they didn't clear their place or got too rambunctious. "James!" they'd yell. "Clean up that mess. That's two laps before gym class." The threat of extra work kept everyone in line.

As I started to sit down with the girls, one of them was saying, "You'll never guess what happened last night."

"You gotta tell us," another said with a giggle. "What? Or should I say *who*?"

The girl started to answer, but then she looked at me and said, "Emily, go away. You don't wanna hear this."

It seems that as soon as the girls want to talk about anything personal, or gossip, or talk about their bodies . . . I actually don't know what they talk about, because they always push me away. They say I spend so much time with the boys that they're afraid I'll spill their secrets if they talk in front of me. I wouldn't do that, but that doesn't seem to matter.

Everyone is changing, and I want to stay the same. So I'm alone.

At least I had football. I loved practice. Once we were in our pads and helmets, it's like the boys forgot I wasn't shaped like them underneath. The games, though, were totally lame. No matter how good I was, I only got the minimum number of plays required by the league. According to the rules of Pop Warner, the tackle league I switched to at the start of sixth grade, my coach had to put me in for eight plays every game, so he put me in for four each half. But he never called for me to carry the ball; I only got to block. Turns out that the dad who coached us didn't think girls should be allowed to play.

One of my teammates ratted him out. "Yeah, you're not imagining it. He doesn't want you on the team. He told us to tackle you so hard that you'll quit."

I believed him. In practice, I usually scrimmaged with the starters, running plays and going out for passes. I was good. I caught the ball more often than most and could juke around the defensive players with the best of them. I felt like I was one of the team stars. After practice last week, I thought, *This weekend's game'll be different. Coach saw how I broke a tackle and ran the ball for thirty-five yards. I was really good. Everyone congratulated me.* One of my teammates even chest-butted me after the play, forgetting that under my shoulder pads, I'm starting to develop.

But when the game came around on Saturday afternoon, I rode the bench for most of it, just like I have every weekend. It was maddening and frustrating and made me want to yell at the coach, "Just give me a chance to play! You'll see how good I can be." But, of course, I didn't. And I'm not telling Mom and Dad because I don't want them to make a big deal over it. Instead, I'll just wait until the seventh-grade school team. Those coaches like me and will let me play.

THE WORST PART is that my body is changing. Puberty. Shoot. It's really difficult for me. The worst moment so far happened during PE class. Coach K stopped me as everyone was heading to the locker room to shower and change.

"Emily, you got a moment?"

My first thought was that she was gonna say I'd done a good job during our basketball scrimmage. I'd managed to shoot five times and never missed a shot. I'd even gotten more than my share of rebounds, which is hard to do because I'm so short.

"Sure, Coach. What's up?" I asked, a little breathless after running around so much.

"I'm going to be blunt," she said. "You can't wear a white shirt anymore unless you're wearing a bra."

What the—? I thought as I stood there feeling as if my whole world had crumbled. My head exploded and I felt crushed.

Why is this so hard? It's not like I don't know I'm a girl. I get that. But somehow I never thought that meant I'd grow up to be a woman. I'm facing this very real thing of my body changing, and I'm not okay with it. It was bad enough being a girl, but I really, really don't want to become a woman.

puberty

I wish I could stop the process. But puberty is happening, and there's nothing I can do about it. I hate every single thing that's happening to my body, the softer curves, my breasts. Everyone around me is excited by the changes, but I dread every moment of it. And there's nobody I can say that to. I can't tell my sister or brothers or my parents. I can't handle disappointing them.

A couple of years ago, Liz and Ben stopped thinking my boyishness was cute. They wanted me to be more girly. It's not like they made fun of me or anything like that. They were just afraid that if I didn't change, my classmates would tease me. So Liz encouraged me to wear makeup, and she picked out some of her old clothes for me to wear. Then Ben would say, "You look great. You should dress like this more often."

I know it was coming from a good place, that they wanted to boost my confidence by cooing over me and telling me I'm beautiful. But every time, it just . . . it sucked. It's like I was getting praised for something that wasn't real. For being someone that I'm not. At first, I went along with the makeovers because I enjoyed the attention. But eventually I got sick of them and wore basketball shorts and T-shirts to school every day. I put my hair in a ponytail and pretended it didn't exist. I let it get gross and didn't brush the snarls out because I just couldn't deal with it.

Jeremy (11) with hair in a ponytail

The worst time was when I had to dress up for our family photo, which we did every year so that Mom could send it out with our holiday cards. We'd schedule it weeks in advance and decide on a theme. My favorite was back in first grade when we all dressed in sport uniforms. That was the year I played baseball and my hair was short and I looked like a boy.

puberty

Ivester family in 1996. L to R: Jeremy (6); Elizabeth (11); Jon (31); Ben (9); Jo (29); Sammy (2)

Other times, though, when Ben and Sammy got to wear slacks and a jacket or a vest, Elizabeth and I had to wear dresses. She never minded, but I hated it. I would have given anything to be allowed to dress like my brothers, but in the years that the theme was "party attire," I wasn't offered any choice. I even had to wear tights and makeup. It was hard to smile for the camera when I felt so uncomfortable.

*Ivester family in 1998. L to R: Elizabeth (13); Ben (11);
Jon (33); Sammy (4); Jeremy in a dress (8); Jo (31);
Grandma Aura (76)*

five

THE "SWOOSE"

—:—

Summer 2002 — Austin, TX
Emily (12 years old)

Sometimes I really do try to be the person that everybody wants me to be. Actually, I do that a lot of the time. A few weeks ago, I saw Liz shaving and said, "Oh, show me how to do that." And she did. But as soon as I was done, in my head I was like, "Well, that wasn't worth it." It took half an hour, and all I got was smooth legs. I didn't even like them. It felt like a waste of time, and I never wanted to do it again.

Now the hair has grown back, and Ben is concerned I'll get teased once school starts up. He mentioned it to Dad, who seemed kind of disappointed. So now I'm shaving again. I could've stood my ground and said, "There's no reason to shave. I don't have to." But instead, I felt this huge amount of guilt.

I'm also trying to wear more girly clothes, at least some of the time. I wear Liz's old sweaters and put on a sports bra underneath. That flattens me out a bit, which is nice, but it still feels unnatural.

Sometimes, I talk with Grandma Aura about it. When everyone else tells me I should look more feminine, she just says, "Darling, you look however you want."

A few days ago, we were sitting in her living room, which is actually a part of our house. You walk through a door from our front hall and you're in her apartment. She's proud of it and calls it the "Queen Mother's Apartment," pleased that when my folks built the house, they set aside a generous area for her, complete with her own kitchen and dining area, and a bedroom, bathroom, living room, and screened-in porch. She asked my parents to paint it pink because she'd always wanted pink walls when she was a little girl. At eighty years old, she feels free to do what she wants.

I'd found Grandma sitting on her couch knitting and watching the news, which she does a lot of the time. She knows a lot about what's going on in the world and often asks me about political stuff that I don't really care about.

I rocked back and forth in the chair nearby and stared at the TV, not really hearing what the newscaster said. Sometimes it just feels good to be in the same room with Grandma. We don't really have to talk. This time, though, I wanted to ask her a question.

"Do you think it's bad, Grandma, that I don't like my body changing?"

"Not at all," she said. "It's okay. Lots of middle schoolers aren't comfortable with their bodies."

"I liked it better when everyone thought of me like a boy, when they didn't care whether I wore a bra."

"You look beautiful no matter what," she answered.

I didn't want to tell her that looking beautiful wasn't what I had in mind, that I would rather look handsome.

When I didn't respond, she went into her kitchen and brought me a glass of apple juice and some Girl Scout cookies. She knows my favorites are the Peanut Butter Patties, even though everyone else in the house likes Thin Mints. Food is her answer to everything.

"You're a swoose, dear," she said as she watched me eat.

"A what?" I asked, not sure I'd heard right.

"A swoose," she repeated. "Half swan and half goose."

I like that idea. I'm a swoose. Not a boy and not a girly girl, but something in between. Maybe that's what I'll be for this school year, for seventh grade. Two-a-day football practices are about to begin, and Ben is encouraging me to go out for volleyball instead of football. Even though I know he just wants me to fit in better with my classmates and play a sport I can continue all through high school, it bothers me when he talks about it. I don't want to play volleyball. I want to play football. Ben's comments just remind me that eventually, I won't be able to keep up. I'm jealous of the boys who are growing bigger and taller than me, and it frustrates me a ton to know that soon I won't be able to compete with them.

Fall 2002
Emily (12 years old)

IT'S BRUTAL PRACTICING OUTSIDE IN THE LATE-summer heat, wearing pads and running around for hours at a time, but it's worth it. Middle school football is so much better than the Pop Warner league, with a real coach, not that dad who'd pretty much benched me during the games. On the first day of practice, all the focus was on figuring out who would be the starting quarterbacks. The coaches already knew that Clay would be one of them because his big brother, Turner, started in that position. The only question was whether he'd make the A team with the bigger guys or play on the B team because he's so little.

Clay did great that first day of practice. The ball flew out of his hand right to where the coaches told him to throw. But the receivers were having a hard time catching his passes because he threw bullets. Over the summer, he'd started throwing a lot harder than he had in flag football. Since he and James and me had played in our front yard almost every day that summer, I'd grown used to it gradually and could still hang on to his passes. But most of the guys couldn't.

After a while, Coach Long yelled, "Hey, Clay, who can catch your balls?"

I grinned as I waited for him to answer, "James and Emily!" But he didn't. After saying James, next on his list was Will. That made sense. He was good and fast. I'd be next.

"Michael."

Wait, wh—?

"Aaron."

I stared at Clay, willing him to call out my name too. I wanted to wave to him, but that'd be awkward. Surely he'd say something to Coach about me. But he didn't. I got this terrible sinking feeling as I realized Clay wasn't gonna let Coach know that I could catch anything he could throw. It seemed like he'd forgotten that I played just as well as the guys. He ignored me. Like I wasn't there.

So Coach made me a running back, which I liked almost as much as being a receiver. I couldn't wait for Thursday afternoon, for the first game, which was at Connally High, twenty miles north of Austin.

The Monday before, Coach pulled me aside and said, "Emily, you're doing great out there."

"Thanks, Coach."

"What do you think about moving up to the A team?" Did I hear right? I was the littlest player on the B team, and Coach wanted me to move up? After basking in the thought for a moment, I worried that maybe it was because he wanted a girl on the A team to make some sort of political statement. I didn't want that.

"Would I still be a running back?" I asked.

"Yeah. You've done a good job with that."

"Would I still start?"

"Uh . . ."

"Coach, I want to play. I'd rather be a starter on the B team than ride the bench on the A team."

"Your choice."

"Then I'll stay on the B team."

Had I really just done that? Turned down an opportunity to be on the A team? To play with Clay and James, who both had made it even though Clay is so little? To watch Ben's face light up when I told him I'd moved up? Yeah, I guess I had. Mostly, I wanted as much play time as I could get. I didn't want it to be like Pop Warner, where I barely got a chance.

And I didn't wanna let my B team friends down. We'd been practicing together, and they were counting on me. I was doing so well that Coach had even made me the third-string quarterback and kicker, in addition to starting me as a running back. For a while, I thought I might start as kicker, too, because I did great during practice, but I choked up during the games, so that's why I was just third-string. *(Jo's note: It was also that Emily was up against some pretty stiff competition. The kid that landed the starting spot on the A team was Justin Tucker, who eventually went on to play for the University of Texas and the Baltimore Ravens and is now the best kicker in the NFL.)*

It turned out that it was okay that I said no to playing on the A team. Ben was really proud of me just for being asked.

When I got to school the day of our first game, I saw that the cheerleaders had arrived early and decorated the halls and cafeteria. There were signs saying, "We're #1!" and "Go Cougars." There were balloons and ribbons, and it felt like a party. When I got to my locker, I saw a sign taped to it saying, "#21 Ivester Rocks!" It was actually happening. My first middle school game.

We got out of school early to suit up. I had to go to the girls' locker room to change, but then I joined the boys for the pregame team meeting. Coach Long gave a speech about how hard he knew we'd worked and that it all was leading up to this first game. That those two-a-day practices had been worth it because we were totally ready. That he knew we were going to get out on the field and make our school proud. Then we all started chanting, "Cougars! Cougars!" and ran for the bus.

As we took the field to warm up, there was a big cheer from the stands. Lots of parents had driven up for the game even though it took almost an hour to get there with the afternoon traffic.

I started running routes with my teammates and could feel the sweat pouring down my face. It was September and the temperatures had dropped from their August highs, but it was still close to one hundred degrees out.

After a while, Coach called us off the field to rest while the home team warmed up. He gave a mini-version of his locker room speech, and then we all circled up to yell "Go, Cougars!" one last time before taking the field.

We won the coin toss and started the game with a series of short passes and quick runs. You could feel the excitement in the stands. Within minutes, we were on the other team's twenty-yard line. Then they hardened up, and we had eight yards to go on the third down. Coach called a time-out, and as we huddled up on the sidelines drinking some water, he said, "Emily, are you up for getting us a first down?"

"Yes, sir!" I snapped back sharply, feeling a lot more nervous than I sounded.

"Eight yards, fast and quick."

"I can do it, Coach!" I said.

It seemed like time slowed down, and my vision grew suddenly sharper as the quarterback handed me the ball. I saw an opening and dashed past the first-down marker. Then I realized there was only one defender between me and the goal. As he tried to tackle me, I juked him out, faking to the left and then running right. In an instant, I was over the goal line and my teammates were jumping on top of me. I had just scored the first touchdown of the season.

Jeremy playing football in seventh grade (12)

I can't remember what happened the rest of the game, other than that we dominated and the final score was pretty lopsided. By the end, my throat felt raw from cheering so much, but I didn't feel tired at all. Just incredibly excited and not sure how I'd be able to sit still and watch the A team play their game.

While they warmed up, I made my way into the bleachers to sit with my folks. I was so pumped up that I ran up the bleacher steps. As I passed some moms from the other team, I heard one say, "There's Number Twenty-One. He's really good." At that moment, I took off my helmet and my long hair tumbled out.

Dad had suggested to me that I could get my hair cut if I wanted. "You always wear it in a ponytail anyways. Wouldn't it be easier to just keep it short?"

"Nobody else does," I'd answered.

"You don't have to be like everybody else. Besides, lots of women cut their hair short."

"Yeah, but only the moms. I don't want to look like an old lady."

When the moms from the other team saw my long hair, they called out, "Hey, Twenty-One, come over here." So I ran up to them, still holding my helmet.

"It's great to see a *girl* playing football."

"Yes, ma'am," I answered, enjoying the praise but not really liking that it was based on me being different from my teammates.

"And you were the best one on the team."

I knew I should say something good about the other players, but instead, I said, "I just like to play."

"That is so cool," said the first mom. "We played basketball, but nobody would've ever let us play football."

"We think it's fantastic that you're out there with all those boys," said the second mom.

It was a nice ego stroke, but I wanted people to admire me for being a good player, not for being the only girl on the team. Coach thought it was a big deal and was always telling the other players that I tried harder than they did, that I was tougher. My teammates ran faster because they didn't want to be shown up by a girl. Even the high school coaches said that. Ben told me one of them joked around with him, saying they were going to trade him with the middle school so I could be on the high school team.

When we're on the field and suited up, my teammates forget that I'm a girl. With my shoulder pads and helmet, I don't look any different from them, and we're all caught up in the sport. But I feel left out because we're no longer friends off the field. I thought sixth grade was tough, but seventh grade is even worse when it comes to not fitting in.

One day as we were hanging out before practice, waiting for the coaches to show up, I walked up to a group of guys who were laughing together. When I got there, though, they all went quiet. Whatever they were talking about, they didn't want to discuss it in front of me. Maybe it was girls, or their junk, but it made me really uncomfortable.

So I climbed into the stands to sit alone, thinking, *It's okay that they don't want me around. I can deal.* But I couldn't. I couldn't make the feeling go away. My throat hurt and my chest tightened, and I felt isolated and deserted as I thought about how long it had been since I'd hung out with my teammates like when we were little kids. I no longer had a social life.

So I found other things to do that didn't include my football teammates. I played basketball and ran track. I joined the art club and even sold a sculpture to the school librarian.

the "swoose"

Fall 2003
Emily (13 years old)

I LOVE PLAYING PERCUSSION WITH THE EIGHTH-grade symphonic band, especially the snare drum, and I'm excited for high school where I'll play in the pit as a freshman and march with the drumline after that. Last year, the high school band was so good that they were invited to the Rose Bowl Parade out in California. There's a rumor that at some point while I'm in high school, we'll get to perform at Carnegie Hall in New York City.

Next year, girls and boys wear the same uniform, and I'm looking forward to that. But for performances with the symphonic band, girls have to wear long black skirts and white blouses. I wanted to dress like the boys in their shirts and slacks, so I went to Mr. Fischer, the assistant director who taught percussion, and said, "It's really awkward to wear a skirt when I'm moving instruments around. Can I wear pants instead?"

What I said was logical, given that the percussion players, unlike the rest of the band, have to maneuver drums and keyboards about in between pieces. But I knew I could make a skirt work. The real reason I asked was that I hated wearing girls' clothing. Mr. Fischer didn't seem to give it a second thought, though, and said, "Sure."

I couldn't stop grinning the whole performance.

Spring 2004
Emily (14 years old)

BAND WAS GREAT AND I PLAYED BASKETBALL ALL winter. I like going to school each day and even got elected president of the art club. But I don't have any close friends. No matter how involved I get in all the extracurricular stuff, I'm lonely.

My friendship with Sammy helps a lot, even though he's only nine years old. I treat him the way Ben used to treat me, teaching him how to play sports, watching TV together, and playing video games. We hang out all the time after school, and he never seems to care that I'm boyish.

I want to continue being buddies with Ben, but that's not happening. I know it's natural for an older sibling not to want a younger one around, but I miss the days when Ben didn't mind me being there with his friends. Sometimes he lets Sammy stick around, which makes me miss it even more, but I know Sammy is still little-kid cute and funny, and I've grown beyond that.

Sometimes Ben teases Sammy the way he used to tease me. You wouldn't think it would feel good to have somebody make fun of you, but it did. I liked it when Ben and his friends used to challenge me to lift a weight that was too heavy for me and then laugh when I'd struggle and make grunting noises. It was great when they wrestled with me. I couldn't pin them unless they let me, but they respected me for trying. Now Ben's decided I've outgrown that, and I feel like, "Hey, you just wrestled Sammy, I want to wrestle too." It sucks.

The hardest part of Ben getting older is that he has

the "swoose"

this brotherly relationship with Sammy that excludes me. Ben imparts words of wisdom about how to behave around girls and the bro code, and I want him to do that with me too, even though that doesn't quite make sense.

So I focused on sports. After the basketball season ended, I signed up to run track. I even placed second in district for running the hurdles. During the last week of middle school, there was an awards presentation for athletics. First Coach Long announced the top boy in each individual sport. Then he presented a special award for the best all-around male athlete.

When he was done, the volleyball coach did the same for the girls. But when she finished with the individual sports, she didn't move on to the best all-around girl athlete. Instead, she said, "I'm going to break with tradition now, and ask Coach Buzbee to join me on stage. You'll understand why in a moment."

When Coach Buzbee took the mic, he described my entire middle school sports career. Then he said, "Emily has been a real asset to the football team. She's the only girl in the history of the school to have played in both seventh and eighth grade, and I'm proud to have been her coach. Emily Ivester, please come up to receive the award for best all-around female athlete."

six

ARE YOU GAY?

—·—

Fall 2001 — Austin, TX

Jo

After her incredible success with sports in middle school, ninth grade seemed a bit of a letdown for Emily. Jon and I weren't quite sure what was going on with her, but we could see she was drifting. She still derived a lot of happiness from sports, making the softball team at school and getting recruited to be the goalie for a recreational soccer team. She played in the drum pit with the school band. But she didn't hang out with anyone outside of her scheduled activities. Instead, she spent a lot of time on her own and didn't appear interested in developing deeper friendships.

I tried to encourage her to socialize more, but she resisted. Over dinner one night, I asked, "Do you want to have your basketball team over for a pool party?"

"No, that's okay," she answered, not taking the bait.

Jon tried as well. "Is it pretty much the same girls that you played with last year? Anyone we know?"

"Some," Emily mumbled between mouthfuls of spaghetti, one of her favorites. We waited for her to elaborate, but she remained quiet.

Jon and I had talked about it the previous night while the kids were away at practice and study groups. It was still warm outside, but I'd built a fire for the ambiance and we were enjoying the peace and quiet after the hub-bub of the dinner we'd managed to squeeze in. Sitting in the family room, we chatted about Jon's day at work and my day subbing at school for one of the math teachers before moving on to discussing how each of the kids was doing.

"She doesn't even know the names of her teammates," Jon said when we got to talking about Emily, both of us worried that something was stopping her from getting close to anyone.

"Yeah," I answered, having noticed the same thing. "It's almost like she's become antisocial."

We found it confusing that Emily was such a loner. Elizabeth and Ben were always surrounded by friends, and we'd assumed that Emily would be the same.

"Do you think something is going on?" Jon asked.

"Like what?" I responded, not really wanting to put my concerns into words, as that made them more real.

"Is she, um, depressed, maybe?"

I didn't think so. Although she stayed by herself a lot, it seemed reasonable that she'd need some downtime. So much of her day was scheduled that she barely had time to stop for meals. We'd actually encouraged her to back off of some of her commitments, afraid that she'd make herself sick playing two sports at once and getting up for band practice before dawn.

"No, but I think it's possible that she's gay," I said in a

rush of words, verbalizing for the first time a thought that had occurred to me a while back.

"Maybe," Jon said, adding that he'd been thinking the same thing. "She's never shown any interest in boys. By this age, Elizabeth was already on her second boyfriend."

"Should we say anything?" I asked, always impatient to take whatever steps were needed to reach some sort of closure so we could move forward.

"I think we should wait," said Jon.

"I just want her to know that we'd be okay with it."

While I waited for Jon to consider what we should do next, I thought about what I'd said. Of course we'd be okay with it. She was our child. When I'd learned in my late teens and early twenties that my brother Charles and sister Connie were gay, I'd found it easy to accept, fairly quickly progressing from thinking it strange to feeling a sense of pride for their willingness to be open about who they are.

Our mother was supportive right from the beginning, although her initial response to Charles was a little strange. He had just turned twenty-one and they were celebrating over dinner in a restaurant when he told her that he had a boyfriend he wanted her to meet. When she didn't respond, he said, "What do you think? How do you feel?"

"Charles," she said, "I will always love you."

"But what do you think about me being gay?" he prodded.

"It's much better than if you told me you'd taken twenty-six children and buried them in a quarry so you could ransom them off." It was 1976, and the Chowchilla kidnapping had been front-page news the week before. The horror of it was still on everyone's mind. "I would hate to be the mother of one of those men."

"But you're okay being the mother of a gay man," he said. "That's better than being the mother of a kidnapper."

"Yes," she'd answered, not catching the irony in his voice. "I'm absolutely okay with that. You're my son. Now, tell me about your boyfriend." With that, she accepted not only that Charles was gay but also that he was in a relationship.

A few years later, Charles invited our mother to join him for the tenth anniversary of the first Los Angeles Pride Parade. When she showed up at the staging ground, the organizers greeted her warmly and asked if she'd mind walking with the first row of marchers. They thought her gray hair and tiny stature—she's only four foot ten—would make people notice her and think, "Aww, how cute." Then they handed her a sign that read, "We Love Our Gay Children!" All through the parade, people kept running up and hugging her. She didn't understand why until one young man said, "Your sign is beautiful. My mother doesn't love me. She says she can't because I'm gay."

Charles had known he was gay long before he came out to our mother. As a child and a teenager, he'd felt rejected by our dad and believed that was at least in part due to what he perceived as our dad's lack of acceptance of him being gay. My brother felt as if he were constantly being judged by our father and said that Dad was "mortified by the thought of having sired an effeminate, weird, and disturbing son."

Charles ran away in the early '70s at only fourteen years old. He bounced around between living on the street and sharing a shack with two other runaways, finding odd jobs to provide a little bit of cash. Although he returned to Miami a year or so later, he never again lived with our family.

Knowing how damaged Charles felt by what he saw as our father's rejection and how he treasured our mother's love for him, it was important to me to be sure Emily knew that we would completely support her, that her sexual orientation was not an issue for us. I kept coming back to the idea and began to see all of her behavior through that lens. I reflected on her friendships the summer before high school, when she'd mostly hung out with our neighbors Karl and Jacob, who were classmates as well as friends. They came over almost every day to shoot baskets with Emily, and I was sure this was their way of flirting.

Jacob was a skinny, long-legged boy with jet-black hair and a soft-spoken manner. His family was from Thailand, and his mom ran one of our favorite restaurants. He enjoyed cooking and often came inside after shooting baskets so that he and Emily could experiment with recipes they'd found online. Usually their results were delicious, though every once in a while they had to throw everything away because it was inedible. Sometimes I overheard them talking. It was always very task-focused, never personal stuff. Just what ingredients they needed and how hot to make the oven.

Back in middle school, I'd often seen Jacob at Emily's basketball games and knew he came specifically to watch her, but she was oblivious to his interest. When I pointed it out to her, she'd said, "He doesn't think of me like that. He likes girly girls."

"What makes you say that?" I asked.

"All my guy friends do," she said.

"Do you want them to like you?" I asked. "Because if you do, you can say something."

"Mom, no!"

"Or give them a signal. You can smile. Or flirt back."

"Just stop. I'm not interested."

Once the school year started, Emily still never talked about boys, even when lots of her classmates were pairing off and experimenting with romance. I truly wasn't bothered by the thought that she might be gay, other than the fear any parent might have that their kid would face discrimination and bullying. What did disturb me, however, was the possibility that Emily was isolating herself because she didn't accept herself, whether because she was gay or for some other reason.

Emily didn't seem unhappy as the fall progressed, but we couldn't ignore her difficulties with her schoolwork. Her geometry teacher called us in for a conference. When we arrived, the students were gone and the room was quiet. Mrs. Wilson, sitting behind her desk and grading homework, looked up and gestured for us to take a couple of seats in the front row. Setting aside the papers, she thanked us for coming and began to talk about what the students were studying.

Letting my mind wander, I noticed the geometric shapes covering the bulletin boards and the colorful three-dimensional models sitting on a table in front. I stared at the dodecahedron, slowly counting its twelve sides, remembering how much I'd enjoyed studying math when I was a child. How could a couple of MIT grads produce a kid that didn't like math?

"I know Emily's smart," Mrs. Wilson said, pulling me back into the moment. "But she won't pay attention. She stares out the window most of the time and draws cartoons instead of taking notes."

Then she handed us a piece of paper from the pile on

her desk. It was the previous night's homework, covered with sketches. We'd seen the same drawings over and over again at home. Emily spent hours drawing pictures of teenage boys. Always boys. She said they were easier to draw than girls. Maybe they were. It certainly wasn't because she was dreaming about boyfriends.

The afternoon following the teacher conference, as I was driving Emily home from soccer practice, I asked, "How's school going?" I wanted to start with something pretty safe.

"Kind of boring," she answered.

"Why's that? Don't you like any of your teachers?"

"I don't dislike them."

"What is it then?"

"I dunno."

This was fairly typical. No matter how I approached it, I couldn't get Emily to talk about school. She didn't seem to care. After driving silently for a while, I commented on soccer practice, observing that I'd seen her make some pretty impressive saves. Finally, after that conversation ran out of steam, I decided the time was right to ask her about her sexuality, ignoring Jon's comments that we needed to let her find her own way.

"Emily," I said quietly. "Do you think you might be gay?"

"Wait, wh—?"

"You never talk about boys."

"Mom!"

"I'm just throwing it out there because Dad and I want you to know that if you are, we're fine with it."

"Ummm . . ."

"And so would everyone else in the family." I knew

that to be true. Elizabeth, Ben, and Sammy were aware of Charles and Connie being gay and were totally accepting of both of them.

For a while, Emily sat there quietly, uncomfortably. I matched her silence, waiting for her to say something, anything.

Then she laughed that kind of nervous giggle she had that could mean anything from "I don't want to talk about it" to "That's really funny."

The laugh broadened, and I relaxed as I realized this was the latter kind. She'd found my comment so strange as to be entertaining. "Mom, I'm not gay."

"Okay."

"I'm not." Then she grew serious again. "I'm just not interested."

"Do you think that might be because you're attracted to girls and haven't accepted that? Is it possible you're in the closet and don't even know it?"

"No, Mom," she said. "I'm not attracted to anyone."

Spring 2005
Emily (15 years old)

IT'S PRETTY COOL THAT MY MOM TALKS WITH ME about all sorts of stuff and asks me questions and listens when I answer. But she went overboard when we were driving around and she asked if I might be gay. When we got home, I found Sammy and Ben up in the game room over our garage. They were playing video games, so I picked up one of the controllers, waiting for a chance to join in. Before the next game started, though, I told them what had happened. "You won't believe how ridiculous Mom was and what she said in the car."

"Well—what?" Ben asked.

"She asked if I'm gay."

I waited for them to burst out laughing or say, "Wow! Yeah, Mom's really crazy." But they didn't. Instead, Ben said, "What did you answer?"

"No, of course."

I was stunned by Ben's question. Time stopped. My brothers started the next game, but I couldn't even try to play. I was frozen, confused. How could Ben not have known? Why did he think it was a possibility that I was gay? What did he and Mom see that I didn't?

I hadn't put it into words before, but when it came down to it, I've known for a long time that I am different from other teenagers. Calling myself a tomboy no longer captures it. And it never really did. Tomboys dress like boys and play with boys, but it is so much more than that for me. I really want to *be* one of the boys, not just be like them.

Fall 2006
Emily (16 years old)

RIDING ON THE BAND BUS, HEADING BACK TO THE high school after a big football win near the start of my junior year, I tried really hard to want to kiss a guy. I was sitting with my drumline friends, five of us, three boys, one other girl, and me. I'm still pretty much a loner except for my band friends, but they seem to like me and we hang out sometimes. During lunch, we sometimes sneak off campus and go to my house to eat and jump in the pool. On weekends, we lie out in the sun or play Ultimate Frisbee at Zilker Park. Liza Baskin is our ringleader. She's a senior and captain of the drumline and is always suggesting pretty silly stuff for us to do.

Like "car surfing." We're usually the last ones in the high school lot after games because we have to put away all the percussion instruments. Before driving home, Liza sometimes says, "Who wants to go?" One of us climbs up onto the roof of her car and poses as if on a surfboard, and then she drives in big loops around the empty parking lot. It feels like she's going fifty miles an hour, though I'm guessing she's barely moving since none of us have ever fallen off.

Kissing on the band bus was also Liza's suggestion. We were on the way home after a football game when she said, "Hey, guys, I've got this wild, crazy idea. Let's play rock, paper, scissors, and whoever wins gets to kiss one of the others."

(Years from now, I will realize that Liza was looking for a safe way to make herself kiss a guy. Sometime during college, she will come out as gay. But now, in high school, she's in denial and trying to make herself be attracted to guys. In some ways, we're feeling the same insecurities and pressures, but for different reasons.)

The boys were all sophomores, and Liza's suggestion seemed pretty harmless.

Matthew, a redheaded boy with curly hair and round glasses, won the game. "Oh, yeah," he said, looking at me. "You're it."

I just kind of stared at him without moving. I didn't want him to kiss me. I was actually queasy but felt like I couldn't say no. More than that, I wanted to believe that I'd be okay with him kissing me. Kind of like when I make myself taste food I've never had before and discover it's delicious.

It was over quick. Matthew leaned in and gave me a quick peck on the mouth, barely making contact. No long look or pretense at romance. We could have been ten years old for all the passion we put into it. I was relieved that it hadn't been anything more.

A few minutes later, he asked if he could try again. But we weren't playing the game anymore, and that made it seem more real, more grown-up. I shrugged and said, "No, I'm not into it." He looked like a sad puppy and I felt bad for him, but I couldn't make myself want to kiss him.

Soon after that, Liza started teasing me in the band dressing room, saying that I'm gay and just don't know it yet. When I told her that I'm not, she said, "You have to be, Emily. I know a girl that likes you. Don't you want to know who it is?"

"Not really," I answered, wondering if she was talking about herself. "I don't like anyone that way."

"You don't have a crush on some girl?"

"No."

"Or a boy?"

"No."

Fall 2006

Jo

THE PHONE RANG AS I RETURNED HOME AFTER dropping Sammy off at Hill Country for his early morning football practice. As a parent, I always fretted about the possibility of sports injuries, but it never occurred to me anything could happen in drumline. But it did. That morning, the phone call was from the nurse at Westlake High. Emily had collapsed during marching band practice.

I tried not to imagine all the different possibilities. She had been tired for weeks, forcing herself to go to band and soccer practices. We worried that she did too much, that we should restrict her activities and not let her overcommit, but she always seemed so confident that she could do it all.

"What happened?" I asked as I sat on her bed an hour later, trying to get her to drink some water. She'd already told me that her stomach hurt terribly.

"I was okay until I picked up my harness," she said. I pictured the twenty-five-pound drum setup that she wore as they marched up and down the football field. I hadn't believed her when she first told me how much it weighed. Not until I picked it up myself and realized she hadn't been exaggerating. "Then I got this stabbing feeling and my knees buckled. My friends half carried me over to the stands, and I lay there for a while until practice was over."

"Why didn't you go to the nurse right away?" I asked.

"I didn't want to make a big deal over it." That sounded like Emily. "It's better now that I'm lying down."

I picked up our six-year-old miniature dachshund, Indy,

and placed her on the covers. She nestled her long body up against Emily and curled right into Emily's side, her short tail wagging, her big eyes closed as if showing Emily how to relax.

A week later, Emily was still exhausted and complained that her abdomen hurt if she moved around. I visited the school and picked up her homework assignments, but she showed no interest in them and just wanted to reread all her *Harry Potter* books. The pediatrician thought it might be an ulcer and sent us to a gastroenterologist. She disagreed but didn't have any better ideas. So it was back to the pediatrician, who sent us to a surgeon.

After exploratory surgery, the surgeon said that Emily had ruptured an ovary. He believed that to be both the cause of the pain and the source of some blood he found pooling at the bottom of her abdominal cavity. We waited weeks to see a gynecologist. She took one look at the surgery photos and said that the ovaries were normal, not ruptured at all. When our pediatrician couldn't think of any other explanations, she recommended a pain specialist. He gave Emily some tools for dealing with the pain—self-hypnosis, visualization, biofeedback, massage—but we were no closer to figuring out why Emily hurt.

Fall 2007

Jo

A YEAR WENT BY, AND WE LOST TRACK OF THE number of specialists Emily had seen. She dropped out of drumline, stopped playing sports, could only drag herself to school about one day a week, and was barely passing her classes. The doctors gave up on a physical explanation and began to talk about depression, anxiety, and stress. They prescribed antidepressants, anti-anxiety pills, and muscle relaxants, all to no avail. Jon and I grew pessimistic and started to believe that we'd never figure it out.

We sat quietly on the living room couch after dinner one night, keeping our voices low so that none of the kids could overhear.

"I'm fighting hard to be hopeful," I said. "But I'm scared this is it, that this is Emily's life now. Am I overreacting?"

Jon put his arm around my shoulder and pulled me in close to him, leaning his head on mine. "No," he said. "Sometimes I feel the same way."

"What are we going to do?"

"I don't know," he said. "I don't know."

"We've run out of specialists."

"We must have missed something," he said. "Maybe there's some underlying cause that's behind both the abdominal pain and the depression."

"Or maybe the pain is causing the depression," I responded. "If we can fix the pain, maybe she'll perk up and start engaging again."

Jon was frustrated that Emily didn't seem interested at all in staying caught up at school. "I don't get it," he said. "She can sit for hours looking at her computer, but she won't study."

"That takes more effort," I said.

We'd had this discussion before. Jon wanted Emily to learn how to live with the pain, to push through it and graduate. He suggested that we get her into some sort of counseling so that she could do that. Her older siblings expressed a similar frustration, Elizabeth from her home in Philadelphia, where she'd found work as a consultant after graduating from Penn, and Ben from Lehigh, where he was a sophomore playing football and majoring in supply chain management. Like their father, they wondered if Emily simply wasn't trying hard enough.

I focused instead on just trying to keep her from going stir-crazy. I took her to the movies when she felt well enough and out for lunch on the few exceptionally good days. I never shared with her that Jon and I worried about the possibility that she wouldn't ever recover and would instead have to live with us her whole life.

I made the hollow promise, "Everything's going to be fine." When she showed me the lyrics of a song she'd composed, "If You Say," I thought that maybe I'd convinced her.

Did you believe what you said when you said things
    were gonna be fine?
'Cause I'm thinking that I'm sinking, falling further
    behind.
I don't know where to go, what to do to resolve this
    mess.
Things have changed, rearranged, and not for the
    best.
But if you say everything's OK,
I'll trust your word that they'll work out that way.
And if you say that you know what to do,
I'll listen close and pin my hopes on you.
So don't let me down.
Don't raise my hopes just to jerk me around.

Was I jerking her around? Was there really no hope? As I sat by her side, I thought, *She'll never graduate from high school or go to college. We'll never be empty nesters. I'm going to grow old taking care of Emily.* It was hard to be okay with that, to give up on my dreams for her of a fulfilling life with a family and a career. It was overwhelming.

seven

THE OLD COLLEGE TRY

—·—

Spring 2008 — Austin, TX
Emily (18 years old)

I expected to be drumline captain my senior year, but I missed too many practices. At first I was named co-captain, with the hope that I could still take a leadership role, but I couldn't keep up, so, oh well. What was supposed to be an awesome year . . . well, it wasn't.

I've gone as long as a month before the pain kicks in again. That's allowed me to stay caught up in school enough to have a shot at graduating on time. I even went to a summer program for a week at Cornell University, just before the school year started. It was for students wanting to major in architecture and my instructors said I had real talent, especially when it came to converting my two-dimensional drawings into three-dimensional models.

Mom helped me investigate college architecture programs, even though I'd pretty much given up on being able to go to college. I've barely been getting by in my classes and for a long time couldn't make myself care about filling out applications. Not just because my body hurts so much of the time. It's also that I'm spending a lot of emotional energy trying to define myself and figure out why I have no interest in dating. It's easy to attribute that to how much pain I'm in, but that doesn't quite capture it for me.

Even if I were pain-free, I wouldn't want to be in a relationship with anyone. What does that mean? Why don't I have the same drives and desires as everyone else? Why do I hate dressing up and feel so much more comfortable in baggy clothes? And why can't I put more effort into my schoolwork and the college search? Even when the pain recedes, it's so much easier to read my books, play video games, and watch TV.

Eventually, Mom insisted that I get the school applications done. She sat by my side, watched me browse through college websites, and didn't leave until I'd submitted several applications. I actually got pretty excited about the possibilities and decided it would be fun to be up in the mountains, where I can go snowboarding if I ever feel well enough. And I'm drawn to the Pacific Northwest, with its outdoorsy culture and laid-back lifestyle. Growing up skiing with my family in the Colorado Rockies makes that a natural choice for me.

During one of the times when I was feeling okay, we flew to Washington and checked out schools there and in Idaho and Montana. While we were on the road, I got an acceptance letter from Montana State University. By the time we arrived at the campus in Bozeman, I already knew that's where I wanted to go.

Jeremy (18) during senior year of high school

Summer 2008
Emily (18 years old)

SOMEHOW, I MANAGED TO GRADUATE AND FOUND a job as a host at Macaroni Grill. The pain isn't as bad, and attending Montana State University in the fall is looking more and more likely. In the meantime, I've enjoyed socializing with my coworkers at the restaurant. They're all in their late teens and early twenties, and it's fun to grab a late dinner with them after the place closes for the night.

After I'd been hosting for a few weeks, one of the guys, Jake, asked me out. I thought it might be fun. He's a couple of years older than me, but not much more experienced at relationships and a little bit awkward. He wears his hair parted down the middle and almost long enough in back to wear a ponytail. He always smiles at me and is kind of sweet.

So even though I wasn't comfortable with the idea of a date, I agreed to go. I could tell all evening that Jake wanted to take my hand. But he was nervous, so instead he kept touching my arm as if by accident, like when he held the car door open for me. After dinner, he drove to this deserted spot looking out over Highway 360. I knew that high school kids sometimes went there to drink and make out. I told myself I could do the same. Maybe if I drank enough wine, I would want to kiss him. I mean, a real kiss. Not like the childish ones with my drumline friends a few years back.

We got out of the car and stepped over the chain that stopped cars from getting too close to the edge of the cliff. We found a big, flat rock and sat next to each other, our shoulders touching. Slowly, Jake turned toward me, his face close to mine. I could smell the wine on his breath and see that he was sweating a bit, even though it had already cooled off for the evening.

Then we kissed. Or I should say, he kissed me, very tentatively. Barely more than his lips dryly brushing against mine. I didn't kiss him back.

Instead, I pulled away. "Ummm . . ."

"What's wrong?"

"This isn't working for me."

"I—I'm sorry. I shouldn't have done that."

"No, no. It's not that. It's . . ."

I couldn't get any more words out. I couldn't explain to Jake that I didn't feel anything. No matter how much I wanted to. No matter how hard I tried. Nothing. He drove me home in silence, looking just as miserable as I felt.

What's wrong with me?

Fall 2008

Emily (18 years old)

I LOVE MONTANA STATE UNIVERSITY. IT'S PERFECT for me in so many ways. I love the old buildings and the mountains that surround it on three sides. Students dress the way I do in practical, androgynous clothing. Jeans and flannel shirts everywhere I look. No girly girl clothes. The Bridger Bowl ski resort is less than a half hour away, and there's a bus I'll be able to take from campus any day I finish classes early enough. That is, assuming I'm healthy enough to snowboard once the season starts.

The percussion teacher doesn't care that I missed my senior year on drumline. When we visited campus last spring, he'd just taken my word for it that I could play and didn't even make me audition. I guess he figured that if I was good enough for a Texas high school marching band, I was good enough for MSU.

Band members start practice two weeks before classes,

so I arrived on campus in mid-August and stepped into an instant group of friends. I desperately want to believe that my fresh start at MSU is going to work. New friends. Not getting behind in my classes. Marching down the main street of Bozeman before each football game, successfully carrying the same twenty-five-pound snare drum that gave me so much trouble in high school. In my first month at MSU, I haven't had to stay in bed for more than a few hours at a time, so I'm letting myself be optimistic.

Winter 2009
Emily (19 years old)

AS I WOKE UP IN MY DORM ROOM, I COULD practically smell the snow that had fallen while I slept. My roommate and fellow drumline member, Jessie, was still asleep and wouldn't get up for another hour. It was Thursday, and I knew I could sleep in as well since my architectural history class didn't start until ten. But I loved the early morning, when it was all so quiet. And the pain hadn't started yet. Each day, I lie in bed thinking, "Maybe today's the day that the pain won't come back."

I was feeling okay that morning and ran out quickly for breakfast. When I got back, Jessie was just waking up. She looked out the window, saw the snow, and said, "Hey, let's go sledding! We've got time before class."

She's our ringleader, just as Liza was in high school. A boisterous girl with long hair and an infectious laugh, Jessie is always suggesting something fun, like sledding when we have no sleds. "Don't worry about that," she said when I pointed that out. "I know where we can find some old boxes. They'll work. You'll see."

It sounded great. I hadn't played in the snow since I was a little kid, and I couldn't wait. The boxes were in the trash room in the basement of the dorm. We each selected the largest, sturdiest one we could find and then stomped on them until they were completely flat. Without even bothering to put on our gloves and heavy coats, we ran up the stairs to the first-floor exit and dashed to the top of a nearby hill, our breath visible in the icy air.

With an experienced flourish, Jessie flicked her box down into the snow and jumped on as it tipped over the crest of the hill. As she slid, she gained speed with each passing second. Laughing and screeching, she managed to stay on for about thirty feet before toppling over and landing facedown. Standing quickly and brushing the snow off, she called back up the hill, "Your turn!"

Slightly more cautious than Jessie, I sat on my box before putting it in motion. Then I pushed off with my hands until gravity took over. With the wind in my face, the mountains almost on top of us, and the sense of exhilaration, I hadn't felt that happy in a long time. As soon as the hill leveled out and I came to a stop, I grabbed my box and rushed back up to the top, not caring that my boots slipped deep into the snow and my jeans were almost soaked through.

Again and again I flew down the hill, my cheeks tired from laughing so hard. Then, all of a sudden, the laughter began to hurt. As if someone had pulled a switch, all the pain from the last two years came racing back, sharper than ever before. I held my left side, frantically trying to will away the nausea and hold back the tears. When my box stopped sliding, I lay in the snow and curled up into a ball.

When I didn't get up, Jessie raced over, worried that I'd broken a leg or something like that. I couldn't talk and felt light-headed. I realized I was hyperventilating, so I cupped my hands over my nose and mouth and forced myself to slow my breathing. Jessie knelt beside me with her hands on my shoulders, trying to get my attention. "Focus," she said, with her face inches from mine. "Tell me what's happening."

"My side . . ." was all I could say.

"Can you stand?"

I nodded. Jessie slipped her hands under my arms and helped me up. Leaving the boxes at the bottom of the hill, she half dragged me back to our dorm room and lay me down on my bed, wet jeans and all.

"You need to go to the clinic," she said.

"It'll go away," I said. "I just need to rest."

"This isn't normal, Emily."

"I know. But I'll be okay. I just need to lie here for a while. You should go to class." With that, I closed my eyes and willed myself to relax, breathing slowly and deeply, trying to figure out why the pain was back and why it was so much worse than it had been during the last bout.

Jessie must have thought I'd fallen asleep because she whispered, "I'm gonna go, but I'll be back in an hour. If you're still feeling rough, we're going to the clinic." With that, she closed the door behind her and I was alone.

There was no way I could go to my architectural history class. I tried to sleep, but I kept worrying that this was the start of falling behind, just as I'd done in all my high school classes.

Two weeks later, I was ready to give up. I'd tried going to a few classes once my abdomen felt a little better, but I couldn't follow what my professors were saying, either because I hadn't studied the material or because I hurt so much that I couldn't concentrate.

Three weeks later, I called to tell my folks I wanted to come home.

They showed up the next day and arranged for a medical withdrawal for me, which meant I'd have a clean record. As far as MSU was concerned, it was as if I'd never enrolled. No incompletes or failing grades. The chance for a fresh start in January, after I was feeling better.

With that as our "plan of record," as Dad said, we left my books and clothes boxed up in a basement storage area, ready to unpack when I returned. I had to believe that the pain would go away and I'd be back for the spring semester.

For weeks, I lay about at home in Austin, reading, playing video games, writing songs, Indy always by my side, the fur around her face a little more gray than it had been when I first left for college. By the end of the Christmas holidays, I felt ready to fly back to Montana and try again.

It's been a month since I arrived back at school, and I've been in pain frequently enough during this time that I've already fallen hopelessly behind. My parents are coming to get me today. This time, they'll pack up my stuff and ship it home to Texas.

I've failed my first year of college.

Self-portrait. Sketched by Jeremy Ivester

Spring 2009 — Austin, TX
Jon

"HERE WE GO AGAIN." THAT WAS MY FIRST REACTION when Jo told me about it. Emily had stopped going to classes, was far behind in her schoolwork, and wanted to come home. The pain had returned.

It was frustrating because I'd thought Emily had

turned a corner, that either the pain had receded or she'd learned to live her life fully despite her chronic condition. All through the previous summer I'd been upbeat whenever she was near, talking about how great college would be as I made pancakes and muffins from millet or amaranth flour, anything but wheat. We'd been told that wheat was causing her pain and if only we'd clear it from her system, she'd get better.

It had seemed to work, and the fall semester had gotten off to a good start. Jo and I had flown to Bozeman to watch Emily parade down East Main Street with the MSU marching band celebrating the start of the Bobcat football season. We'd listened to her stories of skateboarding across campus to get to and from classes, pleased that she seemed to be able to once again exert herself physically. We'd heard about her new friends in the dorm.

I'd felt relieved that I could stop worrying so much about her. In the back of my mind, though, her pain was an unsolved mystery, and I was angry at my inability to help her. And maybe a bit angry with her as well, both for feeling the pain and for not being able to deal with it.

When Emily had called about six weeks into the fall semester and said she needed to come home, neither Jo nor I expressed the fear and frustration we felt. Instead, we did what we'd always done through the years and simply took care of our child. We flew to Bozeman, put on a happy face, worked with the MSU administration to effect a medical withdrawal, packed up Emily's things, and brought her home to Austin.

Once she was settled in her old bedroom, life seemed to stand still as Emily did little more than sleep. I worried that the pain would never subside. That she was going to live a constrained life and have to figure out how to be happy and productive despite it. She wasn't ready for that, not by a long shot. She wanted to be cured, to be normal. She thought it unfair and didn't want to make any compromises with an unfair world. I was desperate, scared that my daughter would withdraw from the world altogether.

Throughout the holiday season, Emily had reverted to childhood, spending her days in pajamas in our family room, watching TV, surfing the web, playing the piano or drawing. Jo and I tried to focus on the positive, assuring her that she would soon return to Montana and that everything would be okay.

She did begin the spring semester, but only a few weeks passed before Emily gave up again. I couldn't stop thinking that she'd actually given up before she even arrived. I was crushed.

eight

"IS THAT EVEN POSSIBLE?"

—·—

Summer 2009

Emily (19 years old)

There hasn't been a whole lot to do since I got home from MSU, even when I've felt well enough to get up. I've been hanging out with Sammy and taking classes at Austin Community College. Mostly, though, I've been writing music. I messed around with a little composing at the piano back in high school, but lately, I've been taking it more seriously, pouring all my frustrations into the lyrics.

Sometimes I write songs about being in a relationship, even though I've never been in one; I'm still waiting to be attracted to someone. I tell myself it's not happening because I'm in pain so much of the time, that I can't think about being with someone else when it hurts just to be with myself. Nobody else knows how much I hurt, though, physically or emotionally. Whenever they ask, which is often, I always tell my parents, "I'm fine."

When I say, "I'll be fine," it means I'm far behind
See I just refuse to give you bad news.
And I just can't stand leaving doubt in your head

So ask me again how I am.
I'm fine, I'll be fine.

When I tell you just go away, it means I want you to
stay.
See I just don't like looking weak in your eyes
And I've convinced myself that I don't need your
help.
When I say it's not that bad, it means I'm hurt and
I'm sad.

I'm fine,
I'm fine,
I'm fine,
I'm lying.

Summer 2009
Jo

JON TOOK SOME TIME OFF FROM WORK SO WE could spend a few days together with Sammy and Emily at South Padre Island, a resort at the southern tip of Texas, a few miles north of the border with Mexico. Emily didn't get out on the beach much, but she did enjoy watching the windsurfers through our window.

The car ride down had been difficult for her. She'd moaned every time we went over a bump. During the ride back, the pain grew worse. She started groaning and laughing and crying all at the same time. She said she couldn't catch her breath, and we realized that what sounded like laughter wasn't that at all.

We stopped at a gas station so Emily could lie down on the back seat while we tried to get her to breathe normally. Thinking she might be hyperventilating, we sent Sammy inside for a paper bag for her to hold up to her mouth. Jon rubbed her shoulders while I kept my face close to hers, breathing deliberately and slowly with her.

A less extreme version of this had happened a few weeks earlier when Emily and I were driving home from the movies. Not knowing what else to do, I'd taken her to an emergency room. The staff hadn't been able to figure out what was hurting, so we'd just waited it out. Given that experience, we waited again that afternoon, just parked at a gas station in the middle of nowhere until the pain subsided.

I had described the previous incident to Jon, but it wasn't until it happened in front of him that he realized how awful it was. Seeing Emily struggle to control her breathing, he began to think there might be a problem with her diaphragm, so he went online to research the possibilities. None of her doctors had mentioned it, but he thought she might have a hernia there.

A FEW DAYS later, Jon told a friend at work, Amy Mitchell, about his new theory. He'd met Amy soon after he left Applied Materials to join a semiconductor start-up called Silicon Laboratories. He ran their worldwide operations, which included buying and managing property. She was the real estate lawyer who'd negotiated the deal when the company grew so rapidly that they'd purchased a pair of buildings in downtown Austin.

Soon after Jon got to know Amy, he said to her, "You

would like my wife, Jo. The two of you would really get along." It wasn't the first time Jon had helped me connect socially with women he knew through work. Whenever he found someone interesting and energetic and smart and caring, he made a point of getting us together. Amy was all that and more, and we'd become good friends, just as Jon expected.

Amy had followed Emily's health issues with great concern for years now and frequently asked if there was anything she could do to help. When Jon shared his theory about a herniated diaphragm, she said, "You need to go see my gastroenterologist, Bob Frachtman. He'll know what to do. He literally saved my life." Dr. Frachtman had identified Amy's cancer when nobody else had found it.

After meeting with him, we felt optimistic for the first time since Emily had dropped out of college. Other physicians had told us there was no physical reason for her pain and that it was due to depression or anxiety. But Dr. Frachtman took the time to identify exactly where the pain was and the motions that made it worse. More importantly, he believed Emily when she said she was depressed because of the pain and not the other way around.

After reviewing all the previous test results and images and listening to Jon's theories, he recommended exploratory surgery with a focus on the upper left abdomen, under the rib cage. He thought the pain was unlikely to be connected to the diaphragm, yet at the same time he was willing to consider that it might not be Emily's digestive system, where everyone else had looked. He thought it could be something entirely different, something not yet contemplated.

Fall 2009

Jo

JON AND I WAITED WHILE EMILY WAS IN surgery with Dr. Brent Victor at the Seton Medical Center. The procedure took longer than expected, and I grew more nervous by the minute. Jon stayed calm. When he said he wasn't worried, I let his soothing voice and words help me hold it together while we sat in the lounge outside the operating room. Finally, Dr. Victor walked in, a sober look on his face. Taking a seat beside us, he said, "Did you know that your daughter has suffered a significant spleen injury?"

"Wh—? No," I answered, confused by his question and not even sure what the spleen did or where it was located.

He pulled out a photo and showed us an image that resembled a cobweb more than anything else. "There's significant scar tissue covering one end of her spleen. It would only be there if she'd taken some serious blow to the area. Usually, we only see this after a car accident or a fall from fairly high up."

"Could this explain the pain Emily's experienced?" asked Jon.

"Absolutely."

"Can you fix it?"

"Already did," he said, his serious expression melting into a smile. "I trimmed away the scar tissue and removed some damaged ligaments. As soon as she recovers from the surgery itself, she should start feeling a lot better."

Was it really this easy? How could it have taken the doctors three years to figure this out? I felt both relieved and furious at the same time. I paced the room frantically, my chest heaving. Jon pulled me back to the couch and we held each other. It was over. After Emily recovered from surgery, the pain would be gone and she could lead a normal life. She could go back to college and play sports and have friends and do everything else we'd been scared was gone forever.

While we waited for Emily to wake up from the anesthesia, my analytical mind quickly moved beyond the emotions and started sifting through memories, trying to understand how it had taken so long to properly diagnose her. Over the next few weeks, Jon and I researched spleen injuries and developed our own theory of what had happened.

Our best explanation was that the afternoon before she'd collapsed at band practice three years earlier, she'd taken a hard kick to the abdomen during a soccer game. We'd watched her lying on the field and figured she'd be out for the rest of the game. But she was such a tough goalie and so strongly committed to the team that she'd gone back into play after resting for only a few minutes. As a result, it hadn't occurred to us that she'd sustained a serious injury, so we never reported it to the doctors.

Once Emily was no longer flying on the adrenaline of the soccer game, the pain had grown worse and worse, and then more damage was done when she picked up her heavy snare drum the following morning. *That* was our focus and it seemed somewhat trivial, so the doctors had never considered a spleen injury.

Each time Emily had felt better and became active, she'd torn scar tissue. Not only had this made the area hurt again, but it also caused blood to accumulate in her abdominal cavity, which was painful in and of itself. She thus experienced an endless cycle of pain and recovery. The surgery was successful at stopping that cycle. As each week passed and Emily grew stronger, Jon and I grew more optimistic and even began encouraging her to return to college after the holidays. We thought that we would be back to normal, whatever that meant.

Fall 2009 — Austin, TX
Emily (19 years old)

RECOVERING FROM SURGERY SEEMED TO TAKE forever, but it really wasn't very long. Right after surgery, the pain was as bad as it had been three years ago, back when it first started. This time around, though, I got better each day. Within six weeks, I began attending Sammy's wrestling matches. As I sat in the stands one day, one of the moms nearby noticed me cheering for Sammy and asked, "Are you going to start wrestling next year?"

I was confused at first and then realized that she thought I was Sammy's younger brother instead of his big sister. Although I didn't like being mistaken for being five years younger than I am, it felt great to have her think I was a boy. With my short hair, boyish clothes, and tight sports bra that flattened me out, it was an easy assumption to make.

A few days after that, I was binge-watching *True Life*, an MTV reality show, when an episode started called "I'm Changing My Sex." I was mesmerized. Whoa! Could people really do that? Was that even possible?

The show starred a trans man, Ted, and a trans woman, Ella. Ted was a twenty-two-year-old student at Kent State. He'd been on testosterone for over two years, and his voice was low and he totally looked like a man. He had facial hair and big muscles. But he still had breasts, which he found devastating. He wore the same baggy pants and sweatshirts that appeal to me, that cover my body—I mean *his* body—and make you not notice the breasts as much. Other than that, though, we were very different. He was a much larger person, with a beer gut, and he always wore a baseball cap. I'd stayed pretty slim as a high school athlete, which helped keep my breasts smaller.

When Ted said that people asked him whether he was a boy or a girl, it felt as if I was asking myself the same question. My mouth hung open when he demonstrated how he gave himself a testosterone shot in his right buttock. He made it look like it was nothing, easy as anything.

Staring directly into the camera, Ted stated that he was changing his gender from female to male. Then he described how when he was a child playing house, he always wanted to be the dad. How he begged his parents to let him wear the same dress slacks to church that his brothers wore. He also talked about how great it would be to go swimming without having to wear a T-shirt. After explaining how awkward that felt, he added how fantastic it would be to go swimming following surgery, once he had a flat chest and no T-shirt.

I related to everything he said. I knew that feeling, remembering how upset I'd been back in middle school when my breasts first started to develop, how it had been years since I'd worn a girl's bathing suit, preferring trunks and a T-shirt to hide my shape. I watched in awe as Ted described how he was about to take the next step and remove his breasts.

I was also extremely jealous, thinking, *Why does he get to do this when I can't? He's changed his body and his life. Is this real? Is it even possible?*

Not for me. Even though Ted made it all seem like the most natural thing in the world, I realized that MTV had picked the topic because people saw it as unnatural and weird. His older brother stated that flat out one night over dinner, objecting to surgery, calling it cosmetic and elective, saying that nobody should do that to their body if they didn't have to. He said it would be different if Ted had cancer and needed surgery to save his life, but that wasn't what was happening. Ted's brother didn't want him to risk dying in surgery for something he didn't believe was necessary. There was no way he could support Ted's decision. His voice cracked as he spoke, and then he stood up and walked out of the room.

I couldn't imagine saying to my brothers what Ted had said to his, but if I did, I could see Ben reacting the same way. I didn't think I could ever persuade him that surgery made sense. I wasn't sure I could convince myself, or that I should. After all, I'd just discovered that it was even a possibility, and I certainly wasn't ready to think seriously about whether it was an option for me.

After Ted's brother left, his mother said that Ted would always be a girl to her. She wanted her daughter, not another son.

I didn't think my mom would say that, but I couldn't be sure.

No matter what Ted said, his family wasn't swayed.

They just stared down at their food, except for his brother, who still hadn't returned. Then Ted looked at the camera and said this was life-or-death for him. He couldn't change his mind based on their concerns.

Life or death. That was another difference for me. Ted and Ella, the transgender woman, both spoke of how their discomfort with their bodies was destroying them. Ella said she was depressed all the time, even suicidal. And that the only reason she didn't kill herself was that it wouldn't be fair to her mother.

That's not me. I hate my breasts, but I've never felt suicidal. Besides, I don't like change, and being transgender would change everything.

Most of all, I don't want to disappoint my family.

Ted didn't want to let down his family either, but he was so confident that it was the right thing to do that he went through with it anyway. The hormones, the surgery. He never looked back. He managed to save a few thousand dollars by working and saving everything he could. He threw a fund-raising party at a nearby bar, complete with dance music and drag kings, which brought in almost another thousand. His family, while still reluctant, contributed enough to reach the goal of $5,600. Scheduling the surgery after that looked easy. A simple phone call. Then a bonfire the night before to burn his binders, the undergarments he'd worn for years to flatten out his breasts even more than my sports bras could do.

The show ended with Ted at a swimming pool, taking off his shirt and saying this was the first time he was going swimming in three years. He was so happy to be going bare-chested and I could just feel his joy. Then Ted laughed and smiled as he got into the water, cringing with the cold, tightening up his shoulders and making fists as he pretended to shiver. From inside the pool, he said that he wasn't ashamed to be transgender, that he just wanted to be able to live his life as a man.

Wow, I thought as the show's credits played. It's actually, truly possible. But is it for me?

I know I have issues with my body and want to be more masculine. But, ultimately, I'm pretty content with everything else in my life. Because of that, I feel like I have no right to want to change like Ted did. It's such a huge deal that I can't even contemplate it, even though I want it, even though I need it.

I've buried any thoughts about Ted's story applying to me, about the possibility of me being transgender, and instead continued on my path of denial, turned my energy to recovering from my spleen surgery. And maybe even to going back to college once I feel completely better.

Sometimes, I talk about the future with Ben. I see him fairly often now because he moved to Houston to take a job in the oil and gas industry after graduating from Lehigh. It's only about a three-hour drive, so he visits us in Austin most weekends. At least, when he's not going to Baltimore to see his girlfriend, Jenn. She didn't move with him because she's working on a graduate degree in pharmacy back in Baltimore.

Jenn is terrific and fits in well with our family. She even looks like Elizabeth with her athletic build and long brown hair. People often think they're sisters. In college, she played both field hockey and lacrosse. That's how she and Ben met. The women's teams often socialized with the football team. The two of them started dating at the end of their sophomore year and have been a perfect couple ever since. Doing the long-distance thing is hard on both of them.

Ben has often said that if he hadn't been able to play football at Lehigh, he would have liked going to the University of Colorado. So I started considering it for myself. Mom and I went to visit and I loved it. Hearing the story of my health difficulties, they admitted me to start in January even though it was past their deadline. I registered as a math and education major, switching from architecture. I'd enjoyed my design studios at Montana State, but the required classroom work had left me bored.

For the first time in what seems like forever, things are breaking my way. I can run around and not be terrified that my pain will return. And after so many years of scrambling to survive academically, I finally have a chance to succeed.

nine

I'M NOT BROKEN

—·—

Summer 2010 — Austin, TX
Emily (20 years old)

My first semester at CU wasn't great academically, but I passed. I made friends at my dorm and even found three women who wanted me to share an apartment with them in the fall. When I tried snowboarding at the Eldora ski resort, forty minutes away from Boulder, the pain didn't come back. I returned to Austin for the summer feeling pretty darn good about myself.

Despite that, though, I still felt awkward and weird about not being attracted to anyone. I could tell that guys were hitting on me at school, but I wasn't interested in any of them. I didn't want to talk with my folks about it. Or anyone else, for that matter. So, I turned to the Internet.

At first I just stared at my laptop, hesitant to type anything, afraid of what I might find. I was astonished when I entered the phrase "not interested in sex" and saw a ton of responses. Blog entries, queries like mine, websites. I explored for hours, frequently coming back to AVEN—The Asexual Visibility and Education Network. People there were asking the same question as me. People wrote from all over the country, from cities and from rural places like Appalachia, and even from other countries like Lithuania and Scotland.

AVEN hosted a chat room for introductions where one person wrote, "I always thought that this whole sexual attraction thing was exaggerated." That's exactly how I've always felt, but I'd never said it before, not even to myself. Not until that moment when I read comments from others like me.

I didn't write anything myself, but it was a relief to discover that I'm not the only person in the world who doesn't want a sexual relationship, and that there's a name for it, asexuality. More than that, there are people who aren't interested in romance either, aromantic people. Now that I realize that other people acknowledge being asexual or aromantic, I can too. I am asexual, not interested in sex. I am aromantic. I don't want a boyfriend. Or a girlfriend.

When I was a little kid, I always found it kind of disgusting to think about people kissing and making out. Everyone felt that way in elementary school. But in middle school, other kids started flirting while I still thought it was gross. I didn't want to be around it. At twenty, I still don't like even thinking about it, let alone doing it. I don't mind hugs, but they have to be in a totally nonsexual, non-romantic way. The physical contact in sports never bothered me, but I don't want to snuggle up to anyone on the couch to watch TV. Or hold hands. I have no need for that kind of intimacy.

It took me a few days to mull everything over, but I finally worked up the courage to tell Mom. She was at her desk in her bedroom, planning out her lectures for the week. She'd stopped substitute teaching when Sammy started high school and instead got hired as an adjunct professor at St. Edward's University. She teaches two classes, Statistics and Operations Management, and is often either grading problem sets or preparing lectures.

I picked up Indy, who'd followed me when I left my room, and I flopped down on the bed, quietly waiting for Mom to become aware of us. I knew it could take a while. When she was working, she often tuned out the rest of the world. She noticed though, when Indy started yapping and barking. Mom glanced over her shoulder, pushed away from her desk, and sat down next to me.

I took a deep breath and said, "Mom, I've got something important to talk about."

"I'm listening," she said quietly.

"Mom, I'm . . ."

Getting the words out was harder than I'd anticipated.

"What, sweetie?"

"I'm not—I'm not broken."

Mom stared at me, waiting for me to continue. Finally, she broke the silence by asking, "What do you mean?"

"I'm asexual," I said slowly, not sure if she'd understand.

She didn't.

"What's that?" she asked.

"Well, you know how you thought I might be gay?"

"Yeah," she said, a little hesitantly.

"I'm not."

"You've said before. Are you having second thoughts? Is that what this is about?" She looked a little confused.

"No," I answered, absentmindedly stroking Indy's tummy. "Being asexual is something else. It's a different sexual orientation entirely." I waited for her to respond, but she didn't. So I added, "It means I'm not attracted to anyone, male or female. I don't want to have sex."

Mom was quiet at first, taking it all in, struggling to figure out what to say. When she finally spoke, she offered a different perspective. "Maybe you just haven't met the right person." She looked at me hopefully, and I could tell that she really wanted that to be the answer.

I took another deep breath to slow my racing heart. "At first I thought maybe that was it. But I don't think so anymore. I've been looking around on the Web, and there are a lot of people like me."

"Okay," she said, not sounding convinced.

"There are. Being asexual is a real thing. You should go to this website called AVEN and read about it."

Mom nodded while I rambled on. I could tell she didn't quite believe me, which was frustrating. I'd spent so much time searching for information that I'd become pretty expert and knew a lot more than she did.

"I promise I'll check out AVEN," she said eventually. "But in the meantime, would you do something for me? Would you see a doctor so they can make sure there's not something else going on? Maybe you've got some sort of hormone imbalance."

I was convinced the doctor wouldn't find anything like that, but I was okay with getting checked out. I'd had so many tests to figure out why my gut hurt for so long that another few wouldn't be a problem. "Sure."

"You'll get through this, sweetie."

"This isn't something to get through," I said, feeling as if I'd hit a brick wall. "This is who I am."

"Oh, baby," she said, her voice cracking a bit. "I don't

want you to be alone. Maybe you can find someone to love that doesn't care if you don't want to have sex."

"I don't *want* to find someone, Mom." Then I told her about being aromantic as well as asexual, that I didn't want a boyfriend, even without sex.

"What about children?" she asked, somewhat wistfully. "You love babies. You've always dreamed of being a mother."

"No, Mom," I answered. "That's *your* dream. You're the one who's always wanted me to be a mother. I do love babies, but they don't have to be mine."

Summer 2010

Jo

AFTER EMILY WENT BACK TO HER ROOM, I LAY on my bed feeling sorry for her, and for me as well. A sense of loss and sadness overwhelmed me. Tears started to flow and I began to cry silently, not wanting Emily to hear. She said she wasn't broken, but she was. How could she not want a life partner? I didn't care who it was or what their sexual relationship was like. I just didn't want her to go through life alone. To grow old alone.

Gradually, my breathing returned to normal and I started to think about next steps, refusing to let myself drown in grief. In a daze, I called the doctor's office to schedule an appointment. Performing that task gave me a pretense of normalcy, but nothing about what Emily had told me seemed normal. Was there really such a thing as being asexual or aromantic? Wasn't it more likely that she was gay but in denial?

I couldn't control my emotional response to Emily's revelation, but I could ignore it for a while by burying myself in research. Pushing my feelings away, I sat at my computer to look for the AVEN website. My disbelief slowly began to fade as I read that asexuality is a sexual orientation just like being straight or gay, and that according to the well-known *Kinsey Report*, published in the 1940s, one percent of the population is asexual. While I found less information about being aromantic, it appeared that it was a real thing as well. If Emily was truly asexual and aromantic, it wasn't that she hadn't found the right person yet. It was that she never would.

Remembering how I'd felt as a teenager, driven to find a relationship both romantic and sexual, I found it hard to accept that others didn't feel the same way, and even harder to understand that my own daughter was one of those people. The more I read, however, the more I had to acknowledge intellectually that what Emily said seemed supported by the medical community. The American Psychiatric Association described it in the fourth edition of their *Diagnostic and Statistical Manual of Mental Disorders*. I didn't like that it was called a disorder and a pathology, but the National Institute of Health presented a literature review by Dr. Kristin Scherrer, a PhD candidate in social work and sociology, that presented it in a more positive light, describing it as "a relatively recent emergent sexual identity."

While Dr. Scherrer's study supported everything I found on the AVEN site, I still felt indescribably sad, with a profound longing for a different life for my daughter, one in which she wouldn't have to deal with the loneliness of being asexual and aromantic, or with the prejudice that was likely to go along with that self-definition.

I also felt a sense of guilt that I hadn't done well by her as a parent. That it was my fault that we hadn't been able to learn about her spleen injury sooner. If we'd only known why she hurt so much, we could have done something about it. And I couldn't help but wonder if it was all connected somehow. Maybe if we'd been able to cure Emily sooner, she wouldn't have given up on school and sports and band and would instead have had a more active social life. Dated boys—or girls—and developed some closer friendships. Maybe then she wouldn't be saying now that she was asexual and aromantic.

Jon wondered about a different connection, having read that people with autism were less likely to be in sexual relationships. He suggested that perhaps Emily had a mild form of autism, which might explain her apparent lack of interest in caring for her body, as well as her isolation in middle and high school. We didn't pursue that explanation, though, since Emily didn't exhibit any other symptoms of autism. Nor did we consider that transgender teenagers were also less likely to flirt and date, for we didn't yet know what it meant to be transgender.

THE ENDOCRINOLOGIST SAID nothing was wrong with Emily's hormones. I was actually disappointed. I'd hoped medication or supplements would increase her desire for a sexual relationship. But they wouldn't. Struggling to accept a future I didn't want for Emily, I pretended that I was okay with it and told myself she was the same person she had been before her announcement. But I couldn't get rid of the deep sense of loss at what could have been, at the fact that she would grow old alone, that she would never know the joy of being a mom. Her reassurances that she would have friends, that she would love her future nieces and nephews, that she could still have a happy and fulfilling life . . . they all sounded empty to me.

ten

INTRODUCING "EM"

==

Spring 2011 — Boulder, CO
Emily (21 years old)

I loved everything about attending CU—except the classes. I somehow managed to stumble through the fall term, but it was rough and I fell behind. Perhaps it was because I spent so much time online and in self-contemplation. I thought I'd nailed it last summer when I began identifying as asexual, but I was still missing something. Thoughts of the MTV episode I saw almost two years ago about a trans man kept swirling about in my mind despite my best efforts to bury them. I didn't want to believe I was trans, but the idea of changing myself physically to match the way I felt inside kept returning, like a boomerang I couldn't escape no matter how hard I threw it. Every time I sat at my computer to do homework, I instead found myself on websites exploring what it meant to be transgender, visiting chat rooms and seeing what people said about it, both good and bad.

I experimented with calling myself *Em* instead of *Emily*.

I didn't know where that was leading, if any place at all. Did it mean that I'm really transgender? That didn't seem possible. I wasn't like the transgender people in the TV show, and I couldn't say that I was a boy born in a girl's body. It wasn't as simple as that. I didn't think of myself as a man, but I didn't feel like a woman either. I was just me.

My education class partner, Matt Getty, had no difficulty calling me Em. He was the first real friend I made at CU, a little younger than me with a clean-shaven, little boy face. He wears his straight blond hair with a strong part and a little longer on top than the sides, and his rectangular glasses give him a studious air. When he smiles, his lips go slightly higher on the left, making him look a bit nervous. He loves talking about cars and is great with little kids.

One of our class requirements was to design and teach a science or math class to elementary school kids. During the fall, we worked with third graders and created a lab where we used sticks and rubber bands to show how joints work. This spring, we developed a math class for fifth graders that involved a dice game we made up. It was fun and we spent a lot of time together. Mom liked our curriculum so much that she ran with our idea and taught a variation of it in her college statistics class.

It was through Matt that I discovered the Forty-First Street house. He rents a room there, along with three other guys, some students, some working. The older brother of one of the guys owns it. It's run-down and usually a mess, but I love it there. There's always music playing and guys sitting around just chilling. Not a whole lot of studying going on.

The first time Matt invited me over, I fit in immediately. We sat around playing video games, watching sports and other stuff on TV, having a few beers. So I was pleased when one of the other guys, Rick, asked me to come back. Like Matt, he's a little younger than me and grew up in the Boulder area. His folks have a condo right downtown, but he prefers living with his friends. He's shyer than the rest of the gang but still a lot of fun.

If I'd gotten to know the guys at the Forty-First Street house during my first semester at CU, I would have tried to live with them instead of with the group of women I met in the dorm. It would have been so much better. I just don't fit in with my apartment mates the way I do with Matt's circle of friends.

Especially Colin. He was there the first time that Matt brought me over to visit, but we didn't become close friends until a few weeks later, when we realized we make terrific partners at beer pong. We also both like to eat out. Whenever he asks if anyone wants to go someplace for dinner, I'm always game, even when nobody else is.

I can afford going out to eat without touching my sav-ings from years of birthday, Christmas, and Hanukkah gifts from my grandmother and parents because my folks pay my tuition and give me an allowance. Colin, although not as comfortably set up as me, makes money working in a physics lab and doing odd jobs as a computer programmer, despite carrying a full course load. He's in a long-distance relationship with his girlfriend, which works out great for me since it means we can be buddies without romance getting in the way. I can talk with him about anything and know he won't judge me. Even the stuff about how I like looking like a boy. Or that I'm asexual. Colin is okay with all of it.

introducing "em"

I THOUGHT THIS spring term might be a turning point academically, but as the March midterms approached last month, I had to acknowledge that my coursework had spiraled out of control and it was time to tell my folks. I hadn't been to class in two weeks, and it was getting more and more obvious by the day that I was never going back.

Putting off calling home, I drove around Boulder for a while and then pointed the car north toward Estes Park, a cool little town about an hour away with a bunch of hiking trails that go up into the Rocky Mountains. Driving helps me think, and I was able to plan out what I wanted to say. I had to tell Mom and Dad that I had dropped out of school again. I could just hear Mom offering to come for a few weeks and help me catch up, like she did at the end of the fall term, but I didn't want to be rescued. I just wanted it to be over. It was also time to share what I'm thinking about my body. That it's all wrong. That I can't stand to see my reflection.

Noticing a gas station ahead, I stopped to fill my tank, even though it was still half-full. Standing by my car with the fuel nozzle in hand, I knew it was time. So instead of getting back on the road, I pulled into a parking space where I could look up into the mountains and called Mom.

"Done with class for the day?" she asked after recognizing my voice.

"Uh, yeah," I said, not sure where to begin.

"What are your plans for the evening?" Mom asked. "A lot of studying?"

"No, actually," I answered, scratching at my head as I tried to find the right words. "Ummm, I . . ."

"Is everything okay?" she asked, picking up on the un-certainty in my voice.

"No. It's not." I waited for her to start asking questions, but she remained silent. "I've got something to tell you and Dad." More silence. "I'm quitting school."

I'd planned on telling her that I'd already dropped out, but I couldn't say that, so I implied that I was still thinking about it. I expected a lecture about how I could get caught up again, how I'm smart and capable. Instead, Mom asked, "Is the pain back?"

"It's not that, Mom. It's just . . ."

"What, dear?"

"It's just that I'm behind again." Not wanting her to start making suggestions about how I could get things un-der control, I added, "I'm never gonna catch up."

"Okay."

"I don't want to catch up. I'm miserable and wasting my time, and I feel guilty about you and Dad spending money on tuition and—"

"Emily," Mom cut in before I could add to the list, "it's your choice. You know that. We'll always encourage you to try, but we don't want you to make yourself miserable. You've been struggling with school for a long time."

Whoa. That was unexpected. I didn't realize I'd been that obvious.

"So what happens now?" she asked. There was the mother I know that always moves too quickly from realiz-ing there's a problem to trying to identify a solution. That had bugged me as a kid because sometimes I just wanted to live with something for a while before figuring out what to do next. But in this case, I'd already given it a lot of thought. "Do you want to come home to Austin?"

Knowing it would disappoint her if I didn't move back, I was hesitant to tell her no. But I'd decided to put everything on the table, so I was brutally honest. "No. I want to stay in Boulder. I've got my home and my friends, and I like it here."

I could barely hear her response over the sound of a trucker gunning his engine just a few feet away from me, but I could tell she was rambling on about what it would be like, how everything would work out.

"Mom, I'm not coming back. I'm staying in Boulder."

"That's fine, sweetie."

"I've already got a job. There's this residential facility for seniors right near my apartment."

"What'll you be doing there?"

"It has a day care center for the staff's children. They advertised in the local paper looking for someone to take care of babies. When I called, they said to come for an interview. They didn't care that my only experience was babysitting and that I hadn't finished college. I got the job. I'm gonna take care of babies."

There. I'd said it. I wasn't a college student taking a break from school; I was an adult with a job and a life, and I was okay with that.

"That's awesome, kiddo. When do you start?"

"Monday. The pay's not great and it'll be a long workday. But it's a terrific job and I'm really excited about it."

"Wow! I'm proud of you, Em. That took a lot of courage to decide to stop being a student. And you'll be good at the day care center. You've always been terrific with little kids. They'll love you."

"You just called me 'Em.'"

"Yeah . . ."

"That's something else I need to talk with you about."

"Don't you like that nickname anymore?" Mom asked. "Should I stop using it?"

"It's not that. In fact, I like it a lot and that's what all my friends call me now. You and Dad are the only ones who say *Emily* anymore."

"Is that okay? Do you want us to switch to Em?"

"No, you don't have to. You can still say Emily. It's just that, well, the reason I like it when people call me Em is that it matches more how I feel."

"I'm not sure I follow."

"I'm happiest when I look the most like a boy," I explained. "When instead of seeing a twenty-one-year-old woman in the mirror, I see a teenage boy."

"You've always been a tomboy."

"This is different. I understand that biologically, I'm not a boy. But I don't feel as if I'm a woman."

"What does that even mean?" Mom asked, sounding confused.

"What does *what* mean?" I answered, a bit defensively.

"That you don't feel like you're a woman. I'm not judging or anything, I just want to understand."

"Okay." I took a big breath to slow everything down and gather my thoughts. "When I was a little kid, it wasn't a big deal. I knew I was a girl and was biologically different from all of my guy friends. But I never thought about my body changing."

"You mean . . . what? Puberty?"

"Yeah. I didn't think about the fact that I was gonna grow breasts and start my period. Until that happened, I could just kinda not think about being different from the boys."

"I get it," said Mom. "Remember, Emily, I was a tomboy too. I was happier looking boyish and liked it when people mistook me for a boy."

"Mom, this is a different," I said, a little too loudly. A car had pulled in right next to me with its windows open and the radio blasting, and I felt all distracted. I really wanted Mom to understand, but I felt like I couldn't find the words to explain it any better than I already had.

"This is much more than being a tomboy. Sometimes I wear a binder."

"A what?"

I wasn't sure whether she hadn't heard me clearly or had just never heard of a binder. So I plunged on. "It's made of this stretchy material, kind of like a sports bra. It compresses my chest and flattens me out completely."

Trying to lighten the mood, she said, "There are a lot of girls with flat chests who would love to swap with you."

Humor wasn't what I needed from her at the moment. Instead of answering, I threw open the car door and jumped out to walk around for a minute.

When I didn't respond, Mom realized I was annoyed. "Sorry," she said. "I do get that this is a big deal."

"Yeah, it's a very big deal," I said, leaning on the car. "I really need you to hear me."

"Okay," she said. "I promise I'm listening. And I'm glad you feel free to talk with me."

"I do. It's hard, but I do," I said.

"So what happens now?" she asked, shifting back into problem-solving mode. "I mean a bout school and all."

I could tell she wanted to fix everything then and there, but that wasn't going to happen. "I guess I just go to work."

"Okay, then. Will you call me after your first day? Tell me how it goes?"

"Sure."

With that, I got back into the car and returned to Boulder, relieved to have finally told Mom that I've quit school, go by Em, and sometimes wear a binder. Relieved, but a little sad, too, because having told her makes it all much more real.

eleven

I'M NOT READY TO GROW UP

==

Summer 2011 — Boulder, CO

Em (21 years old)

M y job at the Take-a-Break day care center has
been great from the beginning. It's located in the
Frasier Meadows Retirement Community, this twenty-acre
campus with a few hundred residents spread throughout
several buildings. Lots of the units have windows looking
out over the Flatirons. Grandma Aura would like it, with
their swimming pool and dining hall, and a huge front lobby
with couches and a grand piano. It feels more like a resort
than a senior center.

The day care rooms are on the first floor of the main
building, just off the lobby. It feels all clean and new, even
though it's been here for around ten years. My assignment
is the baby room, where all I have to do is snuggle four babies all day long. Of course I also have to change them and
give them bottles and walk around with them if they cry.

Almost everyone else working there is part of this one
family, all related to the woman who started it up. They
treat me as if I'm part of the family, too, like a little sister.

They all cheered for me when I finished my infant and child CPR training.

They don't know that when I'm not at work, I dress more like a man, binding my chest sometimes when I'm running errands, especially if I don't expect to run into anyone I know. The more I wear my binder, though, the more I want to look that way all the time.

MY CHANCE TO experiment in front of my friends came on the Fourth of July when I was invited to a party to watch fireworks. Only a few of the Forty-First Street guys would be there, so it was a perfect opportunity. I was both exhilarated and frightened. Could I really do this? Look the way I wanted to look? Would the guys there even notice anything was different? Getting ready to head out, I looked down at my new shape and couldn't help but grin, feeling almost giddy.

The party was awesome. We threw a football around, and I loved the sense of freedom of having my chest completely flat under my T-shirt. I'd found that perfect amount of tightness that made me look the way I wanted but didn't constrain me so much as to get in the way of breathing or throwing the ball. I was a little jealous, though, when some of the guys took off their shirts as we all started to sweat. There was no way I could take mine off and have everyone see the binder underneath.

Despite that, I was incredibly happy and started wondering whether I should bind myself all the time. It definitely makes me look right, but it's uncomfortable and restrictive, and it makes it hard to breathe properly.

THE SUMMER IS almost over, and I'm feeling totally competent at the day care center. I have no difficulty taking care of four babies at once, keeping them clean and fed and entertained. Turns out that I'm a natural and never got bored lying on the floor with them crawling around on top of me.

Whenever I feel restless, I load them into a stroller, walk around the facilities, and end up at the piano in the lobby. I let the babies just sit in the stroller while I play a few songs. Sometimes, some of the residents follow us around and then listen while I play. We form a mini-parade as we head for the lobby. One day a couple of weeks ago, one of the staffers suggested that I do an evening concert.

I played my newest song, "I'm Not Ready to Grow Up," which describes exactly how I feel about having dropped out of college.

I've never been the type to know just what they're after.
I'd rather just skate by, enjoying life, focus on the laughter.
So when you ask about my plans,
I find it hard to look ahead.
Can you tell me what's the rush?
I'm not ready to grow up.
I'll figure out my life
When I'm done wasting time.
You think I'm just a bum,
But fuck you I'm having fun.

For now I'm good with me.
I'm where I wanna be.
I'm not the perfect one,
But fuck you I'm having fun.

For the concert, I changed "FU" to "screw you," thinking about how Grandma Aura would wince at the crude language. I could just hear her reaction. "It's one of your best songs, sweetie, but do you have to say that word?" She used to tell us how she'd respond to her high school students when they cussed. She'd say they should challenge themselves to find something more descriptive and that they should develop the habit of never using foul language because otherwise it could slip out when they'd find it embarrassing, like at a job interview or in front of a date's parents.

Turns out, my audience at the senior residence would have been fine with the original lyrics. After I finished playing, one man in his eighties told me it was his favorite song. "I'm not ready to grow up either," he told me. I guess it was his way of saying that he still felt young and understood what I was trying to express with my song, that I really don't know what I want to do in the long run. That I have to live in the moment. I can't focus on the future when I'm still trying to figure out who I am.

Jeremy (21) at keyboard in 2011

Spring 2012 — Boulder, CO
Em (22 years old)

WHENEVER I'M NOT AT WORK, I HANG OUT WITH my friends at the Forty-First Street house. A few nights ago, one of the guys, Rick, invited me over for dinner and a movie at his parents' place where he was house-sitting. After dinner, we were sitting on the couch together, close but not touching, watching a kung fu movie. After a big fight scene, the hero started walking toward his girlfriend. Rick paused the movie and said, "Do you ever see this relationship going anywhere?"

I knew he wasn't talking about the movie. Instead of answering him, though, I tried to buy some time, asking, "What d'ya mean?"

"You know."

"No, I don't."

"I want us to be more than friends," he said. "Don't you feel that way too?"

"No."

The word just popped out, without even an "I'm sorry" afterwards. I was certain I didn't want a romantic relationship with him. I didn't want to even try. It had been a while since I'd made myself kiss my coworker from the Macaroni Grill, and I never wanted to do that again.

Rick was downcast as he hit the play button and started the movie up again. I wanted to say something to make him feel better, but what could I say? Instead, I pretended to be engrossed by what was on the screen, even though I'd totally lost track of what was going on.

"Why not?" he eventually mumbled.

"I just don't feel that way," I answered. "I don't want to be in a relationship like that—with anyone. Can't we just be friends?"

"I don't know," he said. "Maybe."

It was so awkward that I wanted to leave. But Rick seemed so miserable that I couldn't do that to him. Instead, I stayed and watched the rest of the movie while we sat in silence.

i'm not ready to grow up

Summer 2012 — Boulder and Austin
Em (22 years old)

WORKING AT THE DAY CARE CENTER WAS A GREAT
way not to think about what happened with Rick. Between taking care of the babies and cleaning up while they
napped, I kept incredibly busy. Usually, everything went
smoothly. But one afternoon in early May, I was scrubbing
the floor when my right knee locked and I couldn't move.
It was hours before an emergency room physician was able
to straighten my leg. By then, it had swollen up to twice
its normal size and I couldn't put any weight on it.

Mom flew in from Texas before the day was over. The
following morning, she took me to see a knee specialist. He
thought I'd torn a ligament and would need surgery. I
called my boss to say I couldn't come back to work for a
couple of months. Then, in a whirlwind of activity, Mom
boxed up my stuff and moved it into storage, I gave thirty
days' notice on the lease I'd signed for an apartment near
the day care center, and we drove to Austin.

An MRI revealed that it was only a nasty sprain. Within
a week, I was up and about, enjoying a stress-free vacation.
I could have gone back to Colorado to work and complete
my physical therapy there, but my family was getting ready
to go to Costa Rica for an adventure vacation, and I'd only
have a few weeks before it would be time to leave again to
join my family in Central America. After that, I wanted to
be in Austin for my grandma's ninetieth birthday party.
Besides, I rationalized, I'd told my boss I'd be gone for two
months, so she'd already made plans to cover my shifts.

Anyway, it was much more fun to stay at home and

119

hang out with Sammy, who had just graduated from West-lake High. We spent a lot of time talking about college life. The more we talked, the more I liked the idea of giving school another try. By the end of the month, I had registered for fall classes at CU and told my boss at the day care center that I wouldn't be returning to work.

IN MID-JUNE, Mom and I flew to Boulder to look for a new place for me. On the flight to Denver, I told her I'd like to buy a condo instead of renting another apartment.

"That's a big deal," she said. "That only makes sense if you're going to live there for five years. Do you think you will?"

"Yeah, actually," I said. "All my friends are there, and I'm pretty sure I'll want to stay there after I graduate."

We spent the rest of the flight running calculations to see whether it made sense financially, and I was relieved when Mom said that it did. She and Dad could help with the down payment, and then my monthly mortgage payment wouldn't be any more than if I were renting. And if I got a two-bedroom condo, I could rent out the second one to cover insurance and utilities. I immediately thought about asking Colin to move in with me until his girlfriend, Meg, finished college and came back to Boulder.

Mom's radar went up when I mentioned Colin and she started asking if there was something between us, despite me having told her that I'm asexual and aromantic. I assured her there wasn't and then explained that, if anything, I was growing more confident in my self-definition and told her about my experience with Rick wanting to date me and how uninterested I was.

twelve

ONCE A GIRL, ALWAYS A BOY

—·—

Summer 2012 — Austin, TX
Em (22 years old)

B en took Sammy skydiving. I didn't really want to jump out of a plane with them and my knee still hurt if I stepped wrong, so it wasn't really possible, but it would have been nice to be invited.

It's not that they explicitly excluded me. They just never thought to ask me along. Sammy and I are super close, but he and Ben share this special brother bond they've had since childhood, and I want to be a part of it. But they don't see me that way. I feel left out and mad and relieved not to be skydiving all at the same time.

The day after their jump, they came with Mom and me to Macaroni Grill for lunch. On the drive home, Mom mentioned that one of our neighbors told Grandma Aura that her kid is transgender. Jessie was Jeffrey when we knew her growing up, but she recently started wearing a dress and letting her hair grow long.

I think Mom told us about Jessie as a way of encouraging me to share my own thoughts with Sammy and Ben.

Not about being transgender, because I'm not, but about not identifying as a woman.

It didn't work at first. Nobody said anything while we were still in the car. But once we got home and Mom went inside, Ben, Sammy, and I stayed outside to shoot baskets and Sammy started talking about it. He said there was this kid at Westlake who had said to his classmates, "I'm transgender. Please refer to me with male pronouns and use my new name, Mark."

My immediate reaction was, "Wow. That's so brave. That's incredible." This kid had done in high school what I still couldn't do in my early twenties.

Before I could even consider whether to explain why I was so blown away by Mark's disclosure, Sammy said, "It's just weird. And it's not fair for her to expect everyone to instantly change what they call her. Maybe if she looked like a boy, but she doesn't."

"What does she look like?" Ben asked.

"She wears baggy shirts all the time, and athletic shorts. And she doesn't shave her legs or brush her hair." I looked down at my own clothes and hairy legs. Sammy had just described *me*. My brothers hadn't had the benefit of hours spent on the Internet researching all kinds of issues regarding sexuality and gender. They had no way of knowing that I identified with Mark and felt as if everything they were saying about him was really about me.

Thinking about Mom's comments in the car, I said, "What about Jessie? Could you call her Jessie right away?"

"That's different," Ben said. "Of course I'd call him Jessie. If he says he's a girl, then I'd call him a girl."

"Her," I prompted.

"Her," said Sammy, jumping in. "But this kid at school

hasn't changed her appearance at all. That makes it harder to call her Mark."

"If Mark wants you to use male pronouns and call him Mark, then that's what you should do," I said, with a little more force than I'd intended.

"I don't know," said Ben, shaking his head. "She can say she's a boy all she wants, but she's still got two X chromosomes." With that, he passed the ball to Sammy, who dribbled for a moment and moved in for a layup.

After his successful shot, Sammy grabbed the ball before it hit the ground and turned to face us. "Yeah. That's exactly my point."

"Just because she says she's a boy, that doesn't make her one biologically," Ben called out to me over his shoulder as he moved in on Sammy and swatted the ball out of his hands. The two of them both reached for the ball, shouldering each other out of the way in the attempt, competing roughly, just as they have ever since Sammy grew big enough to hold his own. Neither one got to it in time, and the ball rolled down into the cul-de-sac.

Our driveway rises steeply until it reaches a level area that was once a horse meadow. Glancing around while Sammy ran for the ball, my eyes landed on the tree house Dad started a long time ago. Many hours of our childhood were spent sitting up in that tree, just beyond the driveway. Years later, the structure is still in an unfinished state. Dad made progress with each of the children in turn, adding a rail here and a plank there. When we were little, the tree house floor was just big enough for the four of us Ivester kids; I wasn't sure if it could still hold us as adults.

We'd held many conversations up in that tree. Sometimes we argued. Growing up, I always found it difficult to debate with Ben in particular. Not only was he older, he was also so logical and confident. I knew the discussion about Sammy's classmate Mark wasn't emotional for him and that he wasn't attacking me personally. He was talking about biology, while I was talking about what Jessie and this kid at Sammy's school felt inside.

It was like we were carrying on two separate conversations and not really communicating. I knew that, but with my own insecurities, it felt as if Ben was saying, "I'm right, and you're just being whiny for disagreeing." It was incredibly frustrating because I couldn't tell Ben that I empathized with Mark and Jessie, that I was questioning my own gender identity. I'm sure if he'd realized that, he would have been more sensitive. But I'd never told him that I sometimes bound my chest and introduced myself as Em. He didn't know that even though I didn't think of myself as transgender, I'd taken some baby steps toward being like Sammy's classmate.

"If Mark says he's a man, then he's a man," I tried again. "His chromosomes don't define his gender, just his biology."

"That's what I'm saying," Ben said. "Biologically, she's a girl."

"Right," Sammy added. "If you don't have a dick, you're not a guy."

"That's not tr—"

"Biologically," said Sammy, interrupting me.

"What if he goes on hormones and grows a big, hairy beard and talks with a deep voice. Is he still a girl?" I asked.

"Yup, biologically she's still a girl," answered Ben.

It's not that Ben was trying to be mean. It's just that I

was talking about gender identity and expression, and he was responding with biology. That day, shooting baskets in the driveway, I desperately wanted Ben to say that he understood what it meant to someone like Mark or Jessie to feel different inside from the sex assigned to them at birth, because then he'd be acknowledging who I am inside.

My inability to communicate my need to my big brother made me tighten up so much that it hurt. I needed him to say flat out that he understood what I was saying about gender identity, because I cared about his opinion on everything. Always have. I wanted to impress Ben and make him respect me. When he kept talking biology instead of gender, I felt as if he'd dismissed me, like I didn't know what I was talking about. That hurt, because what we were talking about was *me*.

Knowing I might start to cry if I stayed any longer, I mumbled something about needing a break and escaped inside.

Jo

I KNEW SOMETHING WAS WRONG THE MOMENT Emily walked into the kitchen. She was breathing hard and her face was all twisted up, her lower lip quivering. I guided her to the living room couch, wishing she were a little girl again so I could put my arms around her and hold her in my lap to comfort her.

After a moment, the tears came. I tightened my grip on her shoulder and gently stroked her cheek with my other hand, murmuring, "You're okay, baby, you're okay."

Then I waited.

Looking down at her hands, she finally started to explain. "You see there's this kid at Sammy's school. He said that everyone should start calling him 'Mark.'"

"Why is that a problem?" I asked. "What was his name before?"

"He had a *girl's* name before. When Mark was born, he was a girl."

"So he's transgender, like Jessie?"

"Yeah. But Ben and Sammy won't listen. I tried explaining about Mark, that he's so brave for coming out to the school like he did. But they kept calling him 'she' and saying he's a girl. And that he'll always be a girl."

"And you don't believe that?"

"No. No, I don't," she said emphatically. "Mark is transgender. That means that he's a boy."

"They haven't studied it the way you have. You can't expect them to understand the way you do."

"They don't get that I'm like this kid."

There. She'd said it. She was like this transgender boy. She was like Mark.

"So tell them," I suggested. "Make them understand that this is personal for you."

"I don't know," she said, shaking her head. "It's not like they're rejecting me or anything. They have no idea that I identify with Mark and wish that I were courageous enough to say something about how I feel. He's so young, still in high school." She looked down quietly for a moment before continuing. "Sammy and Ben never have to think about being guys. They've known for as long as they can remember who they are and how they fit in. They get to look the way they feel, and nobody questions it. So they see it as being unfair for Mark to ask everyone else to change."

"Sounds like a reasonable description of their attitude."

"Yeah," Emily said. Then she stood up and paced about. Stopping by the piano, she played a few notes before returning to the couch. "I empathize with Mark, but I'm not transgender," she said, surprising me with her intensity.

"I know. You've said that before," I said, not sure where the conversation was headed.

"But I get how Mark feels. He doesn't like looking like a girl. I'm the same way. It would be so much better if I didn't have breasts."

Where was she going with this? This was a lot more than what she'd said before about being more comfortable dressing androgynously and wearing a binder.

"What does that mean?" I asked, not really wanting to know the answer. "Are you thinking about removing them?" My stomach churned at the thought. From what I'd read recently, I knew it was major surgery. "I thought only transgender people did that."

"That's usually true," she said. "Mom, I'm not transgender, but I want a flat chest."

"But you still identify as a woman, right?"

"No, I don't. Why would you say that? I may not feel like I'm a boy, but I don't feel like I'm a girl either."

"So . . . no labels?" I asked.

"That works," she said. "They just get in the way."

"Can you tell that to Ben and Sammy? Darling, they probably have no idea that you're upset, that what they said hurt you."

"I'll think about it. Yeah."

I had to think about it as well. No matter how much I read about what it meant to be transgender, I cringed at the way Emily said she wanted to remove her breasts. How could she even think of doing that to herself? How could anyone?

thirteen

MAID OF HONOR

—·—

Winter 2013 — Steamboat Springs, CO

Jon

Sitting comfortably by the fire, I rubbed my legs where they were sore from overdoing it on the ski slopes. We were in Steamboat Springs, where we'd been skiing as a family for almost twenty years, always returning to the same slopeside condo. We'd remodeled it recently, with lots of stone and wood and big windows looking out over the gondola. With its mission-style furniture, it looked modern and cozy all at the same time.

My plan for a relaxed afternoon of catching up on my reading was interrupted when Jo came down the stairs and said, "Emily wants to move forward with top surgery." Jo's brow was furrowed and her eyes glossed over as if she were fighting a headache.

"Did she say that specifically?" I asked. "Or is that just based on what she's said before about wishing she didn't have breasts?"

Emily had returned to the University of Colorado at the end of the previous summer and was seemingly happy as a math major. She'd arranged her class schedule to have

Fridays off so she could come to Steamboat for long week-ends. This morning, as I watched her snowboard effortlessly down a steep slope at twice the speed I could handle, it had struck me how happy she looked in her element, how competent and comfortable. I'd had no idea that beneath her smile, she was contemplating something so drastic.

I recoiled at the thought. Top surgery was serious stuff, essentially a double mastectomy. Emily had described it to us almost a year earlier and I'd been reading about it ever since, dreading the possibility that she would want to actually get it done. "Is that what you two have been talking about upstairs?"

Jo nodded, her lips held tightly together. Then she walked into our bedroom and threw herself onto the bed. I sat beside her and rubbed my hand gently on her forehead, waiting for her to tell me more. After a few false starts and a couple of deep breaths, she began to talk. "I thought . . . I really thought Emily was happy enough with her androgy-nous clothes and hair and looking like a boy. But . . . but . . ."

"It'll be okay," I said. Inside, though, I didn't believe that. I had this bubble building inside my chest that told me it wasn't okay at all.

"No, it won't," Jo said. "She's made a decision. She wants to get rid of her breasts."

"She said that?" I asked, repeating my earlier comment, at a loss because I didn't want to believe it. Despite all of my attempts to learn about why some people feel a need for the surgery, I still struggled to understand why Emily would want to cause herself such physical pain and suffer-ing. I thought of teenagers I'd read about who were so emotionally disturbed that they cut themselves, either to punish themselves or to get attention, or just to feel in control. Was Emily like them?

I'd always suspected that her tomboyishness was tied to some sort of self-image issues, but could it be this bad? Was it some sort of self-hatred that caused her to want to mutilate herself? I thought about the Oliver Sacks book I'd read a few years earlier, *The Man Who Mistook His Wife for a Hat.* In that, Dr. Sacks described patients with neurological disorders, people that didn't recognize that their limbs were their own and wanted to amputate them.

Jo pulled me back from my thoughts, explaining more about what Emily had told her. "She says she has 'gender dysphoria,' which means she doesn't feel right about her female appearance. It used to be called 'gender identity disorder,' but now it's not considered a disorder. It's a condition."

"Is that a medical diagnosis?" I asked. "Has she seen a doctor?"

"She has, actually." As Jo moved into her storytelling mode, she sat up and found it easier to talk. "She's been in counseling since last summer. Apparently, that's a legal requirement before you can get top surgery."

"Why didn't she tell us before?"

"She was afraid we wouldn't understand and would try and talk her out of it. She wanted to figure things out on her own first."

I tried to think logically, but this awful sense of dread washed over me. Before I could say anything about how I felt, Jo suddenly threw herself back onto the pillow and started moaning, "Oh no, oh no, oh no," over and over again. I lay down next to her and wrapped my arms around her and she curled up against me.

After lying wordlessly for a few minutes, Jo said, "She's waiting for us now. She showed me a video and wants you to see it too."

"What's it of?"

"Just Emily talking. It's her way of telling us what she's thinking about."

"What did she say?"

"Can you just watch it with me? It's better that you hear it in her words."

"Okay. Are you sure you're up to it?"

"Yeah, I'll watch it again. I want to see it with you."

With that, we walked out to the living room where Emily was waiting for us. She had her laptop out on the coffee table, ready to go. As she started it up, she said, "Can you hold off asking me any questions until you see the whole thing? I recorded myself talking because this is a big deal and I wanted to get it right, and it's important to me that you really understand."

The clip started with Emily looking right at the screen, smiling nervously, scratching at her neck. "Okay, guys. I've made a big decision, and it may be hard for you to understand. I want to have surgery to remove my breasts. It's called 'top surgery' or 'female-to-male surgery,' and it's usually done when a transgender man wants to look more masculine.

"It's not about that for me. I'm not transgender. I'm just really uncomfortable with the way I look. I don't like looking feminine, and that's what breasts make you do. I know this is a serious decision, and I didn't make it lightly. I've been going to a therapist since the summer and she's helped me a lot. It was actually while I was talking with her that I decided to make this video."

Then she stood and stepped back from her computer so that her whole body came into view. "I thought you might find it helpful to see what I'm talking about." She held her arms out to the side and bent at the elbows in a hip-hop pose, her hands pointing right at her chest.

"I'm wearing a binder right now, so my breasts are flattened out. With my shirt on, I look the same as I will after surgery."

She beamed as she moved about so we could see her from all angles, bouncing around the room and sporting the same smile I'd seen earlier in the day out on the slopes. Glancing over at Jo, I saw that she was smiling as well, responding to the sight of Emily practically bursting with joy. It had a powerful effect on me too. The joy evinced by Emily made it impossible to deny the impact that a flat chest had on her mood and attitude.

I had to begin rethinking my reservations. I had to recognize that I hadn't seen Emily this deeply happy since she was a little girl. Sure, she'd had fun playing football or snowboarding or even just hanging out with her friends. But this profound sense of satisfaction with her inner self, well, I hadn't seen that since her body had changed with puberty. As horrified as I was by the possibility of surgery, and despite not really understanding why Emily felt a need for it, I could see how completely gratified she was by the thought of having a boyish physique.

February 2013 — Austin, TX
Jo

I COULDN'T GET AWAY FROM EMILY'S VIDEO. Every time we talked on the phone, she gave me more information, explaining what the procedure would entail. Somehow, calling it a "procedure" instead of surgery made it seem not as big a deal. But it was a very big deal, and I found the thought chilling; my gut tightened whenever I thought about it.

I discovered it to be quite helpful, though, to learn as much as I could about the medical side of the equation. In one of my online searches, I found the *Standards of Care*, which confirmed that breast removal is such major surgery that women getting a double mastectomy were typically kept in the hospital for several days. Yet gender-affirming top surgery—in many ways the same thing physically—was done as an outpatient. How could that be okay?

During my phone conversations with Emily, I peppered her with questions. "What will recovery be like? How will you select a surgeon?"

She generally responded patiently to all my questions, saying she wasn't nervous about the procedure being performed as day surgery, that she'd done extensive research about surgeons and selected one that had a terrific reputation. Unable to trust that my twenty-three-year-old had researched the matter adequately, though, I threw myself into doing my own investigation.

I looked into the ratings of surgeons that performed top surgery and checked to see if the ones Emily was considering had any lawsuits or complaints against them. I asked my cousin Toby to see if her contacts in the medical community of South Florida had anything to say on the matter. Her dad, my uncle, had been a radiologist there and she'd lived in the area for over forty years, so I figured she'd know whom to ask. While I didn't want the surgery to happen, I wanted to make sure that if it did, my daughter would get the best care possible.

During our third conversation about it toward the end of February, Emily interrupted my questions, saying, "Mom, there's something else I need to talk with you about."

"Okay. What's up?" I asked, trying to sound cheerful despite my growing sense that we were about to head into even more difficult terrain.

"You know how I said I'd be Liz's maid of honor?"

"Of course." How could I forget? The wedding was only a month away and Elizabeth had just been in town, meeting with the caterer and the florist, trying on the bridal gown for last-minute alterations, checking out the garden where the ceremony and reception with over a hundred people would take place, finalizing the menu and the seating plan, attending a tasting party to approve the wedding cake, and planning out the rehearsal dinner at our favorite barbecue restaurant.

Dustin had proposed the previous summer, kneeling on a beach in South Texas. Elizabeth had decided pretty early on that he was the one, with his wry sense of humor and thoughtful outlook on life. They'd met three years earlier through a coed soccer team and had started dating almost immediately. She was drawn to the way he encouraged her to think more broadly about life, challenging her to question her assumptions about everything from politics to work to social interactions.

Emily's next comment pulled me back to the moment. "I can't do it."

"Can't do what?" I asked, still thinking about my future son-in-law.

"Be the maid of honor," she said, her voice cracking.

"Slow down," I said in as soothing a voice as I could muster. Emily had been so happy when Elizabeth asked her. What had changed? "Talk to me, sweetie. What's going on?"

"I can't wear the dress."

"Because . . . ?"

"I'm never again gonna wear anything but men's clothing. That's all I wear anymore. When I dress up, I wear a three-piece suit. I even wear men's underwear. That's who I am. I've picked a surgeon, and I'm scheduling my top surgery for this summer."

Oh no! I thought to myself, feeing sick. *When did this happen?* Although I'd grasped how ecstatic she was wearing a binder in her video, I'd never stopped hoping that she'd change her mind about surgery. Clearly, she hadn't. It was actually going to happen.

"Have you told Elizabeth?" I asked.

"About surgery?" she asked.

"No, about the dress," I said.

"I did. Just now."

"What did she say?"

"She wanted to know why."

"Did you tell her?"

"No," Emily said, sounding somewhat wistful about it. "I didn't. I didn't have to. When I told her I couldn't wear the dress, she was actually okay with it. I think she knew this was coming. We worked out that I'll wear a shirt and slacks like the groomsmen, and a vest in the same color as the bridesmaids' dresses."

"That'll look cute," I said, pretending that my head wasn't reeling over the news that she was definitely moving forward with removing her breasts. "Can you tell her that you're going to have surgery so she'll understand why you need to wear something different?"

"Not yet," Emily answered. "I'm not ready yet."

I so wanted her to share with her siblings. I truly believed that they would try to understand, even if it took them some time. And it was important. I didn't want Jon and me to be the only ones who knew. This keeping-a-secret stuff was hard, really hard.

"Sweetie, please give it some thought. You need to tell the whole family. They'll be supportive. Maybe not at first, but you can trust them."

"I know I can. And I will. I promise. Just not yet. Besides, I don't want to say anything to take away from Liz's wedding."

"I get that," I said. "One more question, now that you've decided to go ahead with everything. Is there any way they can leave milk ducts so you can still nurse if you ever have a baby?"

"I don't care about that, Mom," she said, her voice revealing her exasperation. "I'm never going to get pregnant. I won't be breastfeeding a baby."

I knew I shouldn't keep coming back to the subject, but I couldn't help myself. Glancing around our family room, a sanctuary that had seen so many years of children and babies, I wanted to believe that Emily might someday change her mind. Being pregnant and nursing had been such an important part of my own life that I had trouble accepting that it would never be part of Emily's.

Then, contributing further to my sense of despondency, she added, "Carrying a child is, like, the most feminine thing you can do. I can't imagine myself being pregnant. I don't see myself ever having children."

"I get that you don't want to have sex. But there are other ways to get pregnant. Artificial insemination—"

"Yeah, Mom, I know," she said. "It's not for me."

"That could change. I didn't want children until after I was with Dad. It could change for you too. Maybe you'll find someone. I don't mean a sexual partner, but just someone you want to live with and raise children with. It could happen."

"Stop, Mom," Emily said. "Just stop." I could hear the irritation in her voice, despite the fact that she was on the phone and almost a thousand miles away. Then, in a softer tone, she added, "I can always adopt. And a baby can drink formula."

Accepting that I'd taken the conversation as far as I could—maybe too far—I changed the subject once again. "I get that you're not ready to tell Elizabeth, Ben, and Sammy about surgery, but would it be okay with you if I tell Grandma Aura?"

Emily said that I could, knowing how much my mother cared and also realizing, on some level, that I needed to be able to talk with someone in addition to Jon. Emily trusted my mother, who had lived with us since before Emily was born and had influenced every aspect of our children's lives. My friends were often jealous when I described our situation, how when my mother retired from teaching at sixty-five, she moved in with us. It was a win-win situation. We didn't want her to be lonely, and Jon and I needed help taking care of our young children if we were going to continue to devote ourselves to work as much as we did.

My mom was thrilled when we decided to have a third child. She frequently described Emily as her reward for moving in with us, and the two bonded right away. It was my mother who kept Baby Emily distracted while waiting for me to arrive home from work. It was my mother who took Emily to and from childcare each day so Jon and I could go to work a little earlier and stay a little later.

At sixty-five, when Grandma Aura became an integral part of our lives, she was still a fiery, active individual, proud of her knowledge of current events, her support of her gay children, and her ability to gently challenge those with less liberal views. Now, however, she was ninety-one years old, dementia had crept in, and her short-term memory was gone. She could remember the politics of her younger days but was no longer able to wrap herself around new ideas. Emily's decision to have top surgery was beyond her comprehension.

She was so horrified by the thought that it stayed with her constantly, even when she couldn't remember anything else. She couldn't get it out of her mind. Over and over again, she'd say, "I hope Emily doesn't do it. She's so beautiful. Why does she have to do this to herself?"

My mother had accepted relatively easily the revelation that two of her four children were gay. She hadn't fought my own tomboyish behavior and appearance, giving me space to explore my identity on my own. But the thought of Emily removing her breasts was too much for her to handle.

I didn't have a good answer when she repeatedly asked why surgery was necessary. That hurt because it made me recognize how powerless I was. Emily had made her decision and wasn't going to be swayed by anything I said or did. Her surgery was going to happen.

Spring 2013 — Baltimore, MD
Jenn

LIVING WITH BEN IN MARYLAND LESS THAN AN hour from my folks and sister was great, but it would have been nice to live near Liz as well. She and I had been close ever since Ben brought me along on a family vacation soon after we started dating. We quickly became close friends, partly because we shared so much in common. The same competitive drive in athletics. The same love of family. Some people even said we looked similar. So much so that we were often mistaken for sisters. Our families were so much alike that we could have been. Both families were tightly knit, and Ben was as close to his grandmother as I was to my grandparents.

Although we lived on opposite sides of the country, Liz and I talked frequently. She was my go-to source for all things wedding, given that Ben and I were getting married only four months after her and Dustin. We read the same bridal magazines and wanted similar ceremonies, with beautiful gowns, a large bridal party, men in dress suits or tuxedos, a formal dinner, and lots of friends and family in attendance.

Ben proposed to me not long after Dustin asked Liz. He was so romantic, asking me over a champagne picnic dinner at a park on the shore of the Chesapeake Bay.

About a month before her wedding, Liz called and said, "I just finished talking with Emily and need to give you a heads-up because I'm sure you're going to end up with the same conversation. She won't wear the dress I picked out."

"What do you mean? She doesn't like it?" I asked.

"No. Something about never again dressing in girly clothes. Everything has to be androgynous from now on."

"Did she say why? I don't get it. She's worn dresses before."

"I know," said Liz. "I felt like saying suck it up and wear the dress. It's only for a day."

"But you didn't, right?"

"No. She seemed pretty adamant about never wearing women's clothing again. She said it made her too uncomfortable and didn't feel right."

"Could she wear it just for the ceremony and then change for the reception?"

"I actually suggested that," answered Liz. "But she said no."

"So what are you going to do?"

"Emily's going to buy some slacks that are the same color as the groomsmen's, a button-down white shirt, and a vest to match the bridesmaids' dresses."

That evening, I told Ben about our talk, ending with, "You know we're going to have to do something similar."

"Are you okay with that?" he asked.

"Do we have any choice? There's no way Emily will wear a dress. Sounds like she'd drop out of the wedding party first."

"You're probably right," Ben said.

"She's your sister, and it wouldn't be right not to have her up there with us."

"Even if she looks different? You've got a pretty strong opinion about how you want everything."

"That's true," I said. "But we have to figure something out, something like what Liz and Dustin are doing."

"Do you want to offer the same thing they did?"

"In all honesty? No, not really. I want all the brides-maids to look alike, wearing the same color dress. I don't want Emily to look different, because that'll draw people's attention." I was being honest. I knew exactly how I wanted everything to look, and that didn't include having Emily clustered with the other bridesmaids but not matching. "What if we have her stand on your side with the grooms-men and wear the same suits as them? Except she could go with just a vest, no jacket. That way she'll look different from the groomsmen, which is good because she's not one of them. She'll still be a bridesmaid, which is how we've got her listed in the program."

"You would do that?" asked Ben.

"It'll be fine."

"Thanks," Ben said. "I mean that. I know you pictured how everything would be and that you're not getting that. And you're doing it for *my* sister, not yours. You don't have to do this."

I knew that, but I wanted to make it work. It meant a lot to us to have Emily be comfortable at our wedding. We wanted her to be able to enjoy herself and feel a part of everything.

maid of honor

Spring 2013
Em (23 years old)

EVERYTHING ABOUT LIZ'S WEDDING YESTERDAY was so confusing for me. I didn't know how to be a bridesmaid, let alone a maid of honor. But I loved the way I looked, dressed basically like the groomsmen. When I saw myself in the mirror, I was able to step outside of my discomfort with my body because I was happy with what I saw. My short hair. Looking more like the groomsmen than the bridesmaids. My vest hiding my curvy chest.

It didn't even feel strange to be hanging out with a bunch of women as we were getting dressed and helping Liz get ready. I would've liked to join Ben and Sammy and have fun with the groomsmen instead. But Liz is my big sister, and I love her and wanted to be with her. I got to stand by her side and share the day with her, without having to deal with being all girly and feminine.

I had worried that others might say I looked strange and criticize me for choosing not to wear the maid-of-honor gown. People may have thought that, but nobody said anything to me. They seemed to just accept me. Some even told me I was handsome, which felt so much better than when people complimented me for being beautiful. Oh yeah, I was handsome.

Jeremy (23) with Elizabeth's (28) bridal party

Spring 2013 — Boulder, CO
Em

SOON AFTER LIZ'S WEDDING, I STARTED THINKING about Ben and Jenn's, just a few months away. I was touched that Jenn asked me to be a bridesmaid and I said yes, just as I did with Liz. Ben and Jenn haven't said anything to me yet, but I figure they're talking about what I should wear for the ceremony. They know it won't be a dress.

Soon they'll know why. They'll understand more about how strongly I feel about not looking girly. They'll figure it out when I tell them that I've scheduled top surgery and am getting it done less than a month after their wedding.

Finalizing things has made it all seem so much more

real. I told Mom and Dad right away, and although they weren't happy with it, they almost immediately switched gears into discussing logistics. They want to be sure I've picked the best surgeon possible and that I know they're willing to pay for everything. They don't want me picking my doctor based on price.

"We'll take care of the cost," Mom said on the phone one day.

"I know that," I said. "And I appreciate it. But it's important to me to pay for it myself."

"How much are we talking about?" she asked.

"It's about $9,000. That covers the doctor and anesthesia and the surgery center."

"That's a lot, but not as bad as I thought it would be," Mom answered. "Will insurance cover any of it?"

"No," I said. "And I still have to get to Florida and stay in a hotel for a week."

"Please let Dad and me pay for that part of it at least."

That would help. Ever since I was a little kid, I've saved almost every gift from birthdays and Hanukkah and Christmas from my parents and Grandma Aura, as much as $500 at a time. And when I worked at the day care center last year, I was able to live on less than I made, so I socked away some more. Now that I'm back in college, my folks cover my tuition, room, and board expenses, so I haven't had to eat into those savings. I'm incredibly lucky. Other people have to save for years after they decide to have top surgery before they can actually do it. I've been able to schedule it in a matter of months.

"Thanks," I said. "That'd be great." It wasn't just the money. Her offering to help out financially meant that she and Dad were okay with my decision.

"Now that it's definite, are you going to tell everyone else?"

"I'm not sure I'm ready for that," I said.

"Do you want me to do it for you?"

This was her way of saying that I should tell Liz, Ben, and Sammy that I've scheduled my surgery. I know it'll be easy with Sammy, who sees me frequently in Boulder and knows how much I already act like a guy. We've talked about the possibility, and he even knows I wear a binder some of the time. Liz will be more concerned and frightened for me, but also relieved to understand what was behind my refusal to wear the maid-of-honor dress, to know that it wasn't just me being stubborn or not supporting her. She still won't fully understand. Nobody can who hasn't experienced gender dysphoria themselves. But she'll try.

Ben is another story. I haven't been able to let go of the driveway conversation when I wanted so much for him to hear me, when I wanted to open up but couldn't because he just kept talking about X and Y chromosomes. At the time, Mom wanted me to let him know I felt hurt by his words, but I couldn't do that. So the hurt has stayed with me. So much so that I can't just bounce back and trust Ben with the fact that I no longer identify as a woman. Or, more accurately, that I've never identified that way. Deep inside, I'm scared that he's gonna reject me, and I don't think I can handle that.

I SHOULD'VE HAD more faith in Ben. After I finally got up the courage to tell him about the surgery, he asked if I'd prefer to dress like the groomsmen, same tuxedos, everything. Not only that, he offered to have me stand with the men, on *his* side of the wedding party rather than Jenn's. We were on the phone, so he couldn't see me. If he could, he would've noticed my eyes watering. Maybe he heard my voice crack as I thanked him.

I really do appreciate that Ben and Jenn made this incredibly generous offer, that they love and support me even though they don't understand. But it hurt that Ben's response was also to say that surgery is a bad idea. It's not like he rejected me, as I'd feared he would. But in some ways, it was just as bad. He said I must really hate my body to be willing to remove my breasts. And what I heard was even worse. I thought he said that I must hate *myself*.

Ben's words made me feel like there's this barrier between us that he doesn't even know about. I want him to see how I'm hurting. I want him to magically figure it out without me having to say anything. But I know that it's partly on me, that I have to tell him what's going on inside me before we can work it all out, and I'm not ready for that. Plus, it's not right to initiate that difficult conversation when he's getting married in just a few weeks. So I'm trying to let it go and just be grateful that he and Jenn have made this remarkable gesture of saying I can wear the same tuxedo as the groomsmen and stand with the men for the celebration. That's huge. I don't have to pretend. It really feels wonderful.

Ben (26) and Jeremy (23) at Ben's wedding

July 2013 — Baltimore, MD
Jon

WATCHING EMILY IN HER TUXEDO, STANDING with the groomsmen during Ben and Jenn's wedding, totally relaxed and smiling contentedly, I couldn't help but wonder if there was more to her upcoming top surgery than just changing her chest to a more masculine shape. Despite her protestations that she was not transgender, that all she needed was to modify her chest, I began to think that perhaps she really was, and that her desire for top surgery reflected an unstated expression of maleness.

That possibility made me more comfortable with the procedure, which previously I'd viewed as akin to a woman getting breast augmentation. Since I thought Emily looked great just the way she was, it bothered me that she wanted to change her appearance. The thought that it wasn't just about that but about something far deeper—her very essence—that somehow made me feel better.

fourteen

FLYING HIGH

—·—

Summer 2013 — On a Plane
Em (23 years old)

The only nonstop flight on Southwest Air out of Denver took off before eight in the morning. I packed last night, selecting my most comfortable, loose-fitting T-shirts and sweatpants, knowing that after surgery everything will hurt. I'll have huge scars underneath where my breasts are now, and I'll hardly be able to move.

The alarm on my cell phone went off before dawn, but I didn't need it to wake up. I'd already been awake for what seemed like hours, too excited to sleep. Although it's only been a couple of months since I scheduled my procedure, in some ways, it feels as if I've been waiting my whole life.

I'm glad it was Colin who drove me to the airport. He's been part of my surgery from the beginning, from his early acceptance of my asexual androgyny to his recognition that I was distraught and had to do something about my gender dysphoria. He's been there for me every step of the way, so it's fitting that he shared this last step with me.

It's exhilarating to be flying to Florida to meet one of the best gender reassignment top surgeons in the country. *Gender reassignment.* That's what they call the procedure I'm about to get, even though I don't think of it that way. My whole motivation behind transitioning is purely physical, so I don't think of it as gender reassignment. I don't follow the narrative of being a man trapped in a woman's body. I don't necessarily feel like I'm a man. I just don't like having a female body. You know? So labeling doesn't work.

All I can really say is that I am somewhere under the genderqueer umbrella. None of the pronouns feel right. Female pronouns feel weird, but so do male ones. Gender-neutral pronouns don't work either. Nothing fits me. When I first told Colin about my gender dysphoria, he said, "I don't really think of you as any gender at all. You're just you." Maybe that's why I don't feel a need to have a label.

Now that surgery is actually happening, I feel downright giddy, grinning like a little kid looking at a birthday cake. In some ways, the trip to Florida is kinda like my birthday. My big present is that I'm getting the body I want. I'll finally be flat-chested.

I know that once Mom arrives, we'll talk for hours. But right now, on the plane by myself, it feels good to be alone with my thoughts. I'm excited and scared and a little woozy all at the same time.

My therapist says it's okay to have more than one feeling at a time. She's great. I started with her last fall, after I bought my condo. I made an appointment at the student health center to start the counseling that's legally required to qualify for top surgery. The school didn't offer that, but they gave me the name of an independent psychotherapist named Maxine Gower, a clinical social worker with a solid reputation for working with folks anywhere on the LGBTQ spectrum.

Maxine is a little older than my mom and like her in some ways. She wears her hair almost down to her shoulders, dyed brown with hints of gray showing through. She smiles a lot, nodding her head in encouragement as I talk through my issues. I'd heard that therapists never give you answers but instead help you figure things out for yourself. But Maxine is willing to make suggestions, which I really appreciate. She won't make them as strongly as my mom might, but she gets me thinking about different possibilities.

"So, Em, it sounds like you're very confident about moving forward with top surgery, but you're not so certain about the social implications. Is that it?" she asked during one of our recent sessions.

"Kind of," I said, not quite sure what I meant by that. I've been telling myself that the physical transformation is all I need. "I'm wondering how I'll react if people start to view me differently."

"How do you think you'll react?" she asked.

"I'll still be me, just without breasts. What'll it feel like if strangers look at me and see a man? Or will they see me as a woman with a flat chest? Or will they just be confused?"

"You might get all of those reactions," Maxine said. "Are you okay with that ambiguity?"

"I don't know."

"Stay with that a moment. Picture each of these happening, and tell me how it feels."

"Okay. Here's what I'm worried about. If people see me

as a man, will that push me to go on hormones so I can be even more masculine? And will I want to change my name?"

"Will it?"

"I don't know. I have more questions than answers."

Thinking back on that session, I'm realizing that I don't expect my new appearance to be all that different from the androgynous in-between space that I've already made for myself. At the same time, though, surgery is a big step toward the masculine. That realization is more frightening than the surgery itself. What will happen if classmates and teachers assume I'm male? I don't know what that'll be like. I can't know until it actually starts happening.

If it does make me more comfortable embodying a more masculine space and going by a male name, will that make me want to start taking testosterone? Every time my folks ask me about that, I say that hormones and a name change aren't on the table. And that's what I've believed, mostly. I've been assuming that once I have my breasts removed, my gender dysphoria will go away.

During my last session with Maxine, I acknowledged for the first time that I'm not sure about that anymore. I admitted that my previous denial had been somewhat shortsighted. "Once others start to view me differently, that might impact how I view myself," I told her. "I'm going to have a whole world of new stresses post-op."

"You will," she said. "How do you think you'll respond?"

"It'll be difficult to put my assumptions aside, to acknowledge that surgery might not be the end of it."

"I'm really happy you said that, Em. This way of looking at everything is a natural and healthy progression."

"Before, surgery itself was the end game because I knew how much better I'd feel about my body," I said.

"And now?"

"Now I'm more aware that my life may take a drastic turn after surgery. And that scares me."

"It's okay to feel scared."

Yeah. I'm scared, but it really is okay. My main emotion is excitement. In a few minutes, we'll start our descent into Fort Lauderdale. Two days from now, I'll wake up in the surgery center recovery room. This is really happening!

For the first time, I let myself experience this exhilaration. I am so ready to be comfortable with my body.

Jo

I HAD MIXED EMOTIONS WHILE HEADING TO Fort Lauderdale to help Emily through her top surgery. I was happy because she was happy. More than that, she was ecstatic, flying high. And that's what every parent wants. For their kids to be happy.

"Are you going home?" the man sitting next to me asked when we first took our seats. I'd been staring out the window at the terminal, ignoring the book and puzzle magazine I'd brought to pass the time.

"No," I said. Normally, I would have explained further, said whether I was visiting friends or taking a vacation. But what could I say? That it was a medical trip for my daughter to remove her breasts?

"What did you do to your arm?" he asked, when I

didn't offer any more information or politely respond with a question of my own.

"I dislocated my shoulder and have to keep it still for a few weeks," I said.

I was used to people being curious. I'd messed up my shoulder the night before Jon and I flew to Baltimore for Ben and Jenn's wedding. When the emergency room doctor told me to sit still for a few days, I told her why I couldn't. She agreed I could go, though she'd jokingly added, "I'd better not see any pictures of you dancing."

I'd followed her directions, except for the traditional mother-son dance. I couldn't give that up, to stand with Ben and rock back and forth to the Lee Ann Womack song I'd picked, "I Hope You Dance." Sitting on the plane, I thought back to that moment and the lyrics that drew me so. *Promise me that you'll give faith a fighting chance, and when you get the choice to sit it out or dance, I hope you dance.*

That's really what Emily was doing, wasn't it? Choosing to dance? But at what cost? Was it really okay that she was chopping off her breasts? I'd never put it in those terms when discussing it with the kids. Instead, we'd talked about "top surgery" or "the procedure," sanitizing the image of what was about to happen. It somehow made it easier.

After we took off, I stared at the clouds, alone with my thoughts, knowing that Emily and I would see each other within a couple of hours and that surgery was scheduled for the next day. It had all become very real, and I couldn't get that violent image out of my head. It was hard to accept that this is what Emily wanted to do. What she was going to do. I knew I'd ask her one more time if she were absolutely sure. "You don't have to go through with this, Emily," I'd say. "Nobody will fault you if you change your mind or want to delay. Do you have any second thoughts at all?"

I also knew what she'd answer. "I'm good," she'd say. "This is what I want. No doubt in my mind."

And she'd mean it. She'd thought this through beginning to end. She knew what the surgery entailed and how hard it would be to recover. She wanted the end result, to have a flat chest. But just because I knew that she was confident didn't mean that I was happy with it.

It was kind of like when Ben and Sammy went skydiving. They were adults, so I didn't have any choice in the matter, yet I still told them I didn't want them to jump, that I was frightened for them, that it was an unnecessary risk. This surgery with Emily felt so much riskier. It wasn't just that there was always a chance that things could go wrong. It was also that Emily was changing who she was.

Staring out the window and picturing my boys falling through the sky underneath fluttering parachutes, it occurred to me that for my daughter, removing her breasts wasn't like skydiving at all. That was taking a risk for the thrill of taking a risk. Emily was so uncomfortable with her body that she was driven to change it, not because she wanted a thrill, but despite her fear of change. I didn't want Emily to feel as if she had to go skydiving.

Everything I'd read, though, said it was totally normal for her to want to take this step, this leap. *She has gender dysphoria*, I told myself yet again. It was a constant pain and frustration for her to see her body looking different from the way she felt it should. And wearing a binder, her short-term "cure," had dangers of its own. Chest and back pain, bruised ribs, shortness of breath, and the potential for permanent damage to her lungs. A better medical treatment for dysphoria was to modify the body. Knowing this didn't change the fact that it was gut-wrenching to accept the reality of what she needed to do. I hated that she had to. But it wasn't my choice to make.

I had to pull myself together and be a supportive mom, to assist my child through a difficult undertaking. It was time for me to help Emily. For me to leave my negative, fearful thoughts on the plane, or at least not to indulge myself in thinking about them. It was time to be the trooper my mother had taught me to be and to convince myself that it was all going to be okay. I sat up straighter, trying to look outwardly the way I wanted to feel inside.

fifteen

IT'S ALMOST TIME

==

July 2013 — Fort Lauderdale, FL
Em (23 years old)

My pre-op checkup with Dr. Charles Garramone lasted all of five minutes. He didn't waste any time with pleasantries, just got straight to talking about my procedure. No reassurances. No warm bedside manner. I actually found that kind of comforting because he came across as so competent and experienced and professional. Most of the time was taken up by a discussion of what my scars would look like.

"They're going to be big," he said as I sat on the examining table, "running in a slight curve across your chest, right under the place where your breasts are now."

I'm prepared for that. I've looked at so many photos that I can totally picture the scars. One of the reasons I picked Dr. Garramone is that he has a reputation for placing the scars such that if I build up my chest muscles enough, the scars will be in the shadow of my pecs and people won't even notice them. He also appealed because he has lots of experience with people who look like me, people with the same body type and breast size. People who aren't on testosterone. People who don't yet have a lot of muscle mass.

I'm committed to building up my muscles because that's a critical part of making my chest look more masculine. Sammy and Ben are super athletic with their broad shoulders and six-pack abs, compliments of years of football and wrestling and working out in gyms. I've always wanted to look like them, and now that's really a possibility. I'm strong but in a wiry kind of way. Going rock climbing with Colin a few times a week has strengthened me, but I'm still kind of scrawny.

For the near term, that means that my scars will be quite visible. That doesn't bother me. I've seen enough examples of Dr. Garramone's work to know they'll fade eventually. I've stared for hours at pictures of young, smiling men with their flat chests. Men I know had breasts before their surgery.

Mom hasn't focused on the artistic results at all. She's been more worried about Dr. Garramone's medical reputation and wanted to make sure he isn't some sort of a quack. Even though I told her I'd checked him out thoroughly and that he has a reputation as one of the best surgeons in the country for this specific surgery, it was important to her to look up any complaints about him and make sure his licensing is up to date. When I told her he does hundreds of top surgeries each year, is a leader in researching the best techniques, and trains other physicians, she grudgingly acknowledged that maybe he knows what he's doing.

I didn't mind Mom having questioned Dr. Garramone's ability. She's just trying to take care of me. But it did make me feel a bit like she doesn't trust me, like she still views me as a kid. Dr. Garramone and his staff, though, seem to trust me completely and never tried to talk me out of the procedure. Although they did require a therapist's statement certifying that I have gender dysphoria and that top surgery is an appropriate treatment. They had to ask for that because Florida law mandates it. Most states have some sort of requirement for patients to see a licensed practitioner before getting scheduled for surgery. Some even say that you have to be on hormones for a year.

"It's going to be a rough week and you'll hate how tightly we have to wrap your chest in an ace bandage, but we'll do our best to keep you comfortable," Dr. Garramone said, pulling me back into the moment.

"Will I be able to get up and walk around?" I asked.

"Not the first day. Mostly you'll sleep. And you're not going to want to move around that much in any case because you'll have drainage tubes at the incisions."

I've read about the drainage tubes. They'll be a pain to keep clean and will probably hurt. Not everyone chooses to leave them in for a whole week, but Dr. Garramone says he likes his patients to do it, saying the results will be better.

Mom is the one who will have to take care of the tubes. She would have been willing to join me for my pre-op appointment with Dr. Garramone, but I asked her to stay outside in the waiting room. I'm not sure why this time was different, why I didn't want her there. She's traveled thirteen hundred miles to take care of me and wanted to meet the doctor and be a part of everything. But it just didn't seem quite right to have her there when I knew we'd be talking about something as personal as top surgery, about nipple placement and how the scars would look. Don't get me wrong. I'm glad she's here for the week, but I need some boundaries.

Jo

EMILY DIDN'T WANT TO HAVE ME WITH HER FOR her pre-op appointment. I started to join her when they called her name from the doorway, but she stopped me.

"Umm, Mom, you can wait out here if you want."

"That's okay, sweetie. I can come in with you." I glanced at the nurse to make sure that was really the case.

"Actually, I'd rather you not," said Emily.

"You don't want me to?" I asked.

"Not really," she said. "This is all kinda personal."

Had I said something that made her worry I'd embarrass her? I knew I tended to jump in with questions. Maybe Emily thought that would make her feel less in control of the situation, as if I didn't trust her to ask her own questions. If that were the case, I wished she could've just said so. I could have stayed quiet. But then, this wasn't about me. It was about how I could be the most helpful and what Emily needed.

Trying to distract myself, I picked up an old *Time* magazine and started to read. At first I was annoyed that the office didn't keep something more current available. Then it occurred to me that this April edition was still there because the cover article was all about gay marriage. So much for getting my mind off of Emily's choice to have top surgery.

I started looking around the room, imagining the backstory of each of the patients sitting there. Most were young men with neatly trimmed beards. It took a moment for me to realize that they were all transgender and on testosterone. Emily was adamant that she wasn't like them, that she was here only to treat her physical gender dysphoria. She believed that once she had a flat chest, she'd be happy. That all she wanted was to look androgynous, neither male nor female.

I thought there was more to it than that. Emily was in denial. She was more like all the young men in the waiting room than she admitted. I believed she just hadn't accepted it yet. I hadn't said this to her, partly because it was her journey to follow and partly because I hoped I was wrong, that she'd be satisfied with this step and not want to take it any further. That she wasn't like the transgender men in the doctor's waiting room and her life would be easier than theirs. That she wouldn't have to change everything about herself, be completely different, stop being Emily. And that she wouldn't have to deal with the discrimination that transgender people face every day just for being who they are.

I got a little choked up looking around. The patients all looked so young, barely out of their teens. Yet only one had a parent with him. How could anyone know their child was going through such a traumatic procedure and not want to be right there? The one other mom who was there looked as if she wished she weren't. Instead of chatting quietly with her son, she stared off into the distance, only looking his way when he reached out and took her hand.

There was one androgynously dressed older couple that looked more comfortable and even excited. At first, I assumed they were lesbians. It didn't occur to me initially that probably one of them was there for top surgery. I couldn't tell if either or both of them were on hormones, because neither one had facial hair or spoke with a deep voice. Then I wondered, *How do you define them if one of them is transgender? Does that then make them a straight couple rather than a gay one?* I decided it was too hard to apply labels and instead returned to my thoughts about how lonely the younger adults appeared without a parent by their side.

That made me wish that Jon were there, going through this with me. I knew he would have joined us if he could, but he was almost five thousand miles away, on a business trip to Norway. We'd considered having him forgo the trip so that he could come to Florida with us, but with four kids, we were accustomed to splitting up and going in different directions so we could support and help all of them at the same time. Looking back, however, I think we messed up that time. Top surgery was a big deal.

Em

THE PRE-OP APPOINTMENT WAS PERFECT. I loved everything about it. The way everyone treated me. The assumption that I know what I'm doing. Most of all, the awareness that the surgery will be over tomorrow and I'll have the flat chest that I've dreamed about since puberty first gave me breasts that don't belong.

"What do you want to do now?" Mom asked, breaking into my thoughts. "We could go to a movie. Or head for lunch and then explore the Everglades. Whatever you want to do is fine with me."

I glanced over at her behind the wheel of our rental car. Her right arm was in a sling, but she was managing pretty well, holding the wheel with only her left hand. I offered to drive. But she insisted she was okay, saying that I wouldn't be able to drive for a few weeks after my surgery and that she had to get used to it. She told me her shoulder doesn't hurt anymore, but I still see her wince every once in a while.

"I dunno. What do *you* want to do?" My answer was typical middle child stuff. Always willing to go along with whatever anybody else wants to do. I honestly don't care. It's not like I'm sacrificing anything. It just never matters to me what we have for dinner or what's on the TV.

"Let's look for the nearest entry to the Everglades and watch for a restaurant along the way," she said. "Okay?"

"Sure."

After that, she was quiet, which was kind of unusual. I'm used to her asking all kinds of questions and wanting to know how I feel about everything. For some reason, though, she didn't ask me about my pre-op visit.

Finally, I broke the silence. "What did you think?"

Mom knew right away what I meant. That I was ready to talk. And so the questions started. "What did *you* think? Are you still okay with surgery tomorrow? Any second thoughts?"

"I'm more than okay," I said. "This is exactly what I need to do."

"So what did the doctor say? Anything new?"

"No. Mostly we talked about my scars and what I'll look like when it's all done."

"Nothing about tomorrow?"

"Oh, yeah. We talked about that too. The usual. I can't eat anything after midnight. I'll be asleep for the whole thing, and after I wake up in recovery, they'll let you in to see me."

"And they really send you home tomorrow?" She frowned. "It still seems to me that they should keep you overnight, just to make sure you're okay."

"I know that makes you uncomf—"

"This is serious surgery to do on an outpatient basis," Mom said, airing a concern she's mentioned several times before.

"I promise I'll be okay, Mom. They know what they're doing. They've done this hundreds of times, maybe thousands."

"I get that," Mom said. "I just want you to consider asking about it one more time. We'll pay the difference."

She doesn't get it, just like when she wanted me to think about going to Thailand for the surgery. I don't want to be different. Everyone else goes home right after the procedure, so that's what I want to do. It isn't a matter of money. I'm glad that Mom and Dad took care of the airplane and the hotel. I appreciate that and the strong statement of support it makes. But the medical stuff is on me.

"No, really," I said. "I'm not at all worried about it. They're all set up to do this as a day surgery. If something unexpected happens, I'm sure they'll keep me overnight."

Mom nodded, but she still looked unconvinced.

It occurred to me that her insistence might just be her way of dealing with the stress of me having surgery. "You saw how young most of the other patients were in the waiting room?"

"Yeah," she said.

"Insurance doesn't cover this, and most of them have had to save for years to pay for this, working two jobs, taking out loans. Dr. Garramone is doing everything he can to keep the cost down for them by doing it this way."

"I suppose that makes sense," Mom said, sounding for the first time as if she got it.

I sat quietly, watching out the window at the scenery as Mom drove towards the Everglades Holiday Park, and thinking about how incredibly lucky I am. All of a sudden, the houses on our right stopped and it seemed pretty clear we weren't going to find a restaurant before we got there.

"How about if we spend a few minutes at the park and then go get lunch? Sound good to you?" Mom asked.

Now the houses had disappeared completely and we were driving through empty fields. The palm trees yielded to lower-lying shrubs with a few live oak trees scattered about.

"Sure," I said.

It didn't look much like how I'd pictured the Everglades. The water was just the same canal we'd been driving along since we left the doctor's office. The next few minutes were focused on finding a parking space, rejecting the idea of going for an airboat ride, and deciding to walk on a trail that looked like it might lead to something more interesting.

It didn't. It was flat and sandy and we could barely see the water beyond the high grass that surrounded us. There were no trail markers, and I was beginning to think it was just going to continue on in the same way forever. But after we'd gone a few hundred yards, we heard someone hollering. When we looked back to see if they were yelling at us, we saw a park ranger waving his arms for us to come back. Maybe the path wasn't really part of the park. Or maybe there were alligators. In any case, we turned around to head toward the car, walking slowly in the heat.

"So, Emily," Mom said as we made our way back up the path. "I couldn't help but notice that most of the other patients in Dr. Garramone's waiting room looked like men and had low voices and beards. I hadn't thought about it before, but are you unusual getting top surgery without going on testosterone first?"

Clearly, she'd been looking for the right moment to ask me about this. I'd tried to explain all of this before, but I guess she hadn't quite understood.

"Yeah, Mom," I said. "I am. Most of the patients have presented as male for at least a year before having surgery. And, by the way, you shouldn't say that they 'look like men.' They are men."

"But you're not."

"No."

"And you don't ever see yourself making that transition?"

"No. It's purely physical for me. I just want to get rid of my curves."

"That's good," she said.

This took me aback. She rarely made a judgmental statement like that. And this one hit me hard. "Why would you say that?" I asked, not looking at her.

"Because you're really short for a guy."

Glancing at her face and seeing her smile, I realized she was trying to be funny.

"Thanks for that, Mom," I snapped. "Like I really needed to be reminded."

She stopped walking. "Wait," she said. "I didn't mean—"

"It's okay. I know." I suppose it wasn't fair of me to be irritated with her. After all, I'd said pretty consistently that I wasn't transgender, even though the procedure was considered gender reassignment, and even though I'd end up with a letter from the doctor saying that I was eligible to modify the gender marker on my identification cards.

"There's something else I've been wanting to ask you," she said, changing the subject.

"Sure," I said.

"Ben and Jenn's wedding."

"What about it?"

"I know you really liked wearing the same tuxedo as the groomsmen, and standing with them instead of with the bridesmaids."

"Yeah, that was awesome," I said, grinning at the memory.

"Did it bother you at all that they put you at the end of the line of guys instead of right next to Ben and Sammy?"

"Wh—? No! They were incredible for letting me dress like that. And I never thought twice about being at the end. Sammy was the best man, so of course he stood next to Ben."

"You're right, but I worry that you felt . . ."

"What?"

"Left out," she said, struggling with the words.

"I was okay with it. Really."

"You're sure?"

"Yeah. Both weddings were perfect. It was a big deal for Liz and then Jenn to let me dress the way I wanted instead of the way they'd pictured. But I actually felt great about both weddings. I promise."

"I'm glad. I was worried. You looked happy, but—"

"I *was* happy."

sixteen

WHAT'S IN A NAME?

——

July 2013 — Fort Lauderdale, FL

Jo

A different waiting room, just as cold as the one yesterday. This time, though, people weren't watching
for someone to come out of a pre-op appointment. Instead,
they were waiting for word that their partner or friend or
child was waking up. This was it. Surgery. There was no
turning back.

Emily was incredibly excited. I'd gotten up early, but
she was already awake, channel surfing on the hotel TV
set, impatiently moving from one show to the next, unable
to concentrate on anything. When she noticed I was up,
her first words were, "I can't believe this is actually happening. This is so awesome."

I didn't expect to feel the same way, but I did. I was
excited for her.

I was also scared. Not just about the surgery itself, but
also about whether she'd have any regrets and what the
future would hold for her.

Emily was scared as well. But that anxiety was totally

overwhelmed by her sense of joy. Watching her, listening to her, I didn't know whether to smile at how ecstatic she was or cry at her need to take this extreme step. Or do both at the same time.

Once at the Memorial Same Day Surgery Center, I didn't have time to worry about it. From the moment we checked in, the nurses kept us busy with prepping Emily, inserting an intravenous needle, starting antibiotics and hydrating her, checking her vitals, and placing a breathing tube around her mouth and nose. The nurse kept up a constant patter, telling us what to expect. "The procedure will take two to four hours, and then it'll be another hour or so before he wakes up enough for you to see him."

"Him." That's how all the nurses and support staff referred to Emily. I couldn't miss this strong reminder that with the exception of Emily, all the patients were there for gender reassignment surgery. They'd already taken male or neutral names and were using masculine or neutral pronouns.

"When will I be able to take her back to the hotel?" I asked, noticing that the nurse frowned at me when I used a feminine pronoun. I could tell she thought I was one of those parents who refused to acknowledge their child's gender change. I wanted to say, "Wait! That's not me. I'm one of the good guys. Emily and I have talked about this, and she doesn't want me to use a new name and male pronouns. Stop judging me."

"After we're sure he's comfortable and stable, we'll bring you back to the recovery area. We'll want him to stay there for another hour while we monitor him. Then we'll go over all of his medication and give you his post-surgery instructions."

"Are you at all concerned about whether I can handle everything with my arm in a sling?" I asked the nurse, unnerved by a sense that I was no longer in control of the situation.

I never really had been, of course. Emily's decisions had brought us to this point, and now everything was moving forward whether I wanted it to or not.

"I'm not," she said. "You seem to be moving around just fine. Don't worry. And don't forget that we're only a phone call away. Or a fifteen-minute drive from your hotel."

I knew she was right, but I was still nervous. I would have to clean the drainage tubes that would be inserted in Emily's chest, monitor her pain, make sure she didn't have a fever, check her pulse, and help her with basic bodily functions. All with one arm.

Once Emily and I were left alone to wait for the anesthesiologist to stop by, I asked about my pronoun usage. "Sweetie," I said, "the nurses call you 'Em' and refer to you as 'he' and 'him.' Do you want me to start doing that too?"

She couldn't hear my heart thumping as I waited for a response. Was this the moment? Was this when Emily would confide in me that the surgery wasn't just to change her physical appearance but that who she was had changed as well?

"No, Mom. It's okay. My friends call me Em and I don't mind the male pronouns, but I don't need you and Dad to do that."

"Are you sure?" I asked.

"Yeah. Really. It's okay."

Maybe it's like when people grow out of a nickname but still want their parents to use it. A way of hanging on to their childhood. I felt a surge of relief when Emily turned down my offer. Changing her name seemed even bigger than top surgery. The medical procedure was physical. Her name was her very essence.

"What about pronouns?" I asked next.

"Not necessary," she said. "Even though it feels good when people call me 'he,' it would feel weird if you guys switched."

After that, the waiting was over. The anesthesiologist stopped by and introduced himself. Moments later, they wheeled Emily off to surgery. I watched as she disappeared down the hallway, wishing once again that this wasn't happening, choked up at the sight of her lying on the hospital bed with an IV dripping fluids into her arm and a breathing tube attached to her nose and mouth. My last image of her before this massive change. Feeling helpless to do anything but be supportive.

"See you soon," I said as I waved goodbye. Now, all I could do was wait.

"YOU CAN SEE him now," the nurse said.

"How's she doing?" I asked.

"*He's* doing just fine," she answered, looking down at me with disapproval. I couldn't deal with it at the moment. I just was eager to get to Emily and make sure she was okay.

"Is she awake?"

"On and off. We're trying to wake him up completely so you can take him home."

Home. The Residence Inn, where we were staying for a week. My stomach tensed as I thought again how unprepared I felt to take care of Emily on my own. My anxiety didn't go away when I finally saw her lying on a bed in the recovery area, looking very frail, an ace bandage wrapped tightly around her chest with drainage tubes coming out on either side.

I sat down next to her and held her hand. Her eyes fluttered.

"When are they going to start?" she asked.

"It's all over, baby. You're done. You made it."

"Really?"

Before I could answer, she fell back to sleep. It really was all done. Underneath her bandage, Emily had a flat chest.

While Emily slept, the nurse went over all the discharge paperwork with me. "He can't be alone for the next twenty-four hours. We don't expect any problems. But we need to know right away if he starts bleeding a lot."

"What do I do if that happens?" I asked.

"Bring him back in. It's unlikely to happen, but that's the biggest risk," she said.

"Got it," I answered, willing myself to believe that Emily would be one of the patients who had no difficulties in the first few hours post-surgery. "Anything else?"

"We do see complications in about 10 percent of the cases, but it's not typically urgent. One more thing. He shouldn't lift anything more than five pounds during the first few weeks."

"I don't think she'll be tempted to try," I said. "I imagine she'll be in a fair amount of pain."

"Not necessarily," the nurse said. "He'll be uncomfortable, but you've got a prescription for medication that should keep the pain under control."

How was I supposed to get the prescription filled when I wasn't supposed to leave Emily alone? Before I could ask about that, Emily woke up gagging.

"Uhhh," she said. "I feel awful. I'm gonna—"

The nurse handed her a little tub and she threw up. Good thing she hadn't eaten since the night before.

"All done?" the nurse asked, gently.

"Yeah, I think so."

"Can you give her anything for that?" I asked.

"We already did. I put something in his IV that should start working soon. Don't worry. It's just a reaction to the anesthesia."

My poor baby. I wanted to hug her and tell her everything was going to be all right. And I wanted someone to hold me and tell me the same.

AFTER STOPPING AT a grocery store to fill Emily's prescription while she slept in the car, I drove straight to our hotel. When we got there, the walk from the car to our room seemed to take forever. She could barely move. As soon as we got in the door, I helped her into bed, saying, "Go back to sleep, darling, and you'll be okay when you wake up." I wanted to believe that.

Once I was sure she was asleep, I read through all of the post-op instructions again, noting that I was supposed to watch for swelling as well as bleeding and that I had to make sure the suction drains were properly collecting fluids. The nurse had shown me how to clear them if they got blocked, but I wasn't sure if I remembered all the steps.

After setting the medications on the kitchen counter, along with a pad to keep track of when I gave them, I returned to Emily's side, leaned over, and kissed her on the forehead. Gently tucking in her blanket under her chin, I noticed how pale she looked, her lips pressed tightly together, even in her sleep. I wanted to hug her but knew that if I did, I might wake her up. Instead, I smiled down at her, willing her to come through her experience as easily as possible. Then I fell into my own bed, exhausted.

Several hours later, once we'd both had our fill of sleep, we started to talk. A week is a long time. When you're trying to make the time pass quickly as you recover from surgery, that's what you do. You talk. Emily shared with me once again all that had gone into her decision to have this surgery and what she expected to happen next.

"I had to do it, Mom," she said.

"I know you did, sweetie," I said. "I know you did."

"I can't wait to see how I look once the bandage comes off."

Then she nodded off again.

While she slept, I checked that her tubes were draining properly, pleased with how quickly I'd learned the basics of taking care of her. Then I slipped out of the bedroom to cook her childhood go-to meal when she wasn't feeling well, matzo ball soup. Molding the matzo meal into little tiny spheres was a welcome distraction; it made the time pass more easily than when I thought about Emily molding her body into a new shape.

Forty-five minutes later, when the soup was ready, I went in to see if Emily was hungry.

"I was thinking about what you said earlier," she mumbled.

"What did I say? Which comment?" I asked.

"Just in general. You don't have to call me 'Em' like my

friends do, because I don't see myself as a man. I don't expect to do anything beyond removing my breasts. But if I do change my name, I don't want to choose one that's a popular baby name today. I want something you and Dad would have picked when I was born."

"Are you really thinking about changing your name? Does that mean that you're trans after all?"

"I dunno. I haven't figured it out. I just want to know what my name would've been if I were a boy."

"That's easy," I said. "Sammy. But you can't use that because it's already taken."

Emily laughed out loud and then squawked in pain. "Don't make me laugh," she said. "It hurts too much." Catching her breath, she added, "But what's another name you would've picked? What would fit with Liz, Ben, and Sammy?"

"They're all from the Old Testament. That was important to me, a way of acknowledging my Jewish heritage. But the names don't sound religious, and they're common in mainstream America. They're also family names."

"Who are we named for?" she asked.

I'd told her many times before, but it was always nice to think about our relatives, so I happily repeated the story. "Elizabeth is Grandma Aura's middle name. Benjamin was Dad's grandfather's middle name. And Dad's middle name, David, is where we got Ben's middle name. David was Grandma Teddy's father and brother. Samuel was Grandma Aura's dad. And Sammy's middle name, Austin, was Dad's other grandpa. By the way, there's a quiz when you wake up in the morning."

"I'd forgotten about all that. So how does 'Emily Amber' fit in? Was I named for anyone?"

"Not really. We just thought it would be fun to pick a name that started with 'E' to match Elizabeth. And since her middle name is 'Jade,' we thought it would be a nice parallel to have your middle name be a gemstone as well."

"So no story behind it?"

"Sorry. Not really."

"So what's another name like Liz, Ben, and Sammy?"

I thought for a while, but nothing came to mind. "Give me some time," I said.

The next day, when I was standing in line at the grocery store picking up some pasta to cook for dinner, I noticed a book of baby names at the checkout counter. I considered purchasing it but decided against that, aware that Emily might think I was moving too fast.

It surprised me that I was excited by the prospect of picking a new name and not bothered in the least by how surreal it felt. How many times does a mom get to name her baby twice? Skimming through the book while waiting for the customer ahead of me to pay, I turned to a section of biblical boys' names and found one that looked interesting, Ember. The first syllable matched the first half of Emily's name, and she could easily keep the same nickname, Em. The last three letters were the same as the second half of Emily's middle name, Amber. The only problem was that it wasn't mainstream American.

"SO WHAT DO you think?" I asked as I unpacked the groceries.

"Never heard of it," Emily answered.

"Yeah, me neither," I said.

"And it sounds kind of girly."

"I know, but I did find it in the boys' section of the baby name book."

"Doesn't really work for me," she said, summarily dismissing my suggestion.

I wasn't ready to give up so easily. The next day, when I went back to the grocery store, I picked up the baby name book again and returned to the entry about Ember. As I read more, it was obvious why it was unfamiliar; it was Hungarian. In that language, it meant human being. It was also a variant of the name "Jeremy," which was in turn a version of "Jeremiah."

"Jeremiah" sounded religious to me, kind of nineteenth-century. But "Jeremy" could work. And it had been popular when Emily was born. It was the name of one of the little brothers of her best childhood friend, James. It even had the same meter as "Emily," and the same vowel sounds.

When I got home and suggested it to Emily, she said, "I'll think about it." Then she grinned in that sweet way that said, "I'm not convinced, but I don't want to disappoint you. So I won't tell you that I don't really like it."

I dropped the idea and went back to putting away groceries, struggling to hold the refrigerator door open with my body, since I still couldn't use one arm.

Jon

I WISH I COULD HAVE BEEN WITH EMILY FOR her surgery, but I was in Europe instead, helping to make sure my company's integration of a recently purchased Norwegian firm went smoothly. Was that more important than being by my daughter's side for such a critical moment in her life? Emily had assured me she didn't mind. And Jo, even with her arm in a sling, was more than capable of providing support, both physically and emotionally.

As it turned out, everything had gone smoothly at the surgery center and Emily was already feeling somewhat better. At least I knew I'd be with her for the weekend.

When I first saw her in the hotel room, her torso wrapped up tightly in bandages with bags of fluid hanging from her sides, I was struck by how fragile she was. She was in pain, unsteady, and obviously wounded. At the same time she was confident, forward-looking, and happy. These two contradictory images were hard to reconcile.

Trying to keep both descriptions in mind, I worried that she was obsessed with body modification for its own sake, that the thrill of surgery would dissipate soon and she'd begin contemplating further changes. Top surgery was one thing, but what else might she want to do? Where was this journey going to end?

Em

IT WAS A TOUGH WEEK. MUCH HARDER THAN I expected. I was miserable, groggy all of the time, and sick to my stomach from the anesthesia. The ace bandage was incredibly tight and itchy. Sometimes I felt overwhelmed. The pain meds helped. Mom cooked matzo ball soup almost every day.

I'd been so focused on the discomfort that I hadn't really thought about what it would be like to have the flat chest I've craved for so long. It didn't hit me until my follow-up appointment yesterday, a week after surgery. Not until I was actually in the doctor's office, watching as he slowly unwound the ace bandage. I held my breath, my heart rate rising. I glanced at my mom, sitting in a corner watching, smiling as if to reassure me. But her smile only reached the lower part of her face; her eyes looked anxious. When she noticed me looking her way, her grin grew bigger, but I didn't know whether she shared my excitement or was just trying to give me strength.

I felt as if everything was moving in slow motion and the doctor took forever removing the bandage, layer by layer. Although he spoke, I didn't hear his words, just the soothing sound of his voice.

Finally. The last layer. Instantly, the pain was gone. For the first time in a week, my upper body stopped screaming at me. In the silence that remained, I became absorbed in the anticipation. What would I look like? Would I be happy with the results?

Letting my eyes drop down to my chest, I focused on the area where my breasts had been.

They were gone. They were really, truly gone.

All the hours I'd spent waffling over whether to take this step had led to this. To this moment. To this life-changing, awe-inspiring, magnificent moment. All I could think was, *Holy crap!*

Except for the two furious scars running in curves under my chest and the little bandages covering my nipples, my chest actually looks ordinary, but kind of prepubescent. Real skinny with no muscle definition. That's okay. I wasn't expecting any because I'm not on hormones like most top surgery patients. My pecs will look better once I start

working out hard, which I plan on doing as soon as I recover from surgery.

For the moment, I just love how normal I look.

seventeen

I'M AWESOME AT DENIAL

—·—

August 2013 — Boulder, CO
Em (23 years old)

T oday, at ten days post-op, I threw away my binders
and sports bras. I even considered burning them in
some sort of a ceremony, but that was too reminiscent of
the women's liberation movement and I didn't feel a part
of that.

Mom asked about my bras when she was packing my
suitcase at the hotel in Florida. "Do you still want these?"
she asked. "Should I throw them away?"

Yes! I screamed to myself. *Oh yes!* My insides were
cheering, but what came out of my mouth was, "No, wait!"

I got this sense of panic as Mom started to put them in
the trash. Would I really never need them again? I looked
down at my chest with a sudden sense of satisfaction. But
what if the doctor tells me to wear one instead of the ace
bandage to keep the swelling down as I start to get better?
Would he say that? In my pain medication–induced haze,
the question seemed too complicated to answer, so I punted
and said, "Pack them."

I should have known that I'd never wear them again. At the time, though, I thought they might be more comfortable than the itchy ace bandage to keep the swelling down. But that was totally unrealistic. I would've hated everything about wearing a bra, even if it was more comfortable than the bandage.

Once Mom finished packing, her arm still in a sling, we faced the problem of how to get our luggage to the car. We stood by the door, looking back and forth at the two suitcases. If Dad had been able to stay longer, he would've taken care of everything. But he had to get to work on Monday, so Mom and I were on our own.

"I'm not supposed to lift anything over five pounds," I said. "And the nurse said I shouldn't even pull a suitcase on wheels."

"I'll make two trips to the car," Mom said.

"What about at the airport?" I asked.

"We'll get a skycap. No problem."

That was a nice idea, but when we got to the Hertz Return Center, there wasn't anyone around to help. We had to get all the way to the Southwest Airlines check-in desk on our own.

"Wait here," Mom said, and rolled one of the suitcases to a spot about twenty yards away. There, she leaned it against a pillar before returning to grab the other one. We walked together to where she'd left the first suitcase and then I rested while Mom continued on for another twenty yards. It took half a dozen leapfrogs and one elevator ride before we reached a moving sidewalk and then an escalator that took us the rest of the way.

I got some nasty looks as people watched what looked to be a perfectly healthy young man stand by while his mother struggled with one arm to handle their luggage. Actually, I probably imagined the nasty looks. Nobody really noticed or cared what we were doing. Though maybe they did perceive me as a young man. That was a cool thought.

TODAY, AT TWELVE days post-op, I took my first shower. That may not sound especially exciting, but it meant that I got to take off the bandage for an hour, and that felt terrific, partly because it was a relief to remove the pressure for a while, but even more so because I got to look again at my flat chest.

Some people get post-surgery blues where they mourn the loss of their breasts, but I've been ecstatic this whole time. I've dreamed about having a man's chest since before I knew it was possible, back when I was a little kid who preferred short hair and boys' clothes and toys. Since before I knew that someday I'd grow breasts. Since the day they started growing and I tried to flatten them out with my hands and pretend they weren't there. Maybe I haven't gotten the blues because I hated my breasts so much that I never looked back. Whatever the reason, I'm happier than I've ever been before.

At the same time, now that my chest looks like I want it to look, I'm becoming more aware of the rest of my body. Previously, I'd been so hyper-focused on my breasts making me look feminine that I ignored everything else. Now that my chest looks right, though, I keep looking at my hips. They're too wide. I'm like scrawny, scrawny, scrawny, and then boom. Hips!

Fall 2013
Em (23 years old)

AS THE FALL SEMESTER STARTED AT CU, I planned to introduce myself as Em when given the chance, but I knew that some professors take roll and might call me Emily. I was especially concerned about my German class because gender is more important in that language than in English. Every noun is considered to be masculine, feminine, or neuter. It's not that the language is sexist. It's just that everything is defined. Rocks are masculine and airplanes are feminine.

On the first day, my German professor did indeed take roll, reading from her class list. Some students responded with their nickname or by correcting her pronunciation. *Should I say anything?* I wondered. I kept changing my mind as she called out names. She was halfway through the class by the time she got to me. As soon as I heard her start to say my name, I interrupted and said, "I prefer Em."

A few minutes later, the professor taught us how to count. She had us repeat out loud, *"Eins, zwei, drei."* Then she asked the women to stand and say their name and count off.

I didn't stand. I waited until she said for the men to get up. Then I said, *"Mein name ist Em,"* and I stood with the men. Nobody questioned me or said a word about it or looked at me funny. It wasn't weird at all. It was unweird, if that makes sense.

AT TWO MONTHS post-surgery, I started rock climbing with Colin again. I can feel the skin on my chest stretching as I reach for an outcropping, but there isn't any pain. Even if there were, it was still worth it to have had the surgery because I so like the way I look. The scars are healing nicely, and God, my whole chest looks so much better.

I keep messing with my hair, trying out new styles. I even experimented with having it stick straight up. I kind of liked that, but I worried it made me look less boyish and more butch, something I don't want. That's fine for other people, but it's not who I am.

I first recognized that last summer when I visited Aunt Connie and Aunt Susan at their B&B in Amherst, just after Ben and Jenn's wedding and before my surgery. Amherst is a small city in western Massachusetts where lots of hippies gathered in the 1960s to attend the University of Massachusetts and never left. Connie and Susan are part of this older lesbian community there, and several of their friends present as very masculine. Hanging out with them made me realize that's not where I want to be in forty years. I've never looked at an older woman, butch or otherwise, and thought, *I want to look like you when I'm your age.* Not once have I thought that.

I do with men, though, all the time. I'll see an older man who presents well and looks put together, a man that clearly makes an effort with his appearance, and my reaction is, *I hope I look as classy as you when I'm fifty.*

That can't happen unless I start taking testosterone and continue taking it for the rest of my life. It's time to return to my therapist, Maxine, to deal with my thoughts about hormones and gender identity and all those things that I've tried not to think about until now.

I've tried, but I can't stop myself from watching videos of people who have transitioned. I want what they have. Not that I want to be a man. It's just that I see how masculine they look and I want that. I want those changes. I want slimmer hips and to be able to build muscle.

It's hard to want my body to change while not necessarily wanting to be a man. It doesn't make sense to have those opposing feelings, but that's how I feel. I can't get away from the struggle, can't decide what will make me happiest. I am so scared of change. It's daunting to contemplate. So I avoid thinking about it. I'm really good at denial. And repressing my thoughts and desires. Yeah, I'm awesome at both.

A FEW WEEKS into the fall semester, I gave up on school and decided to hunt for a job instead. I didn't even bother to tell Mom and Dad. I just stopped going to class.

When I started dropping my résumé off at all the coffee shops in town, I realized that people are seeing me differently now that I've had top surgery. I used to get read as a lesbian or a masculine-presenting woman. I didn't like that because it's not who I am, but it actually gave me an advantage when it came to job hunting because where I live in Boulder, queer people are sorta put on a pedestal. Employers wanted me on their team.

Now that I get read as male, I've lost that edge. Instead of being seen as this cool commodity, people think I'm a fourteen-year-old boy, not a prime candidate for a barista. I imagine the guys at the counters where I turned in my job applications saying to themselves, "Look at this *kid* who wants to work here. How cute!"

Despite my concerns, Vic's invited me for an interview. It's only three minutes from my condo and has this laid-back, '80s-style vibe with bright colors and a casual feel to the place.

I liked the manager, Todd, immediately. He's about ten years older than me, knows what he's doing behind the coffee bar, and doesn't seem to care how I look. He didn't blink an eye when I introduced myself as Emily (I used my legal name because I thought that's what you're supposed to do during a job interview and that's what I'd put on my application). No double take as he realized that I wasn't a teenager. Maybe he knew to expect someone in their mid-twenties because he'd read my application. For whatever reason, he didn't talk down to me at all like people sometimes do with teenagers.

IT'S TAKEN ME a while to figure out how people are responding to me post-surgery. Sometimes they treat me like a kid because I look so young. At other times, I get more respect because I look male. People listen when I speak and don't interrupt me. They expect me to take more responsibility than they did when they assumed I was female. Folks ask me how to do things, whereas before, they'd look around for a man to show them what to do.

It isn't fair that I suddenly have all this power; it's just ingrained in our society. I've ended up with something I never asked for. White male privilege.

eighteen

HONORARY BRO

—·—

October 2013 — Boulder, CO

Sammy

Em and I got together every couple of weeks to listen to music or hang out with my friends. I'd always been able to talk with her about everything, including whatever girl drama was going on in my life. Once she started working at Vic's, she had more cash all of a sudden and started treating me to lunches and dinners out.

"I don't understand," I said in between mouthfuls at our favorite Middle Eastern restaurant. "What are girls thinking when they act so warm one day and so cold the next?" We were talking about my current fling, a girl I'd been seeing for a few weeks.

Em thought for a moment. "Well, if I were to guess, I'd say they're thinking . . ."

"What?" I asked. "What's going on in their heads?"

"I dunno. I don't actually know what girls think any more than you do when it comes to this stuff." I hadn't really thought about that before, but it made sense. Em never really dated around or had romantic interests, and she seemed to think more like my guy friends than my girl ones.

After dinner, we went back to my place and lay on the bed in my basement room in the house I rented with a bunch of friends. We were playing with my new dog, a German shepherd mix I named Dakota. She still had paws that were too big for the rest of her and sharp puppy teeth that could break the skin if I let her play too roughly with me. Em was careful not to let Dakota jump on her, still protective of her chest, even though she was already working out again. Perhaps that made her think about her surgery because suddenly, kinda out of the blue, she asked, "So, do you wanna see what my chest looks like?"

"Sure," I answered, more curious than anything else.

When Em pulled off her shirt, all I saw were her huge red scars. "Whoa," I said, taken aback by how raw they looked. I was so engrossed by them that I hardly noticed that her chest was flat. "Those must be painful."

"It's not so bad anymore," she said. "You should've seen them a few weeks ago. It'll look better once I build some muscle."

"You're climbing again, right?" I asked.

"Yeah. Colin and I have been going since the beginning of October. That's helping, but it'll be hard to develop serious pecs without being on hormones."

"Is that something you're considering? Last time we talked you said that surgery was as far as you were gonna take it."

"It *was* all I was planning originally, but now I'm having second thoughts."

"What'll it be like if you go on hormones?" I asked.

"My hips will flatten out, and I'll get stronger."

"Hormones can do that?"

"Yeah. But I dunno. It's a huge decision."

Then Em got quiet and focused on Dakota, who was nuzzling her for a belly rub. I picked up my guitar and played a little bit from a song I was writing.

After a few minutes, Em looked up from my dog and asked, "Does it bother you that I've got my shirt off?"

"Nah," I said, meaning it. "Not at all."

Em

TODAY—A FEW DAYS AFTER I SHOWED SAMMY THE results of surgery—we hung out in his backyard with a few friends, drinking beer. It's late October, and today was one of the last warm afternoons of the fall before it will drop into the fifties, so we took it all in, throwing sticks for Dakota to fetch, listening to some music.

Toward the end of the afternoon, just before we started up the grill, someone pulled out a beer bong and Sammy and his friends started taking turns chugging whole cans of Rolling Rock. Not something I've ever been good at. When it comes to chugging, half the can usually ends up all down my front.

Wanting to avoid that, I pulled my shirt up over my head and took it off, just as most of the guys had done. I had this fleeting moment of fear wondering how Sammy's friends would react, but I was already feeling pretty good with a beer buzz and so I just kept going. Evan Pratt, Sammy's roommate from freshman year, said, "Oh, gnarly scars. What are those from?"

By the time Evan got his question out, I'd already started chugging. Afterwards, as I felt the sticky beer all over my chin and chest, I looked at him and half-mockingly said, "Really?"

He said, "Oh yeah," and then we spent the next ten minutes talking about my surgery, keeping it all real casual and matter-of-fact-like. Evan is one of Sammy's closest friends, outgoing and kind of goofy. He looks a little like Sammy. Clean-shaven, short light-brown hair, athletic, but taller. His major is integrated physiology, which is just as demanding as Sammy's field of chemical and biological engineering. His questions reflected his interest in biology.

Later, when I caught a moment alone with Sammy, I asked him if that had been weird, me taking my shirt off and talking so openly with his friends about everything. "Dude," he answered. "If they weren't cool about it, they wouldn't be my friends."

His comment, combined with the beer, got me feeling sentimental. This group of guys has accepted me as one of them. I've become kind of an honorary bro. Sammy might not describe it that way, but that's how it seems to me.

Winter 2014 — Denver, CO

Jo

SAMMY AND EMILY MET JON AND ME AT THE Denver Airport so we could drive up to the mountains together in Em's car.

"Hey, Momma," said Sammy, reaching down to hug me as we stepped off the escalator into the main terminal.

"How was your flight?" asked Emily, taking my brief-case from me. I remembered the last time we were in an airport together and she'd been unable to help at all with the luggage, let alone sling a book-filled briefcase up onto her shoulder.

"You're looking good," I said. Gone was the poor pos-ture with her shoulders slumped forward all the time. No more baggy shirts hiding her shape. She was quite dapper, with new clothes that showed off her slim, flat figure. And she stood erect with her shoulders thrown back and her chest out, the image of self-confidence.

Em (24 years old)

A HOT SPA AFTER A DAY OF SNOWBOARDING IN the Rockies. A glass of wine in my hand. Watching skiers on their final run of the day in the late afternoon, just be-fore dusk. Life doesn't get much better than that. The only thing that would have made it more perfect was if I could feel the hot air bubbles pushing against my bare chest.

But my chest wasn't bare. I wasn't quite ready to leave my T-shirt behind while hot-tubbing with my folks. It didn't feel weird with Sammy and our Boulder friends. But my parents? Not yet.

Drying off in the sauna afterwards, I tried to explain my hesitancy to Mom, but she misunderstood and thought I was saying something else entirely.

"It'd be strange to go around shirtless when you still identify as female," she said.

Warning lights went off in my head. I wanted to say,

What on earth makes you think I identify as female? But I didn't, because I could see why she was confused. When she asked recently if I wanted her to switch to a different name and use male pronouns, I told her I'm fine with her calling me Emily. In her mind, that meant that I identify as a woman, despite everything I've said to the contrary. So I tried to clarify things.

"People don't see me as woman," I said.

"Maybe," Mom said, "but you're too cute to be seen as a man."

That was brutal because it's true. Around the time when I was recovering from top surgery and liking my body's new shape, my face started to change and people started telling me that I looked better. Although they didn't say it, I could tell that what they meant by that was that I'm getting more beautiful. I hate this. It's frustrating, and I don't know how to react. I can't stand that I'm being seen as womanly despite my flat chest. So I cut my hair even shorter to look more masculine.

Now I'm thinking yet again about going on testosterone. What stops me is that I know my life would be easier without this massive change. It's hard for me to even consider it because change is too scary. But I've finally realized just how far I am outside of the binary system that classifies people as either men or women. On the scale from feminine to masculine, I'm somewhere in between. I don't really know where. Maybe that's a step forward from total denial.

It'd be easier to change now than it was when I worked in day care. Then, I couldn't start testosterone and transition because men weren't allowed to change diapers. I would've lost my job. Working in a coffee shop, though, makes it simpler. I can just go to the manager and be like, "Hey, can you change my name on everything? I'm going on hormones and no longer feel comfortable getting called Emily." And if that doesn't work, I can just leave and get a job elsewhere as a man.

My friends have accepted me without trying to define me. They don't consider me either gender but instead view me as androgynous. Colin said flat out that he doesn't think of me as either a man or a woman. It wouldn't be a big push to go on hormones and tell everyone to use masculine pronouns and a new name. Some of them kind of expect it of me, like they're just waiting for me to say something. Especially Colin. The other day we were talking about it and he said, "You've been transitioning in your appearance for a long time, taking baby steps."

Colin still shares my condo with me, but now there are three of us. After Meg graduated from the University of Washington, she moved back to Boulder and took a job with Whole Foods. I miss the days when I had Colin to myself as my best friend, but Meg has become a really good friend as well. We were already close, even before she moved in. She's just as athletic as Colin and has gone camping with us many times. She knows how to scuba dive and is just as likely to put on flannel shirts with blue jeans as she is to wear tight leggings. And she supports my gender expression without hesitation.

"Em," Colin said, interrupting my thoughts about Meg. "Baby steps are okay. But are you ready for more? Do you want me to start calling you Jeremy and referring to you as a man?"

Jeremy. I'd told him about my conversation with my mom and how if I ever did transition, that would be my name. I told him, even though I still haven't told Mom about that decision. "No. Not yet," I answered.

I'm not ready to transition, but I know that if I ever decide to move forward, I can do it fast. So yeah, I could do it. I'm scared of making the commitment, taking the final plunge. I'm not ready yet. But it could happen.

nineteen

MORE BABY STEPS

—·—

February 2014 — Boulder, CO

Em (24 years old)

Baby steps. That's what I've been taking so far. Still in denial, I've convinced myself that how others read me plays almost no part in my desired transition.

Wait. Did I just think *desired* transition?

Yeah, that's definitely how I'm feeling. I want to be comfortable in my own skin. I used to think all of this had nothing to do with societal ideas of being a man or a woman. That it's just that I want my body to look masculine. A matter of how I look more than who I am. My gender expression rather than my gender identity. But it's time for me to acknowledge that it's more than that. This is so much bigger than the top surgery I had done the previous summer. That was epic, to be sure. But coming out as transgender will be even more life altering.

I keep thinking about the last time I had lunch with my folks and Sammy in Boulder. After Mom and Dad ordered, the waiter turned to Sammy and me and said, "What can I get you boys?" I could tell Sammy was curious as to how

I'd respond. He's used to waiters assuming I'm a boy, but that was the first time it had happened in front of Mom and Dad. I grinned at him, like we were in on a secret together, and then I just ordered, as if nothing was different.

But something *is* different. I don't want to hide anymore, even though I'm scared to say even to myself that I'm trans. I'm frozen, unable to make a decision. The thought of change is terrifying. Can I do it? Will I disappoint everyone if I do? Oh, God.

March 2014 — Austin, TX
Em (24 years old)

I WAITED UNTIL MOM WAS IN BED TONIGHT before telling Dad I was heading out for a walk. I didn't say that I was planning to go to Rain on 4th, a gay bar a few blocks from their new apartment in downtown Austin. They sold the big, suburban house I grew up in once Sammy went off to college and moved to a much smaller two-bedroom apartment. I'm staying with them for the week, taking care of Mom while she recovers from shoulder surgery.

I dressed carefully in one of my favorite outfits. A relatively new pair of dark jeans that make my hips appear small and emphasize my slim waist. A freshly ironed man's button-down shirt. A colorful tie, one that said, "I'm here and I look good." Combing my hair as I stared in the mirror, I saw a young man. If only everyone else would see the same thing.

I nodded at my reflection, thinking about my therapist's encouragement. How she had suggested that I don't have to make any big decisions. That I can continue with baby steps by introducing myself as Jeremy to complete strangers. Whether or not I'm ready to completely transition, I can at least go that far.

I promised myself that when I got to the bar, I'd introduce myself as Jeremy. I'd been eyeing the place all week, walking by slowly each evening, watching customers laughing and partying as they entered, the music loud every time the door opened. For the first time, I would be Jeremy the man, not Emily the androgynous person. I would be free!

Entering Rain about ten minutes later, all I could think about was the name on my driver's license. Emily. As soon as the guy at the door checked my ID he'd notice my name and see me as a pretender. He'd think to himself, *Oh, this isn't an underage teenage boy trying to get in, this is a twenty-four-year-old woman.*

But I wasn't pretending. I was dressed as me.

Turned out that nobody cared. Nobody judged me. The bouncer probably never even read my name. All he cared about was the date of birth and whether I was old enough. I ordered a beer at the bar and then found a spot near the lit-up dance floor, crowded with gay men and women. A lot of the guys looked like me, kind of cute and short and small. That was comforting because I worried that my height would give me away, that it would feminizes me since I'm only 5'4", maybe 5'5" if I stand perfectly straight. That's short for a guy. But not at Rain. I fit in easily there, a place where everyone understood what it was like to experiment with wearing a new skin, with trying to be more open.

After a few minutes, some women came over to me

and one of them grabbed my hand and dragged me out onto the dance floor. They were all dancing together and I joined in. I love to dance and I'm good at it.

We could barely hear each other talk, but at one point, one of them leaned in close to me and said, "What's your name?"

"Jeremy," I said, with some trepidation. How would she react? I waited for her to say something about having thought I was a woman, but she didn't. She kept dancing and never questioned my gender. It was incredibly empowering.

Moments later, a couple of men started dancing with us as well. For the next hour, we went back and forth from the dance floor to a table. Conversation was hard over the music, but when we did talk, I got the sense that everyone saw me as male. When I finally said I had to take off, one of the guys said, "Hey, Jeremy, you're really cute."

That was an incredible ego boost. This guy who was gay and was attracted to men found me to be attractive. Yeah! It felt great, even though I wasn't tempted to do anything in response. It's not like I was looking to hook up or anything. But it was nice to be appreciated. And it was especially nice to be appreciated by someone who appreciates men.

I was flying high the whole walk back to my folks' apartment. I was Jeremy. I'd been Jeremy for three whole hours!

As I opened the door, Dad called out from the living room, "Hi, Emily. How ya doing?"

Even though it's been a long time since any of us kids have lived at home, whenever we visit, Dad reverts to his old habit of staying up until we're all in for the night. He knows we're perfectly capable of taking care of ourselves and that he doesn't have to do this, but he can't help himself.

Actually, I was kinda glad he was up because I was excited and wouldn't be able to fall asleep for hours. It would be nice to have someone to talk with.

I sat down next to him on the living room couch as he closed his book and laid it on the coffee table. The furniture in my parents' new place is all the same as what I grew up with, a well-worn mission-style couch, a southwestern dining table with a tile top, my mom's writing desk in a corner under a window, and the same pictures on the walls and rugs on the floor.

"You seem happy," he said, sipping his Manhattan.

"I am," I said. "I had a great time."

"You want one?" he asked, gesturing to his drink.

"Sure. Looks good."

I sat quietly while he worked in the kitchen, watching as he measured out the whiskey and sweet vermouth. He's perfected his recipe over the years, and I savored the moment of companionship as we sat together in silence, enjoying our drinks. After a few minutes, I decided the time had come to share.

"So Dad, um . . ." I found it difficult to continue.

"Yeah?" he asked.

"I went to a gay bar and presented as male," I said, proud that I'd accomplished what I set out to do, though a little timid when it came to telling my father about it.

"How'd it go?" he asked simply.

"The bar was great. Better than I expected. I was worried that people would see me as a butch lesbian, and that's not who I am."

"I don't think you have to worry about that," he said.

"Why not?" I asked, curious as to his reasoning.

"You don't dress the part."

"I don't?"

"No, not at all. You look more like a gay man, not a masculine woman."

"Cool," I answered, happy with the thought.

"And you're okay with that?" he asked, probing a bit.

"Yeah, I am."

It felt good to have Dad say I looked like a gay man. In a way, he was paying me a compliment, saying I dress well. More than that, Dad was saying that he had no problem seeing me as a male. My mood soared even higher than it was before, and it occurred to me that maybe he and Mom are ready for me to talk with them about the whole transition thing.

Maybe I'm ready as well.

"EVERY TIME I went out this week, people saw me as a man."

We were sitting around the dining table having breakfast the morning after I went to Rain.

"I've been getting read as male, which only happens about half the time in Boulder. Maybe because being androgynous is kind of a thing in Colorado, folks don't worry about figuring out what gender everyone is. Not in Texas. In Austin, it's less common, so people have to choose a side."

"What does it mean to be read as male?" Dad asked.

"Stuff like waiters in restaurants say, 'What can I get you, sir?' and when someone knocks into me on the sidewalk, they say, 'Excuse me, sir.' I didn't anticipate that would feel so satisfying."

When Mom and Dad nodded supportively, I thought, *Can I do it? Can I tell Mom and Dad that I'm transgender?*

"Now that I see that it's possible to be consistently seen as a man, I guess I'm more willing to admit that it means a lot to me," I said. "It's been super validating."

As we finished breakfast and cleared the table, I went for it. "Hey, guys, do you wanna see my videos? I've been using them to think through all this stuff. They'll help you understand everything."

As I pressed the play button, I was excited at the idea of my parents watching and hearing me say the words I'd thought through so carefully.

I'm looking more and more at men and trans guys and being like, "Oh, I wish I had that. I want that for myself." Just seeing men's bodies and how they're put together and how they're different from mine. That appeals to me much more than what I have. All kinds of little things that I see in men that I want.

I paused the video when it reached that point to see how my folks were reacting.

"Is that it?" Mom asked, not sure why I'd stopped.

"No, there's more. But are you okay with this?" I asked.

"Actually," she said, "I am. You've been saying this for a while now. It's not new."

That kind of surprised me. Here I thought my folks didn't understand that I'd been thinking about hormones pretty seriously, but it turns out that they were ahead of me in some ways. "So you wanna see the rest?" I asked.

Dad nodded.

The idea of actually changing my life, going through with this monumental change, terrifies me. That's definitely what's holding me back. Not anything else. I want the physical changes. I think I've accepted that I am trans. Maybe not. I don't know. It's the going through with the change that is so, so terrifying to me. Yeah, it is, it's scary. But yeah, I don't know. Oh, God.

That was the end of the recording. I'd watched it a few times before coming to Austin, and every time it was difficult. How could I not know what to do? I needed my parents to tell me what they thought.

"I'm trying to understand," said Dad. "You say that you've accepted that you're trans, maybe, but don't know if you can go through with the change. Does that capture it?"

He sounded so logical, cutting right to the heart of my dilemma. "It does," I said. "I don't know what I want to do."

Mom wrinkled her brow, trying to figure it out for me. "You don't have to do anything if you don't want."

"There's no rush, but it's okay if you want to start hormones," Dad added.

Wait! Wh—? I hadn't decided myself if that was okay, and Dad was actually suggesting it.

"I've understood for a while that you physically want to look like a man," Dad continued. "But this video is the first time I've heard you say that you are transgender. Am I right that this means that you identify as a man? Not just that you want to present as one? And you don't identify as a woman?"

"Yeah, Dad," I said. "That's exactly what it means."

"So are you still questioning whether you're trans?" Mom asked. "Or is it that you've accepted that and just don't know what you want to do with that recognition?"

I nodded. "I'm scared," I said quietly, barely getting the words out.

Mom moved closer to me on the couch and hugged me. "It's okay to be scared. This is a big deal," she said. "Whatever you decide, we're with you. If you want to go on testosterone, that's okay. If you want to change your name, that's okay too."

"Until now," Dad said, changing the topic, "I thought you felt as if you've got the wrong shape but still identify as a woman. So it bothered me that you wanted to change your body. Instead, I wanted you to accept it. When you decided on top surgery last year, I thought you were just being stubborn."

I shook my head. "It was more than that."

"I can see that now from your videos. They clarified a lot for me, and I'm glad you shared them. If you decide you need to transition, well, then that's what you need."

My folks were actually okay with the possibility of me changing everything. They were more okay than I was.

twenty

TERRIFIED

—

April 2014 — Boulder, CO
Em (24 years old)

At eight months post-surgery, my scars have flattened out and will soon start to fade. I showed Sammy the progress today and he said, "Every time I see your chest, it looks more regular."

"Cool, Sammy. That's what I like to hear." I'm pleased with how normal everything ended up looking, like I was born as a guy and never had surgery.

Then I told Sammy about showing Mom and Dad the videos and how they'd reacted.

"You know you could've just told them everything straight out," Sammy said.

"I do. But I like sharing with the video because I can make a new recording if I don't like the way something came out. I can pause while I find the right words. It feels safer somehow, gives me a little distance."

"So what did they say?" Sammy asked.

"They were pretty supportive, saying stuff like, 'It's not at all difficult for us to think of you as a guy.' It was almost like there was this role reversal, as if they seemed more certain than I am that hormones will make me happy."

"Was that weird?"

"Big time. Weird, but pretty awesome too. It made me feel confident that if I go ahead and transition, I'll have a powerhouse support system."

"You're still saying *if*," Sammy pointed out.

"Yeah, I'm still saying *if*."

————————

Em

HORMONES. I CONSTANTLY SAY TO MYSELF, *I'M gonna do this. I'm gonna do this.* Then it's, *Oh, crap, that's scary.* Then, *I want this. Let's just get it done.*

The other night, Colin and I were talking over a couple of beers and he said, "It seems as if your life's on hold right now."

"What do you mean?" I asked.

"No judgment, but you seem so lost in self-contemplation and what you want to do with all this gender stuff that there's no room for anything else."

"That may be true," I said, somewhat tentatively. Yeah, it was true.

"You dropped out of school and now you have a job that doesn't challenge you."

"I guess," I answered. "I don't have a lot of ambition right now. School didn't seem that important, and being a barista, well, that's not my ultimate goal."

"You're not working toward anything right now except figuring out who you are."

"I get what you're saying," I said. "But it's not just that. I have no idea what I want to do in the long run, so school seems like a waste."

"Maybe it was just too hard to work at your classes when you had all this other stuff going on."

Colin doesn't pull any punches. That's part of why I appreciate him so much. I can count on him to tell me what he's thinking, even when it's hard. When it comes down to it, I agree with him. I don't like thinking about the future because I can't picture what I'll be in five years. I didn't even know what gender I'll be.

Late April 2014
Jeremy

I'M TERRIFIED OF CHANGE, AND THE ONLY THING I'm more scared of is, you know, not changing.

I'm frozen. The next step is huge, but I want to do it. I tell myself, *I'm gonna start taking hormones.* Once I've decided for sure, then I'll tell everyone else. They all know it's coming. My family and friends have known for a while even though I've been denying it to myself.

My therapist, Maxine, said yesterday, "Don't think of it like a jump. It's just one step. You can tell a few friends to call you Jeremy and see how that feels. Then you can decide if you want to go any further."

That gives me a way to start, to go back to baby steps until I'm more certain. It'll be baby steps, true, but it'll still be moving forward. Maybe if I like being called Jeremy and having friends use male pronouns, then hormones won't feel like such a giant leap from where I am.

I have to do something to get unfrozen. Where I am, well, it isn't a good place to be. It's not . . . it's just not.

Early May 2014
Sammy

THE LAST SEMESTER OF MY SOPHOMORE YEAR WAS pretty brutal, with a tough engineering course load. One night during finals week I was cramming for my differential equations test when I got a text from Em. *Wanna jam?*

An hour later, we were sitting in my basement bedroom, Dakota and Indy curled up on my bed, Em picking out some chords on the portable keyboard she'd brought over, and me sitting with my guitar, playing "My Sound," a song I wrote last year with my roommate, Evan; the lyrics were mostly mine.

> *I must write it down now, no time for contemplation,*
> *'Cause contemplation only leads to exaggeration,*
> *And all I really want is just a little relaxation,*
> *And so I write it down, one line after one line,*
> *Let it all out till the struggle is no longer mine.*

Em and I were seeing if we could come up with something like that together, kind of mixing my hip-hop style with her folksy, singer-songwriter stuff, going back and forth between the two.

After a few minutes, Em stopped and swiveled on her stool toward me and said, "So, uh, Sammy, you know how I've been thinking about changing my name and going on hormones?"

"Yeah, sure," I said.

"I'm gonna do it."

"Now?" I asked.

Em nodded.

"So, what happens first?"

"I guess you start calling me Jeremy. That's the name Mom chose."

"Jeremy? Cool name. I like it."

"You can still say Em if that's more comfortable."

"Doesn't matter to me, whatever you want. Pretty sure I call you 'dude' more than anything else anyways."

"Great. Thanks."

I glanced down at the dogs for a moment and when I looked up, Jeremy was looking away, kind of avoiding meeting my eyes.

"Are you really okay with this?" Jeremy asked, breaking the silence. "It's not too weird?"

"It'll take me some time to get used to it. And I'm sure I'll mess up a lot, but yeah, of course."

"I also want you to use male pronouns if you talk about me."

He spoke so formally that I could tell he'd worked out his phrasing, maybe even practiced. He acted like it was a big deal, but it wasn't so much. Although Jeremy described himself as presenting androgynously for the last few years, really he'd been dressing like a guy since before I started college.

"And I'll start on hormones as soon as my doctor gives me a prescription."

"Badass! That's huge," I said.

"Yeah, I don't know what kind of hoops they'll make me jump through, but once I start taking testosterone, it'll essentially put me through male puberty."

"Nice, so like full-on voice change and facial hair and all that?" I asked.

"Yup. I'll go through everything you did back in middle school."

"Have you told Mom and Dad and Ben and Liz?"

"Mom and Dad know I've been thinking about it, but they don't know I've made a decision. I'll call them later tonight. And I'll write to Liz and Ben."

"None of them will be shocked," I said.

"No." Jeremy shrugged. "It all fits."

"You're not scared?"

"I am. I'm terrified. But not transitioning is worse. I can't . . ."

"You can't what?" I asked.

"I can't keep putting it off. It's not like I set out to do this. I didn't decide one day, 'Oh, I want to be a man.' This is just who I am."

"Okay then, *Jeremy*," I said, using his new name out loud for the first time. It felt kinda good and mixed up and a little bit scary, all at the same time. "I guess I gotta start calling you bro instead of sis."

Jeremy grinned and his eyes teared up a bit. Then he nodded a few times.

twenty-one

CALL ME JEREMY

——

May 2014 — Boulder, CO
Jeremy (24 years old)

T oday, I sent an email to Ben and Liz and spelled it all
out to them.

Hey guys,

*I'm not sure how in the loop Mom has kept you on
what's been going on in my life since the last time I
saw everyone, so I thought I'd give you an update. I've
decided to move forward with hormone replacement
therapy. Which means sometime in the next month or
two, I'm going to start taking testosterone, which will
essentially put me through a male puberty. My voice
will drop, my face and body will start looking more
masculine, I'll grow more body and possibly facial
hair, and everything else that a teenage boy would go
through.*

*I'm also going to start going by Jeremy, though
you guys are welcome to continue calling me Em. And
I'm going to start asking people to use male pronouns
when referring to me (him, he, his).*

*I know this may seem very sudden to you guys,
but I've known that this has been a likely possibility
since deciding to go forward with surgery a little over
a year ago. I've been seeing my therapist, trying to
suss out whether or not moving forward with
transition would be worth it for me. Obviously, I've
decided that it is.*

*If either of you wants to talk, I've got Thursday off
work, so feel free to call me or Skype me or something.*

*I hope this didn't come as too much of a shock to
you.*

Love, Emily

At the end, I added a postscript. "This will probably be
the last time I sign my name as Emily. I'm going to start
using a different email address that has Jeremy in it."

Liz wrote back that evening, calling me Em and saying, "I love you and am 100 percent supportive of your
decision." When I forwarded Liz's response to my folks,
Dad flagged to me that Ben was out of the country so I
wouldn't hear from him quickly. Then Dad added, "I'm
proud of you for your bravery and your honesty."

It felt good to write to Ben and Liz, like I was finally
getting some momentum. Next goal is to talk with my
coworkers at Vic's.

MY PLAN WAS to take some time off and get a fresh start
someplace new after transitioning. That fell apart, though,
because I got promoted to barista and didn't feel right
about quitting.

So I had to let everyone know. When I told the two

coworkers on my shift last week, it was easier than I expected. That helped me gear up to tell my boss, Todd. I
texted him, saying I wanted to discuss how to work the
logistics for something I needed to announce to everyone,
and during my next shift, he approached me.

"What's up, Emily?" he asked, gesturing for me to sit
at one of the tables.

I wasn't too worried about explaining my transition to
Todd. He isn't a whole lot older than me and seems pretty
laid-back. But I still stammered a bit. "It's, um, it's actually
about the schedule," I said.

"What d'ya need? A few days off or something?"

"No, I'm good," I said. "Can you change my name on
the schedule?"

"How come? Doesn't matter. Yeah, I guess." He nodded. "No big deal."

"Actually, it kinda is," I said. "I want everyone to start
calling me Jeremy."

He didn't say anything for a moment, and then he
started nodding again. In Boulder, what I'd just said didn't
seem that unusual to him. "Sure. Sure, thing."

"Do I need to do any paperwork or anything?" I asked.

"Nah," he said. "No problem."

All that worrying for nothing. "Thanks," I said, really
meaning it. "And one more thing."

"What's that?" he asked.

"I'm going to start taking hormones, so I'll be going
through male puberty soon. My voice'll change, and I
might get facial hair."

"So, are you gonna say something to everyone? You
gonna explain it?" Todd asked. "How about you put a note
on the bulletin board? Will that work?"

So that's what I did. It was pretty straightforward. I wrote, "Emily here. From here on, my name will be Jeremy on the shift schedule. Can you start calling me that?" Then I signed it, "Jeremy Ivester."

It wasn't just my coworkers who could see the board but also any customers that came in. Word was out.

Mike, the owner, pulled me aside after he saw the note a couple of days ago. "So then, Emily—" he said.

"Jeremy," I reminded him.

"Yeah, of course. Jeremy. Just make sure you don't make people uncomfortable."

"Of course. I'd never want to do that. I want to do everything I can to help people be okay with this."

"That's good," Mike said. "But once you get extra testosterone, maybe you'll get aggressive. I don't want you getting mad at everyone and challenging people if they don't use the name you want. Don't be getting all radical about it."

That was so not me that I had no idea what to say, so I just nodded.

Everyone else has seemed pretty cool with the news. Everyone I know has started calling me Jeremy. It's mind-blowing to realize that I'll never again introduce myself as Emily.

My close friends got it right away. Some even said, "Yeah, I figured you'd be changing your name eventually." They're willing to just go with it. Maybe if I'd transitioned a couple of years ago I wouldn't have had nearly the support. But after two years of me looking and acting in a masculine manner, everyone is used to it, so a name change doesn't seem like a big leap to anyone. Me included.

Within days of starting to tell my friends, I felt ready

for the next step, so I found this nonprofit clinic that actively reaches out to the LGBT community. That appealed to me because I wanted a doctor who had some experience working with transgender patients. I didn't want to be an experiment.

Once I made an appointment, it all happened really fast.

After the doctor came in and introduced herself, she said, "So, Jeremy, I take it you want to start testosterone?"

"Yes, that's the plan," I answered.

Then we moved on from there. She told me what would happen to my body, and it was all stuff I already knew. She said I'd go through male puberty, just like I'd told my siblings. Then she said, "Normally, I like to do this medication by injection, starting at fifty milligrams per week. I'll order the prescription today. You'll pick it up from the pharmacy and bring it back here. Then I'll give you your first injection, and, if you're okay with it, I'll teach you how to do it yourself for the future."

"That's what I want," I said. I'd read about people who weren't comfortable giving themselves a shot and had to go back to the doctor every two weeks. "I think I'll be okay."

"If you're not," she said, "another option is to bring a friend and I'll teach them how to do the injection."

When I mentioned that to Sammy today, he was very cool with it. We were sitting around in the yard with Evan and a couple of other guys, watching Dakota chase squirrels, talking about plans for the weekend, and listening to some music.

"So hey," I said, trying to sound more casual than I felt. "I'm gonna start testosterone in a couple of weeks."

"Do you get a shot?" asked Sammy.

"Yeah, and I'm gonna have to do it every two weeks."

"That's tough, man," Evan said.

"For the rest of my life."

"Ouch," said Sammy. "You sure about this? It sounds like a pain in the butt, literally."

"In the leg, actually. But, um, the doctor said that some people find it hard to give themselves the shot. It freaks people out because it's this real long needle. So he said that if I didn't think I could do it, I should bring a friend to lear—"

"I'll do it," Sammy broke in. "It sounds kind of cool."

I'M SO READY to get started. My friends have been super positive and a few texted me, saying stuff like, "Hey, I support you," and "I'm so proud of you for doing this."

The strangest times are when I'm in situations in which some people know to call me Jeremy but others don't. At one party this weekend, I overheard a woman say, "Why is everyone calling Emily 'Jeremy?'"

I didn't have to say a word. Colin's girlfriend, Meg, an-swered for me. "He goes by Jeremy now."

"Oh, okay," the woman said, and she started using my new name and moved on like it was nothing. Inside, I was beaming. She hadn't just accepted my new name. She had accepted me.

It's time to let the world beyond Boulder know what's going on. It's time to post on Facebook.

June 2014 — Boulder, CO
Jeremy

My Facebook post:

Hey everyone,

You all may or may not have noticed that I changed my name on here. That's because I'm about to start hormone replacement therapy, meaning I'll be taking testosterone in order to put myself through a male puberty.

From now on, if you are not already doing so, please call me Jeremy and use male pronouns to refer to me.

I'm happy to answer any questions if people want to message me.

Thanks,
Jeremy

I wasn't quite sure what to expect after I put my announcement out there. I knew most people would be like, "Yeah, man." But I was kind of speechless at the number of responses and just how positive they all were. And how everyone just immediately switched over to calling me Jeremy.

"Great name! We love you," commented Sarah, a cousin from Massachusetts.

"I'm so happy for you that you're taking this exciting new step," wrote Naomi, a cousin in Arizona.

"Congratulations on your brave choice to be you," from Claire, a friend in Boulder.

One of Dad's former colleagues wrote, "To your own self be true. Best wishes, Jeremy, as you listen to your own drummer. Keep your smile!"

Uncle Charles added, "Jeremy, everybody in the family is so very proud of you! The future looks grand!"

"Love you, Jeremy! So happy for you," said Amelia, yet another cousin.

So many supportive cousins! Nobody in my entire extended family had anything negative to say. My grandparents had all passed away by then and maybe they would have had some reservations, but my parents' generation and my cousins were terrific.

The comments all meant so much to me. But it was especially satisfying to see what my parents posted.

Dad wrote, "Your bravery is inspiring. I am very proud of you."

Mom was the most sentimental of all. "I'm pleased to tell the world that I now have *three* sons. Jeremy, you are continuing on the amazing journey that was started when you were little more than a toddler. You are such a strong young man that you are willing to see this adventure through to wherever it leads. Know that your family is with you every step of the way. We are bursting with pride for your courage. And we couldn't love you more."

twenty-two

MOM'S STORY

June 2014 — Austin, TX

Jo

When we welcomed Jeremy into the world in 1989, we thought we had a baby girl. As he grew into a preschooler and beyond, we called him a tomboy, which is also what he called himself. At twenty-three, he removed his breasts. A year later, he was about to begin taking the hormones that would influence his entire body. His muscle mass would increase, and he would lose fat. His voice would deepen, and he would develop a male physique.

He asked that everyone use his new name and male pronouns. And he announced this on Facebook, which made it suddenly much more real. Of course we would do exactly as Jeremy asked. He was our child. Whether he was Emily or Jeremy, he was the same person and we loved him. Fiercely.

We were barely beginning to understand what it meant for someone to be transgender, but we had to trust our son to know what he was doing. He spoke about it as if it was some miraculous adventure.

Jeremy told us recently that as a child, he'd go to bed each night hoping that when he woke up, he'd have magically changed to a boy. In a way, that hope was being fulfilled. Except that in a way, he wasn't really changing at all; he'd always been a boy.

The fact that we supported Jeremy didn't mean that it was easy to accept that he was starting hormone therapy. The hardest part was that I'd never let go of my dream of him having a baby someday. I'd always assumed that he would be a parent even though he said that he couldn't be a mom. I would have been okay with him being a daddy instead. Despite having had several years to adjust to the idea of him not having children, I could practically feel his baby in my arms.

"Would you consider harvesting some eggs before you begin treatment?" I asked, naively thinking he hadn't realized that was possible.

Without hesitation, he answered, "No. I wouldn't want a baby from my eggs. That's the ultimate statement of being a woman, and just the thought of it makes me really uncomfortable. And I don't want to raise a baby by myself, to be a single dad."

That was the first time I realized how completely Jeremy had thought this through. With nothing further to say, I let the sadness wash over me. It wasn't just because I'd never have that grandchild I wanted. It was also because my daughter Emily was truly gone. In fact, she'd never really existed. I had raised a son, and now I knew that my son would never have a child of his own.

Moving beyond the grief I felt tied to Jeremy's announcement, I allowed myself to feel joyful that he was able to accept who he is. I progressed so rapidly to this joy that I buried my sadness, so much so that when people asked if I'd ever grieved over the loss of Emily, I said I hadn't. I believed myself. I guess Jeremy wasn't the only one who was awesome at denial.

The Facebook post I wrote in response to Jeremy's had a far greater impact than I anticipated. My brother Charles, who had over 1,800 Facebook friends due to his success with his *Storming Bohemian* column about cultural life in San Francisco, shared what I wrote, adding, "This is for all my queer friends, whatever your journey, to remind you that sometimes things are very, very good. Jo and Jeremy, I am very proud of you both!"

Within hours, I started receiving messages from Charles's friends and followers, many of whom were gay, thanking me for being a supportive mom. Dana Hopkins, a remarkable woman who had adopted trans individuals when they had nowhere else to go, posted, "This is how we can love and support our trans youth!" One of her contacts responded, "This is parenting done right. Seriously, I'm kind of in awe. I hope you know how much your public support means to your son."

Then I started to hear from friends of friends of friends. Some simply thanked me. Others said they wished their parents had been as accepting when they came out. I tried to respond to every one, saying something like, "I want to let you know that there's now one more person in the world who supports you. I truly wish the best for you."

It wasn't long, though, before the feel of the messages turned dark. I heard from young transgender men for whom Jeremy's story resonated. Young men who had been disowned by their families and thrown from their homes when they came out. They couch surfed when they could and lived on the street when they had no other option. Some spoke of dropping out of school. One man wrote, "My family won't have anything to do with me. I try so hard but don't get a lot of affirmation and love." A teenager said, "I'm basically homeless." Then there was the heartrending comment, "I just want someone to wish me happy birthday in a motherly fashion with my preferred name."

Jon and I threw ourselves into becoming familiar with the difficulties faced by transgender individuals and were dismayed by what we discovered. As many as 40 percent of the homeless youth in our major cities had been disowned by their parents and thrown out of their homes because they were somewhere on the LGBTQ spectrum. Over 40 percent of transgender teenagers had tried to take their own lives. Not just contemplated suicide, but actually tried it. We read about a father in Texas who discovered his son was trans when he went through his child's room following a suicide attempt and found a note explaining that the boy could no longer live if living meant being a girl. I couldn't begin to fathom the heartbreak of finding such a letter.

We decided that it wasn't enough to support Jeremy. We wanted to become advocates and help increase acceptance for all transgender individuals. Jeremy appreciated our efforts and helped us to define our roles as allies. At the same time, however, he was uncomfortable with me saying that I had a better understanding of what it meant to be transgender as a result of my childhood experience as a tomboy. My brother Charles really got me thinking about that when, soon after Jeremy came out, he challenged me with the question, "If our society had been different when we were children, would you have identified as transgender?"

When I told Jeremy about Charles's question, he said, "There's a difference between being a tomboy and being transgender."

He was right, of course, but I was pretty extreme. When I watched romantic moments on TV, I didn't want to be kissed by the handsome teenage heartthrobs; I wanted to be like them. At school, I wanted to stand with the boys when we lined up to go outside for recess. When we learned to square dance in gym class, it didn't seem fair that the boys got to lead while the girls had to follow.

I had logical reasons for wanting to be like the boys. Societal expectations were strong even though my parents said I could be whatever I wanted. Boys got to be policemen and firemen and super heroes. Girls got to be rescued. So it wasn't about who I was. It was about the freedom I craved.

WHY DID MY brother ask whether I might be transgender? Because he's the one who first figured out when I was twelve years old that I was pretending to be a boy. I was so good at it that my best friend didn't know I was a girl.

It started shortly after my family moved to Miami in 1969. Because my dad was on the faculty at the university there, my brothers and I were allowed to hang out at the student center and use the facilities—a swimming pool, a bowling alley, some pool and Ping-Pong tables, pinball machines, a cafeteria, and several lounge areas.

On one of my first days there, I handed over my newly

printed ID card at the activities desk and asked for a pool cue. A twelve-year-old boy stood behind me in line, also wanting to play pool. Had he realized I was a girl, he might never have invited me to join him for a game. Junior high school–age boys rarely regarded girls as playmates, viewing us instead as another species, an intriguing one that they dreamed of dating someday, yes, but not a potential buddy.

David had heard my name, Jo, and assumed there was an "e" on the end of it. As we walked toward the room with all the pool tables, I was careful not to say anything that might blow my cover. Before I knew it, it wasn't just David and me playing pool together; it was his entire circle of friends. They welcomed me into their clique, never questioning my gender.

Jo at twelve years old

For the first week or so of pretending to be a boy, I avoided public restrooms. There were no family or unisex bathrooms back then, so I had to make a choice. Should I use the men's room, going where girls were absolutely forbidden? Should I use the women's restroom?

I came up with a bold strategy. When I had to go, I challenged David to use the girls' room, knowing that he would laugh and dare me to do the same. And that's exactly what happened. I felt a tremendous sense of relief, both physically and emotionally, when I managed to pull off my deception.

One day, Charles joined David and me for lunch at the student center and was surprised when David asked, "What was he like as a little kid?"

"Did you just say *he*?"

"Yeah, why?"

"You do know that Jo's a girl, right?"

I froze with my fork halfway to my mouth, frantically trying to figure out what to say to salvage the situation.

"Of course," David said.

I was stunned. I was sure he thought I was a boy.

"That's why I call him 'Mary' all the time," he said, laughing.

When we'd first started hanging out, David had teased me by saying "Mary, Mary, quite contrary." That was before we became good friends. The teasing had since stopped, but he still sometimes called me Mary, just to be funny.

Charles didn't know what to make of David's response, with his confirmation that he knew I was a girl coupled with his description of me as "him." So he tried again. "I'm serious. *She's* a girl," he said, emphasizing the pronoun so as to directly contradict David's use of the word "him."

David ignored Charles at that point and moved on to making plans for the afternoon.

As our friendship deepened, David and I started talking on the phone at night and my parents assumed he was my boyfriend. I protested, saying we were just friends, and I meant it. Neither of us was interested in dating. We talked about girls sometimes, and I pretended to share his growing interest. But that was it.

We saw each other every day over the summer and most weekends once the school year started. As David's thirteenth birthday approached and he began to prepare more aggressively for his bar mitzvah, he invited me to join him in his studies. I helped him memorize the Hebrew and even met with him and his rabbi as he delved into what it meant to become a man within the Jewish community. We spent hours discussing what he was learning, often while sitting by a creek with fishing poles in our hands.

Not religious myself, I still viewed the rabbi as having some sort of magical, mystical power and was terrified that he would see through my ruse and bring down the wrath of God on me for posing as a boy. As the bar mitzvah grew closer, the family began to plan a role for me in the celebration. I was to be honored as David's best friend and given an opportunity to read a brief passage in Hebrew. My parents were invited as well even though they'd never met David or his family; I had carefully kept the two families apart, lest I be discovered.

Despite my fears, I felt as if I had no choice but to accept the invitation. I couldn't disappoint David. I told my parents I would go, but I knew I couldn't. My parents would expect me to wear a dress for the occasion, and everyone would know I was a girl. I couldn't face that. So I pretended. For weeks leading up to the event, I acted as if I were going. I learned the Hebrew words I was supposed to say. I met with the rabbi. And then, on the morning of David's bar mitzvah, I pretended to be sick.

Everyone believed me. David's mom even called the next day to ask how I was doing. I found out later, though, that she'd had her doubts about whether I was really ill. David told me that she'd wondered whether I was embarrassed to come because of my hormone problem.

"Wh—?" I said, not quite understanding what he'd said.

"Oh, don't worry. We know."

"What are we talking about, David?"

"My mom says you have a hormone problem and that's why it looks like you've got boobs."

All that time and I thought they hadn't noticed, that I'd successfully hidden my shape under those heavy jackets. I tried to respond but couldn't find the words. "She said that because your dad's a doctor, you were probably getting some sort of treatment and we shouldn't tease you."

"Y—yeah," I sputtered, not knowing how to answer, feeling guilty about my deception.

Things got worse rapidly after that. One day after school, I stopped at the University of Miami bookstore en route home, still dressed in the skirt required by my junior high's dress code. While leafing through a book in the current best-seller section, I heard a woman gasp. "It's you!" she said, covering her mouth with her hands.

When I looked closely, I saw that it was the mother of one of the boys I'd hung out with all summer. Our eyes met, but I pretended not to know her, hoping that if I didn't respond she'd think she was mistaken. But she definitely recognized me.

"You're a girl," she said, accusing me.

I tried to brazen it out, acting like I had no idea what she was talking about. Then I walked away, deeper into the store. She followed me, telling me over and over again that I was sick.

A few days later, the unthinkable happened. The conversation that I'd hoped would never take place. David's mom and my mom got together on the phone. I sat on the living room couch and listened, hoping that neither one of them would use a pronoun.

For the first few minutes, I heard my mother say "Jo this" and "Jo that" and I thought that maybe I'd gotten away with it. And then . . .

"Did you just say *he*?" my mother asked.

I flirted with the thought of running away, too embarrassed to face my mother.

"You do know that Jo is a girl, don't you?"

Clearly, David's mother didn't answer, for the next thing I knew, my mother was saying, "Hello? Hello? Are you there?"

I couldn't listen anymore. Instead, I went to my bedroom, shut the door behind me, and lay facedown on the bed. I felt as if I had done something terribly wrong and had no idea what the consequences might be.

A few minutes later, my mother walked in, sat on the bed beside me, and began stroking my hair. "It's okay, Jo. We'll make it all right."

Until then, I'd held off crying. But feeling my mom next to me, not hearing any anger in her voice, I couldn't stop myself. The tears flowed and my head began to ache, my breaths coming in quick gasps. I rolled over and tried to talk, but no words would come.

My mother reached out and pulled me to a sitting position and then embraced me. "Shhh, shhh," she said, rubbing my back with one hand and holding the back of my head with the other.

"Mom," I choked out. "I'm sorry."

"For what?" she asked.

"I wanted to tell David, but I didn't at first, and then it just got harder and harder."

"I know, I know," she murmured.

"I never want to see him again," I mumbled, unable to meet her eyes.

"But he's your best friend."

"Yeah, but he won't be after his mom tells him about me."

"Actually," Mom said, "she and I already spoke about that. The four of us are going to get together this weekend to go bowling."

"Mom, no!" I said, cringing at the thought.

"Why not?"

"I dunno."

"Will you try?" Mom prodded. "Maybe you can still be friends."

I did try. So did David. He said he understood. But that day at the bowling alley was the last time I saw him.

I THOUGHT THIS childhood experience allowed me to understand more deeply what Jeremy and other transgender people had to deal with. There's no question that it helped me to recognize the terror trans individuals feel when they are first presenting as their true gender and are scared that someone is going to out them. To some extent, though, it actually got in my way because I assumed that Jeremy was like me when he wasn't.

So what to make of Charles's question? Would I have identified as transgender as a child, had the vocabulary and medical understanding been there?

My first reaction was to think, *Would I? Is Charles onto something?*

I looked up the eight criteria presented in the 5th edition of the American Psychiatric Association's (APA) Diagnostic and Statistical Manual of Mental Disorders to see how they described gender dysphoria. In children, it involved at least six of eight characteristics that lasted more than six months, and that resulted in distress or difficulty functioning. I matched with many of the criteria. I preferred boys' clothing and chose to portray boys in fantasy play. I liked the toys and activities that our society perceived as boyish. Most of my friends were boys. I refused ballet lessons and gymnastics classes, not because I wasn't intrigued by the activity but because I didn't want to wear a tutu or a leotard. Given all of this, I could certainly see how Charles thought that maybe I was transgender and we just never defined me as that.

But there was a critical difference; I never disliked my body or wanted a boy's anatomy. Most significantly, I neither wanted physically to be a boy nor insisted that I was one; I did play at being a boy and fooled people rather successfully, but I didn't go to sleep at night wishing I could turn into what I pretended to be. I didn't conform to society's definition of how a girl should look and act, but as Jeremy likes to say, I was just being me.

twenty-three

A NEW START

===

July 2014 — Boulder, CO
Jeremy (24 years old)

Four weeks after starting hormones and still no visible changes. My voice feels different, but it's not actually low enough yet for people to hear any difference. It's more out of my control, squeakier than it used to be. Sometimes it'll drop down for a moment and I'll be like, "Whoa, is that me?"

Nobody else can see it yet, but my muscles are changing, too, gaining some definition. That makes my arms and legs and abs look more masculine. Even my calves are more toned, which is cool. I'm a bit hairier too. The peach fuzz I've always had over my whole body has grown longer. That's a good sign that eventually that peach fuzz will turn into hair. I know it'll be cool when I need to shave, but I'm not there yet.

My sex drive has gone up pretty drastically. I've read stories from trans guys that theirs exploded once they were on hormones. I'm still not attracted to other people sexually, but something more is definitely going on down there. I'm hoping that settles down because it feels weird and I'm not sure how to handle it.

The appetite thing is starting to come under control. When I first went on hormones, I could never fill up. I remember when Sammy hit puberty and it seemed as if he never stopped eating. Grandma Aura used to say, "Where does he put it all?"

I wish Grandma Aura were still with us so she could see the changes in me and how happy I am, but she passed away almost a year ago. She was disturbed by the idea of me having top surgery, but I don't know how she would have reacted to hormones. She was pretty open-minded and might eventually have accepted that it's the best thing for me.

———————————

August 2014
Jeremy

AT FIVE MONTHS POST-SURGERY, PEOPLE ARE routinely thinking of me as Jeremy and using male pronouns. At first, they had to correct themselves a lot and I could see them struggle. That was uncomfortable for me. Now, though, my roommates and colleagues and close friends hardly mess up at all.

Folks that see me less often have more trouble. At first, I try either not correcting them or whispering "Jeremy" so it won't be awkward. If that doesn't work, I get more aggressive about saying something. I don't like doing that, but I need to drive the point home so they'll get it right.

Rick, the friend who wanted to go out with me, is especially bad about it, maybe because he's still hurt by me rejecting him that night at his parents' condo. I wanted to stay friends after that happened, but that hasn't worked very well. We do see each other fairly often because we both hang out at the Forty-First Street house, but we never talk or do stuff together like we used to.

One evening Rick was out with Colin, Meg, me, and the rest of the gang at a bar at the south end of town, sitting on the deck because it was so perfect outside. Beer and munchies. Then Rick said, "Hey, Emily, send those fries this way."

As I passed him the french fries, I caught his eye and mouthed, "Jeremy."

He nodded, but it wasn't one of those "oh, sorry" nods. It was more like, "Okay, I'll humor you, but I don't like this."

A few minutes later, he called me Emily again. This time, Meg, who has taken on the role of my advocate when it comes to my name and pronouns, slammed her beer mug down on the table and said, "Rick!"

"Oh, right, Jeremy," he corrected himself.

I was thinking, *C'mon, man. Just try. This isn't a little thing. It's a big deal. Make an effort. Don't make it seem like I'm doing this for fun or that you're only humoring me. This is a real change that's happening.*

And it is. The peach fuzz on my face and chest is getting darker and longer. I even have the beginnings of a beard. My voice has finally deepened enough so that I get "sirred" on the phone almost all the time.

I started experimenting recently to see if I can sing the songs I've written over the years and discovered I can't reach all the high notes anymore. I can still sing the high harmony on the songs Sammy and I have been working on together, but that won't last long, so we wrapped up recording a couple of songs in the past couple of weeks, wanting to get it done before my voice gets too low.

As I've reworked my old songs to match my new voice, I've thought a lot about their lyrics. I composed a song called "Pinch Me" a few years ago. It ended up being really dark and kind of hopeless and depressed.

Pinch me. I can't seem to wake.
Take me far away from this place.
Tell me everything's okay.
Hold me. Make it go away.
Stop this throbbing in my brain.
Thoughts are driving me insane.

When I'd first written the lyrics, I asked myself, *Where did that come from?* Looking back post-transition, their source is pretty obvious. I wrote the song back when I'd convinced myself I didn't need to change. When I was burying my feelings of discomfort in my own skin. When I was trying to believe that those feelings didn't matter. Back when I was in a pretty intense state of denial.

The lyrics of "Pinch Me" are about wanting to escape. About being trapped and wanting to hide. About feeling broken. Before, I never acknowledged how unhappy I was —except in my songs—but now that I've transitioned, I can tell the difference. I can recognize joy when I feel it.

Winter 2015
Jeremy (25 years old)

WITHIN WEEKS OF ANNOUNCING MY NEW NAME and gender identification on Facebook, I submitted a request for FBI and Colorado Bureau of Investigation background checks so I could change my name legally. I drove to Denver to get fingerprinted and happily spent my days off doing whatever I needed to do, looking forward to the moment I would hold a new driver's license in my hand, one that had an "M" for male in the space identifying sex.

While I was waiting for the background checks to be completed so I could petition for a court date, I decided I needed a new start at work. Everyone at Vic's has been fantastic, but they all knew me as Emily, and I want to work at a place where my coworkers see me as a man, not as a transgender man.

The other day, I found an advertisement for the perfect job, a clerk at Men's Wearhouse. I could easily picture myself as a salesman, helping people decide what to buy, spending my time immersed in the clothes that make me feel so right.

Getting an interview wasn't difficult. On the scheduled day, I selected my outfit carefully. Dress slacks and a button-down shirt with a striped tie. Glancing in the mirror, I was pleased with the ensemble, thinking I looked just like the customers in the TV and newspaper ads for Men's Wearhouse.

I walked into the store, résumé in hand. It had been incredibly satisfying to update it with my new name front and center, to fill out a job application as Jeremy for the first time.

The store manager, Danny, was expecting me. A guy in his early forties, he was dressed a lot like me, minus the tie, his hair parted carefully on one side, short enough to present a conservative air. I introduced myself as Jeremy, and his only reaction was to smile and shake my hand. No hint of doubting whether I was a man. The only thing that was awkward was that he thought I was younger than I am.

"So, Jeremy, do you go to Boulder High?" he asked.

"Actually," I answered, "high school was a while ago. I was at CU for a while, but now I'm looking to work."

"Great, great," Danny said, nodding. "That's what we need." Then he read over my résumé and saw my birth date. "Wait, you were born in '89? So you're what, twenty-five?"

"Yeah."

"Sorry about that. I thought you were younger."

"That's okay," I said. "I get that a lot."

Danny was pleased that I was a little older than most of his applicants and had several years of work experience. He called that same evening to offer me a position as a customer service associate. It paid barely more than minimum wage, but I could get by on the salary. And the benefits were good, including solid health insurance, which is important, given that I'll be taking testosterone shots every two weeks for the rest of my life.

I returned the next day to complete all the paperwork. While I waited for Danny to look everything over, I glanced around at all the men's clothing in the store. My employee discount combined with the end of winter sale would make it possible for me to pick out some nice sweaters as Christmas gifts for my dad and brothers, and maybe even one for myself.

Danny interrupted my daydreaming, saying, "All I need now is your driver's license and social security card."

I should've anticipated that, but I hadn't. I was so happy to be job hunting as Jeremy that it hadn't occurred to me that a new employer would need to see my identification. And probably do a background check on me as well.

"Um," I said, stalling for time. "About that."

"Yeah?" Danny asked. "Is there a problem?"

"Kind of. Well, not really. More of a heads-up."

I started talking fast, trying to get all the information out before I had a chance to think any more about it. "My ID doesn't say Jeremy on it. It says Emily."

Danny looked at me blankly, as if my words weren't quite registering with him.

"I'm changing my name," I said.

"So what do I enter into the database, Jeremy or Emily?"

"Jeremy. That's my name now." With that, I handed him my license and social security card.

I waited for him to ask why I'd changed my name, wondering if he even knew what it meant to be transgender. I didn't want to explain. This was exactly the conversation I'd been hoping never to have again. I'm Jeremy. I don't want to be someone who used to be Emily, or Jeremy the trans guy. Just Jeremy.

Colorado state law said that Danny couldn't discriminate against me because I'm trans, but I knew that people have been fired elsewhere for exactly that. Just a few months ago, a transgender woman, Aimee Stephens, filed a complaint with the Equal Employment Opportunity Commission because she was fired from her job at a funeral home in Detroit. After six years as a funeral director there, she'd sent a letter to the owners saying that she had a gender identity disorder and was going to have sex reassignment surgery. Two weeks later, she was fired. The American Civil Liberties Union represented her in the resulting lawsuit. We're still waiting to hear what will happen in the US District Court.

I didn't think I needed to worry about that happening

to me, living in Colorado, but I couldn't help but worry as Danny looked over my identification cards.

"So, uh, I don't know if this can work," Danny said, raising his right eyebrow.

"What do you mean?" I asked, fearful that he was about to withdraw the job offer. I didn't want to argue. I just wanted the job.

"It looks like I can't enter 'Jeremy.' What I put into the computer has to match your driver's license and your social security card."

"But I'm in the process of getting those changed," I said, hoping that he could use my real name and let the paperwork follow.

"Are we talking next week?" he asked.

"I dunno," I said. "I have to wait for a federal background check before I can file a petition with the court. It's been a while now, but it could take up to six months."

"Well, how about if we put in all your old info for now, and then change it later?" He was clearly trying to be helpful.

"I'd rather not," I said.

"Nobody else needs to know," Danny said, his tone apologetic.

"Okay," I answered, still hesitant but feeling as if there were no other choice.

After Danny spent another moment entering my data into the system, he leaned back in his chair and looked up at the ceiling. "Hey, sorry about this, but because the computer system has you in as Emily, that's what's going to show up on the shift schedule."

"And everyone'll see that?" I asked, hoping it wasn't true.

"Yeah. There's kind of no way around it. Given that, do you want to make an announcement or something on your first day?"

No! No! I didn't. That's not what I wanted at all.

After waiting a minute for my response and getting none, Danny said, "We've gotta explain or everyone will get confused. They'll be saying, 'Who's this Emily?'"

"Isn't there anything you can do?" I asked.

"For your login name, I can use your initials. Then at least when people see you on the computer, they won't see the name Emily. Would that help?"

I nodded.

"What's your full name?"

"Jeremy Andrew Ivester." I hadn't actually decided on my middle name yet, but I'd been thinking about Andrew ever since Mom suggested it a while back. So I made a split-second decision and it felt right. "Can you maybe use 'JAI' for the shift schedule as well?" I asked.

Danny shook his head no.

I wasn't quite ready to give up. He'd shown me a sample schedule, and I noticed that he was listed as Danny, which was probably a nickname. I couldn't see why he couldn't do the same for me, treating "Jeremy" like a nickname as well.

When I asked about that, Danny again shook his head. I really wanted the job, so I decided not to push any further.

I STARTED MY new job today. When I arrived, Danny pulled me aside and said, "Hey, heads up. I told everyone about your name change, and they're all okay with it. Thought you'd want to know. Okay?"

"I guess so," I answered, not sure what else to do.

Although I'm furious that Danny outed me to my new coworkers, I know he was trying to be supportive and just didn't know any better. But that doesn't stop me from feeling boxed me in, helpless to proceed with my new life, my old one still anchoring me to a person that's not me.

I WAS CAREFUL not to let my health insurance lapse as I moved from Vic's to Men's Wearhouse, but I didn't pay close attention to the options available and ended up unable to stay with the physician who prescribes my hormones. More stress. Would I be able to get a new prescription before I ran out of the old? If I couldn't, the medical implications were significant. My body would almost immediately begin returning to its previous state, and I didn't want that to happen. So the moment my new insurance with Kaiser Permanente activated, I scheduled an appointment to get my testosterone.

I was nervous going into my first appointment with the new doctor, scared that he wouldn't accept me as a patient because I'm transgender, or that he'd want to change my prescription. My anxiety level increased when he said, "I'm happy to work with you, but I should tell you that I don't have any experience with trans patients."

"But you're okay with it?" I asked, looking about the exam room and seeing lots of signs about how to avoid spreading a cold and the importance of getting an annual check-up, but nothing about gender-affirming treatment.

"Sure. Hey, one of my kids has a friend who is transgender."

That seemed a strange thing to say, as if he was suggesting that made him an expert. It didn't, but at least he sounded somewhat accepting.

"What about my hormones?" I asked. "Are you okay keeping me on the same prescription?"

"I don't have any reason to change it. We'll keep every-thing the same and monitor your levels like your old doc-tor did."

Whew! That was huge.

Next, my new doctor asked me all these questions about how I know that I'm transgender and how old I was when I transitioned. It didn't seem like he was just getting my medical history because he didn't ask about my spleen injury and surgery and stuff like that. Instead, it was more like he was curious, almost a voyeur, and that didn't feel right.

Another problem arose a moment later when he went to put my prescription into the computer system. "Uh-oh," he said. "You're in the database as female, and the computer won't let me prescribe testosterone for you."

My head started spinning. There had to be a way out. Before I had a chance to get upset, though, he said, "That worked."

"What?" I asked.

"I just overrode your sex in the system and put in an 'M' instead of an 'F.' Now it's accepting the prescription."

"Thanks," I mumbled, relieved that it had been so easy. At the same time, though, I was annoyed that I'd been marked as female in the first place. Must have been the human resources office at Men's Wearhouse, based on my driver's license.

"Eventually, though, you'll probably want to get a hys-terectomy. At that point, I'll have to change the coding

back to female. If the system won't let me prescribe testosterone to a woman, I'm sure it won't let me schedule a
hysterectomy for a man."

I suppose someone else might have found the irony
entertaining, but I was annoyed that the computer system
was so constrained by gender. No matter how supportive
the doctor tried to be, the impersonal software on the
computer was not.

twenty-four

JEREMY'S DAY IN COURT

—–—

April 2015 — Boulder, CO
Jeremy (25 years old)

I t was three minutes to ten by the time we reached the Boulder County Combined Court lobby. Following the signs to Courtroom E, we literally ran down the hallway to make it on time. Even though I was wearing a new blue dress shirt and tie, I felt all disheveled, not at all the way I wanted to be for this event I'd anticipated for so long.

As we ran, Mom said breathlessly, "We're okay. There's probably a lot of people there, and we'll have to wait for them to call you in any case."

Nope. We walked into the courtroom and it was empty except for the judge sitting up at the front on a dais and a court recorder at a stand-alone desk.

As we entered, Judge Stavely said, "Are you my ten o'clock name change?" He didn't wait for me to reply before gesturing to the podium and saying, "Come on up."

As I walked to the front the room, Mom slipped onto one of the benches. I glanced at the door to see if Dad had made it, but he was still parking the car. Mom was grinning, which was reassuring. Not that I needed re-assuring. I'd thought this through and was as prepared as I'd been for anything in my life. I knew exactly what I'd say when the judge asked why I wanted to change my name. I'd explain that I'd been living as Jeremy for almost a year and was confident that this is what I want to do.

I never had the chance to say any of that. The judge, a friendly-looking man in his mid-sixties with salt-and-pepper hair and a bushy mustache, said, "Please state your legal name."

"Emily Amber Ivester," I answered firmly, aware that this would be the last time I would ever say that name. As I spoke, Dad walked in. He nodded to me as he walked down the aisle toward Mom. I watched him long enough to see that he took her hand as he sat down.

The judge pulled me back to the moment. "What is the name that you are petitioning to use from this day forward?"

"Jeremy Andrew Ivester."

I looked over at Mom, realizing all of a sudden that this was the first time she'd heard my new middle name, which actually was a pretty big deal. She'd asked me months ago to consider Andrew, reminding me that her middle name is Ann, named for my great-grandmother. Elizabeth, Ben, and Sammy all had names to honor parents and grandparents, so Mom thought it would be cool if I did as well. She actually got real sentimental about it.

I didn't give her an answer at the time, just said I'd think about it. But the idea grew on me. I meant to tell Mom about it because I knew it would mean a lot to her, but in all of the excitement, it just slipped my mind. When she heard me say "Jeremy Andrew Ivester" to Judge Stavely,

I could see that she was all choked up and smiling at the same time. I'm not sure whether it was just that she got emotional about the whole name change thing in general or whether she was reacting specifically to my middle name and the connection with her, but it felt good to see her so happy. It underscored for me how excited my parents are about my transition. I could feel their pride and was glad they'd come.

"Are you changing your name to avoid creditors?" the judge asked.

"No."

"Are you changing your name to commit fraud?"

"No."

"Having read and considered your petition, I find that the statutory requirements for a change of name under the Colorado Revised Statutes 13-15-101 have been met."

Judge Stavely looked down as he signed the order, and then, glancing up, he smiled. "Congratulations, you are now Jeremy Andrew Ivester."

It was done, almost anticlimactic after all the months of waiting. But I felt all warm and fuzzy inside and knew that I was beaming.

Then Mom, never one to be shy about making requests, spoke up. "Excuse me," she said to the judge. "Would it be okay if I take a picture?"

"Go right ahead," Judge Stavely said, gesturing toward me.

"No, I mean with you," Mom said.

I was pretty embarrassed, not wanting to impose on the judge, but he just grinned and said, "Sure."

So I stepped up to the bench, we both smiled, and Mom got her photo. Then the judge handed me my paperwork and reminded me that before everything could be finalized, I'd have to publish notification in the local newspaper for two weeks.

Next stop, the *Colorado Daily*. I already wrote out what needs to be printed and actually think it'll be pretty cool to see my name in the paper.

Jeremy (25) in court with Judge Stavely

April 2015

Jon

WHILE WE WERE driving to the *Colorado Daily* offices, Jo said to Jeremy, "We should have planned this before, but would you like to have your friends join us for a celebration dinner tonight?"

"We'll host everyone at a local restaurant, maybe get a separate room and make it a party," I offered.

"Can Sammy come too, and maybe some of his friends?" Jeremy asked.

By the time Jeremy finished his business with the newspaper, Jo had made a reservation for ten at the Rio Grande and had already told Sammy about it. That's Jo, always taking action before the rest of us even know that we've made a decision.

Looking about the table that evening, sipping margaritas, I was pleased with the group that had come to support Jeremy. There was Jan from his old coffee shop, the woman who'd helped him figure out how to come out at work. His new coworkers from Men's Wearhouse, who treated Jeremy's new legal status as the most natural thing in the world. Colin and Meg, staunch allies since before Jeremy knew he was transgender. A couple of other guys from the Forty-First Street house. Sammy's friends, Evan and Dustin, who had always accepted Jeremy as one of the gang. And, of course, Sammy himself, Jeremy's constant companion since they were kids, always accepting, always supportive.

I choked up when Jo made a toast.

"Here's to Jeremy. Congratulations on your new legal

status. May your new name bring you great joy and happiness. To all your friends," she said, looking around the table, "you are here tonight because you have *always* been here for Jeremy. I know that means a lot to him. And as his mother, it means the world to me."

twenty-five

A BOOK? REALLY?

—:—

April 2015 — Austin, TX

Jo

In the midst of all the excitement about Jeremy's top surgery and name change, I was on an adventure of my own. For eight years, I'd been working on my first book, *The Outskirts of Hope*, and it was finally getting published. It was a memoir about my family's time living in the Mississippi Delta, where my dad ran a clinic.

Outskirts was more my mother's story than my own, telling of her days in the 1960s as the only white teacher at Kennedy High in Mound Bayou. She filled several notebooks with anecdotes about the family, her students, my dad's patients, and the civil rights movement. When she was done, I asked if I could expand on her work. What started as a writing project developed into an honest conversation about all that had happened. I learned things about her that I'd never known, and vice versa. Bit by bit, her anecdotes evolved into a deeper story, exposing the fears and joys of a traumatic time in our lives. Rarely do mother and daughter get to share so openly.

I wasn't able to finish *Outskirts* before my mom passed away. Within a year of her passing, however, I completed my manuscript and found a publisher. By April of 2015, I was busy getting ready for publication day. I wrote articles, updated my author web page, responded to my publicist every time a question came up about my upcoming tour, did radio interviews, and enjoyed all the exhilarating activities associated with publication.

My emotions bounced around from a fantastic high as my launch date grew close to an unnerving foreboding that I wasn't prepared, that questions would come up that I couldn't answer, that people would say, "Who the heck is she to write a book about the civil rights movement?" Not letting my fears stop me, I began touring the country to share stories and soon realized that doing so was a true form of advocacy. By making Mound Bayou come to life for my readers and listeners, I helped them to broaden their comfort zones, even if they'd personally had very little interaction with people that were a different race or religion or national origin from them.

Naively believing that once *Outskirts* was published, I would no longer be spending a lot of time on it, I began thinking about what I wanted to write next. Having watched Jeremy's journey through its ups and downs, and seeing how unfamiliar most people—myself included— were with what it means to be transgender, I started envisioning a second memoir, one that focused on Jeremy's story. I believed that in the same way I was helping people to understand racial relations from a more personal perspective, I could increase awareness about the transgender community and thus build acceptance.

Jon and I were both already involved in the battle for

transgender rights in our personal lives. Just after returning from Colorado following Jeremy's day in court, we
joined a phone bank with the nation's largest LGBTQ civil
rights organization, the Human Rights Campaign (HRC),
participating in their attempt to call every member in
Texas and encourage them to contact their senators and
representatives to ask that they vote against any discriminatory bills.

For Jon, our focus on the trans community began to
dovetail with his professional life when the executive director of Texas Competes, Jessica Shortall, approached him
about getting Silicon Labs to join other businesses to make
a statement for LGBTQ acceptance.

Jon was initially reticent to become politically active at
work, believing it inappropriate to bring politics into the
professional setting, not wanting to make his colleagues
uncomfortable. After listening to Jessica's arguments and
observing the Texas Legislature's attempts to pass discriminatory bills, however, he changed his mind, convinced
that a non-accepting environment made it difficult to re-
cruit top talent and thus was bad for the company.

The big launch for Texas Competes happened on the
same day as my book launch, April 14, 2015. Jon showed
up to observe the press conference and then returned to
Silicon Labs and talked folks there into signing on to the
program.

Given our own involvement, it was an easy step to in-
vite Jeremy to join the struggle. When he arrived in town
for my launch party, we did exactly that.

April 2015
Jeremy

ABOUT A HUNDRED PEOPLE STOOD BY THE NORTH steps of the Texas Capitol. Every TV station was there, along with the local papers. People carried signs and cheered the speaker. As we approached, someone offered us signs to hold. Mine said, "Don't Indiana My Texas." Indiana had just passed a new law called the Religious Freedom Restoration Act, which made it legal for someone to use their religious beliefs as an excuse to discriminate against gay and transgender people.

The rally at the capitol was a response to Texas trying to pass a similar bill. When she heard about it, Mom invited Aunt Connie, Uncle Philip, and me to join her there. We're all in town for her book launch, and it seemed appropriate to do something political. I've never been politically active before, but I appreciate that Mom is involved. She's always been interested in social action. For me, just living my life is a kind of activism. But I know that sometimes it's good to do more.

As we got closer, we heard a woman speaking about her transgender son, a kid still in elementary school. She accepted her child's gender identification when he was only five years old. She and her husband observed his boyish behavior as a preschooler and sought medical advice. Following an evaluation, a psychologist declared him "gender variant" and advised the parents to allow him to play and dress as he liked. By the time he was six, he'd adopted a boy's name. A year later, the child psychologist said he was transgender. I loved seeing how happy this family was with their decision, how totally normal this kid seemed. It made me glad we had come to the rally.

Jeremy (25), Jo, Connie, and Philip at the Texas State Capitol]

I'D NEVER BEEN to a book launch before last night. It's hard to believe that Mom's book is actually going to be in bookstores and that people will buy it, people we've never met. The launch party, though, was mostly for friends and family. It was at BookPeople, the biggest independent bookstore in the state, which also happens to be walking distance from my parents' apartment in downtown Austin.

It was a surreal experience for me because it was the first time I'd seen a lot of folks since transitioning. Mom asked me to be the bartender, which just meant pouring wine for everybody. She knew that mingling with people isn't really my thing and that it would be good for me to have something to do during the party. It was actually kinda fun watching folks do a double take as they realized I wasn't an employee of the bookstore but was actually the person they used to know as Emily.

Mom and Dad speak openly about me to their friends, so nobody was hearing about me for the first time, but I guess it was different seeing me in person. Everyone was supportive and lots of folks congratulated me on my transition. In general, it was pretty cool, but it did feel weird when all these people I didn't know kept hugging me and saying how brave I am.

This morning, Mom and I were sitting around in the living room and she said, "I've got a question for you."

"Shoot," I said.

"I think I know what I'd like to do for my next book. Would you be okay with me writing about you?"

"What would you write?" I asked, somewhat incredulous that she might write about me being transgender.

"Your story," she said. "Who you are and what it's been like for you, going back to when you were a little kid."

"So, another memoir, like you did with Grandma about Mississippi?"

"Exactly," she said. "I'm just starting to think about how I'd structure it. But I'm guessing I'd start with when we thought of you as a tomboy, before you knew you were trans."

"Um, uh . . ." I stuttered, thinking about how I want to stay stealth at work, not let anyone know I'm trans.

"I won't do it if you're not okay with it," Mom said. "And I'd want you to review everything and make sure it's right and that you're comfortable."

The thought was terrifying. Being out for the whole world to see. Talk about invading my privacy. And what about all the violence against transgender people? I haven't found any solid statistics, but the websites I've explored suggest that trans people—especially black and Latina women—are more likely to be attacked. Did Mom know that? Did she realize that exposing me in a book could be dangerous?

"I think it could be important," she said. "It would help build awareness and acceptance. It would tell about your journey, and of our journey with you."

Clearly, she was focused on all the positive things a book could do, not on any of the problems.

"I could say if there was something I didn't want you to write about?" I asked.

"Absolutely," she said. "You'd have veto power over everything."

Mom really wanted to do this. And I understood why. Before I had a chance to change my mind, I said, "Okay."

"Is that 'okay,' you'll think about it? Or 'okay,' I can do it?"

"You can do it. You can write about me."

Then she started to backpedal a bit. "You don't have to answer right away, kiddo. And if we do this, you can always tell me you've changed your mind and I'll drop the project."

"It's really fine, Mom," I said. "I get why you want to write about me. And it's not like people will start recognizing me on the street. It won't really affect me at all."

"Okay then. Now here's an even tougher question: Will you do it with me?"

"Sure," I said. "If I don't have to write."

I'd made Mom so happy that she started pumping her fists in the air. "You won't have to write," she said. "I've got all your videos, and that can be your voice in the book. And anything else I write in your voice, you can modify it to make it yours."

"I'm good with that," I said.

And just like that, I committed to working on a book with my mom.

twenty-six

I JUST AM

=·=

Summer 2015 — Boulder, CO
Jeremy (25 years old)

It's taken a while for me to resist spending my whole paycheck on the clothing I sell at Men's Wearhouse. With my employee discount, everything seems like a great bargain, and I've been able to purchase a fashionable male wardrobe. Although some of my favorite items are still thrift store purchases and hand-me-downs from Sammy, I love picking out a new tie or the perfect sweater from the bastion of masculinity where I work. I wore boyish blue jeans and T-shirts in the past, but I always admired professional threads as well. Now that I've transitioned, I revel in each article of clothing that was denied to me as a child and a teenager.

We alter suits here in the store, hemming trousers and letting out waistlines. Stephanie is the operations manager, which means she's in charge of all the rentals and the tailoring that goes along with that. I'm her assistant, among other things. Because she came on board after my legal name change, she never saw my old name in the computer system, so I've always been Jeremy to her.

If Stephanie knows I'm trans, she's very good at pretending she doesn't. She's a second-generation American whose family emigrated from Laos. In her early twenties, she loves partying and electronic dance music, and she gets lost in the heavy percussive beat. She's always talking about going to raves with her boyfriend. Even at work, she wears heavy makeup, and she dyes her hair in bright colors.

Everyone loves Stephanie, and she flirts with everyone. Not seriously, because she has a boyfriend, but she smiles a lot and always tells folks how pretty or handsome they look. She says stuff like, "Your cleavage is looking good today." And she's very touchy and giggles a lot.

I like working with her and that she flirts with me the same way she does with all our male colleagues. "Have you been working out, Jeremy?" she'll ask. "Your shoulders are looking really broad today. It looks good on you."

That's a great ego boost because I *am* working out and trying hard to grow into my more masculine physique. When Stephanie compliments me, it's like she's saying, "Jeremy, you're succeeding. You look like a manly man." It feels good to have a woman find me sexy and attractive. It's a whole lot better than what I usually get, which is, "You're cute."

Sometimes she says stuff that other people might find inappropriate, kind of blunt and ridiculous. It never bothers me, though, because she's so outgoing and is just being funny. The other day in the store, there were no customers, so we were hanging out in the back. I was sitting on the edge of a table while she measured some pants. Every once in a while, she cracked the tape measure like a whip and then laughed at the sound it made.

Kind of out of nowhere, she said, "What would you do

if I just hit you in the balls?" Then she snapped the tape measure in my general direction. Not in a mean or harassing way, just being silly.

"Uh . . ." I stammered. I had no idea what I should say.

"No, really," she jumped in. "You know, I always wondered, what's it like for guys to have a penis in their pants? Like, what's that about?"

I've wondered the same thing myself, but I certainly wasn't going to say that.

"What does it do when you're just sitting there? Or, like, when you walk around?"

All I could do was laugh. Stephanie didn't expect anything else from me. She was just saying what came to mind, no matter how absurd. What made me feel good was how she so totally took for granted that I'm a guy. The more I thought about that, the more I realized that I've been taking it for granted as well, no longer hyper-focused on my gender identity. I used to worry that I would never feel like a man, that I would always feel as if I were pretending. But now, I'm like, "This is just me."

This change in my attitude happened very quickly. I'm no longer fixating on being trans. That's only 5 percent of my identity, so I don't want people to think of me as "Jeremy, the trans guy." I want them to see me the way I do, which is just "Jeremy, the guy." Or maybe "the guy who can make a sale even though he's still an assistant," or "the guy who's good at football," or "the guy who writes music."

That's not to say that being trans isn't still important to me. It is. It's shaped my life and affects me every day. But it isn't something that I think about all the time. Because I just . . . I just am.

Fall 2015 — Austin, TX
Jo

BY SEPTEMBER, JON AND I WERE REGULARS AT THE HRC phone-banking effort to save Houston's Equal Rights Ordinance, known as HERO. A couple of years earlier, the Houston City Council had passed an ordinance that made it illegal to discriminate against over a dozen groups, including veterans, the disabled, and transgender individuals. There was one problem. A group of four pastors gathered signatures and petitioned for a referendum.

Those opposed to the new law were successful at framing it in terms of "the bathroom ordinance." They argued that its reversal was a way to protect women in public restrooms. They said that HERO allowed predators to enter restrooms to assault women and children. They aired commercials showing men doing exactly that. By explaining their concerns in those terms, they pretended that they weren't discriminating against transgender people but were instead ensuring everyone's safety.

It was maddening to watch that political battle unfold. We spent hours placing calls to remind HRC members of the importance of voting, imploring them to protect the rights not only of transgender people but also of all the other groups listed in the ordinance. Everyone we called expressed their support. Without exception, people thanked us and promised to vote.

It wasn't enough. The opposition succeeded, much to the dismay of the entire LGBTQ community and its allies. Discrimination against our son was once again legal in Houston.

After that loss, focus group interviewing determined that one of the best ways to advocate for transgender rights was to have parents speak out. While many people were unfamiliar or uncomfortable with what it meant to be transgender, just about everyone understood a parent's love for their child. When Jon and I heard about this research, we joined the emerging group of parents of transgender individuals showing their support. We spoke at meetings and called our senators and representatives to share our family's story.

At the same time, we grew increasingly active with the Anti-Defamation League (ADL), a hundred-year-old organization created to "secure justice and fair treatment to all." I'd initially become involved with the ADL as a result of their program aimed at stopping bullying in schools, No Place for Hate. The program fit in well with the outreach about racial relations I engaged in following the publication of *The Outskirts of Hope*. I hadn't realized prior to my book launch that book-related speaking engagements would become an opportunity to make people more comfortable talking about race. But that's what happened.

With that experience behind me, I decided I didn't need to wait for my new book to get published before I could start giving talks about it. In fact, I came to believe that raising awareness about the transgender community was so critical that I had to speak out.

December 2015 — Boulder, CO
Jeremy (26 years old)

AFTER A YEAR AND A HALF ON HORMONES, I'VE GROWN comfortable with myself. I know that if someone is talking to me, they aren't seeing some front I've put on because of everybody's expectations. They're seeing *me*. I no longer have to live a pretense and am thankful I'm in a time and a place that's accepting and that I have the ability to live my life as myself. I am lucky. Not everyone gets to do this.

The physical changes have slowed down a lot. It's no longer like in the first year when my doctor increased my testosterone dosage and suddenly my voice was an octave lower. In the last six months, my progress has been so slow that I didn't notice things changing until suddenly it was like, "Huh, my pants don't fit the same way. I need to get these taken in." My hips are smaller and my butt has changed, not as wide and flatter than before hormones. More masculine somehow. I'm totally good with that.

I'm disappointed, though, because even with the changes, I'm still fairly curvy. I wouldn't be this way if I weren't trans, if I'd been born a guy. Still, when it comes down to it, I'm thrilled with what my body is doing.

February 2016 — Dallas, TX
Jeremy

IT FEELS STRANGE TO VISIT MY FOLKS IN DALLAS. They moved here when Liz was seven months pregnant so

264

they could help out with the new baby. At first, Dad com-
muted to Austin for his job with Silicon Labs, but he retired when my new little niece was a couple of months old.

I adore Baby Ellie, the way she smiles and interacts
with me. It makes me incredibly happy just to sit and hold
her. When I recently shared those thoughts with Mom, she
jumped on the opportunity.

"So," she said. "Does this mean you'll move to Dallas?"

We were sitting on the bed in my parents' guest room,
where I stay whenever I'm in town. Their place is walking
distance from where Liz and Dustin live over by the
Southern Methodist University campus. They moved there
when Dustin was offered a job coaching men's soccer at
SMU. Liz stayed with HP and works out of their office in
Plano, about a forty-five-minute drive north from their
house. Mom and Dad followed a couple of months before
Ellie was born.

"I can't move here," I said.

"Sure you could," said Mom. "They've got Men's Wear-
houses here. You could transfer pretty easily, and then you
could see Ellie all the time."

"I'm not worried about getting a job."

"What is it, then?"

"It's Texas," I said.

"What do you mean?" she asked.

"I can't move back to Texas. Who I am is illegal here."

"You mean because you're trans?"

"Yeah. Colorado has an anti-discrimination act that
protects me."

"And Texas doesn't."

"No."

"But Dallas does. Austin does. As long as you live in

one of the big cities, you're okay," Mom said, trying to convince me. "I get it, though. You shouldn't have to make a decision between living close to family and being protected by state law. It's not right."

We sat there quietly for a few minutes. Then I said, "Hey, there's something else I've been thinking about."

"What's up?"

"I've been researching phalloplasty."

"Um, creating a penis?"

"Yeah." I was hesitant to go into detail, but it was too late. I'd already opened up the discussion. "I'm just beginning to think about it."

"I've read a little about it," Mom said. She looked kind of worried and sad. "Sounds pretty experimental and high risk. And recovery is terrible."

"It's not like I've made any decisions or anything," I said, not wanting her to be concerned. "It's just that I know I could work out the logistics pretty easily. I could take a medical leave from my job, and my insurance would pay for it."

As I spoke, I realized that it sounded like I'm ready to actually move forward, which I'm not. I just like to understand my options, not only medically but also in terms of how they would affect my life. "I'd still have to figure out who would take care of me and where I'd stay while recovering."

"Dad and I will be there for you. You know that." As she said that, I could almost hear her thinking, *When will this end? Jeremy's done top surgery, and gone on hormones, and legally changed his name. Why does he have to do anything more?*

Sometimes, I ask myself the same questions.

Despite any misgivings I have about it, though, I know my folks will be there to support me if I go this route. But first, I have to do some soul-searching. I know I'd feel better with a more male anatomy down there. And I really think it would get rid of my lingering dysphoria. But while I definitely would prefer the results of phalloplasty to what I have, I'm not convinced it's worth all the pain and hassle. It's a really big surgery with a long recovery time and a high potential for complications. It's a lot to go through, much more intense than my chest surgery and with much nastier scars.

I've watched videos made by trans men who've had bottom surgery, and they all seem happy with it. But then I know of others who've never had bottom surgery and don't feel a need for it. I'm already happy with what has happened with my body. When I take my shirt off and examine myself in the mirror, I'm like, *Yeah, I look really good.* I feel attractive.

But then when I strip down to my underpants, all that positivity just disappears. There's this pouch there, and something is supposed to be filling it, but it isn't. It's just sad and empty and looks wrong to me.

Mom's next comment pulled me back into the moment. "You know that we'll support you. But why is this important to you? Before, you said you didn't think that bottom surgery would be necessary."

"I still haven't decided anything, Mom," I said. "But to answer your question, it's a visual thing. When I see the lack of anything there, it's a weird disconnect with my body."

"Is it the same as the dysphoria you felt about your breasts?"

"Basically, yeah. I'm still trying to figure it out."

"Okay," she said. "No need to rush."

Mom didn't know it, but I'm not rushing. I've been thinking about this for a while. I even pack some of the time. At first, I stuck a sock in my underwear to create a bulge. Nothing super obvious. I didn't want people looking at me and saying, "Wow, he's hung like a horse."

Then I decided to just lay it out for her. "Uh, Mom, do you know what 'packing' is?"

"I take it you don't mean getting ready for a trip."

"No, Mom," I said, laughing. "I mean I've started packing." As I said this, I gestured with my hands, pointing down below my waist.

Mom looked confused for a moment, but then she grinned. "You mean, umm, that you, uh . . ."

"Yeah."

Her eyes looked quickly down to my crotch and then back up to my face. "So, right now, are you . . ."

"No, Mom, I'm not packing at the moment."

"So when do you? *Pack*, I mean," she said, trying to use the word as if it were the most natural thing in the world.

"Not when I'm just hanging out," I responded.

"So to speak," she said, never able to pass up a pun. Then, somewhat sheepishly, she said, "Sorry about that."

"Yeah, that was pretty bad," I said, but I was laughing at the same time. "I don't bother packing if I've got on loose-fitting pants, because then it doesn't make a difference. But when I'm wearing tight skinny jeans, you can tell if nothing's there."

Since Mom didn't seem too weirded out by the whole discussion, I decided to show her. "Do you want to see what I'm talking about?"

"Sure," she said, and I could tell she was interested not only because I'm her kid but also because she was genuinely curious.

I reached over to the nightstand and pulled my silicone penis from the top drawer. Bouncing it up and down a little as if I were weighing it, I said, "I chose this type because it looks and feels realistic and it's the right size."

"That's awesome," Mom said.

Awesome? Yeah. Not weird or creepy or anything else bad. My mother thinks it's awesome that I sometimes wear a fake penis in my pants. How cool is that!

twenty-seven

MAKING A DIFFERENCE

—·—

Spring 2016 — Dallas, TX

Jo

I felt dazed the other day when Jeremy described bot-tom surgery. I tried to be matter-of-fact about every-thing he said. But I wasn't. I didn't want him to do another round of surgery, one that would be a whole lot tougher than what he'd already been through. I told him that I hated the thought of the physical risks involved and how difficult recovery would be.

What I didn't share was that I didn't understand why it was so important to him to be anatomically male. I was afraid that if I did, he wouldn't feel supported. Did that make me dishonest? Sometimes I wouldn't acknowledge even to myself that I didn't completely comprehend what was going on. I wanted to be the mom who got it, so I acted as if that was the case even when it wasn't.

In the midst of this ever-increasing need to demon-strate parental acceptance, both for ourselves and as role models for others, Jon and I received a call from Cookie Ruiz, the Executive Director of Ballet Austin. We'd been nominated to receive the Austin ADL's Maislin Humanitarian Award at their 2016 Torch of Liberty Dinner, coming up at the end of March.

"We'll take care of everything," said Cookie. "All you have to do is show up. Oh, and give a speech."

The Maislins, for whom the humanitarian award was named, were the founders of the Austin-region ADL and, coincidentally, the parents of our good friend, Amy Mitchell, the lawyer who had connected us with the doctor who figured out that Jeremy's abdominal pain was tied to a spleen injury. The Maislins had created an endowment so that all honorees could direct a $1,000 donation to a nonprofit organization of their choice.

STANDING NEXT TO Jon and looking out at our friends, colleagues, and even complete strangers, I was thrilled that our family was there to share in everything. Our four children had come in from North Texas, Colorado, and Oregon. My dad's wife, Audrey, and her brother, Pedrito, had arrived earlier in the week.

As I spoke to the room, which was packed with close to seven hundred people sitting around elegantly set tables, dining on a gourmet dinner and sipping wine, I explained why the ADL's mission was personal for me. That I'd been raised in a family involved in the civil rights movement. That I had a gay brother and a lesbian sister. That my dad and his black Jamaican wife had faced discrimination as an interracial couple. That my nephews from that branch of the family had grown up being taught how to conduct themselves in a white world to avoid getting beaten or killed. And that our son is transgender.

Jon picked it up from there, saying, "My experience as

a business leader taught me that fairness, respect, equality, and love are both more absolute and more subtle than I realized as a child. Fairness doesn't only occur at the level of the individual, but at the system level as well. Justice must be measured by outcomes, not just by intent. And the way to help create a world that is better for my grandchildren is to build a world that is better for everyone's grandchildren."

Then Jon made a statement about how we wanted to direct the $1,000 honorarium that came along with ADL's Humanitarian Award.

"Jo and I have chosen the Equality Texas Foundation, which advocates for the LGBTQ community. We did this in honor of our son Jeremy, whom we welcomed into the world twenty-six years ago as what we thought was our daughter. We are committed to fighting the personal and institutional hate directed against him and other transgender people."

I was glad I wouldn't have to speak again, as I'm not sure I could have made a sound. I could see audience members wiping tears from their cheeks.

"Nobody should be rejected by their family for who they are or how they identify," Jon continued. "Nobody should be kicked out of their homes or communities for being gay or transgender or anywhere else on the LGBTQ spectrum. Nobody should lose their jobs because of their gender identity or sexual orientation. Everybody should be free to love the person they want to love. And I am proud to say that I love my son."

Then Jon added something that wasn't in his notes. Looking directly into the darkness where he knew Jeremy was seated, he said, "Jeremy, I love you."

The room erupted with applause, and the entire audience rose to their feet. Our children and Audrey and Pedrito stood, pounding their hands together, along with everyone else. We began to make our way down the stairs from the stage, moving slowly toward our family. Jeremy didn't wait for us but instead left our table and practically ran toward us, almost knocking Jon over as he embraced his father and wouldn't let go.

Jeremy

WOW. JUST WOW. BOTH OF MY PARENTS HAVE always supported and accepted me, but it's usually Mom who speaks in front of groups to raise awareness about the trans community. Dad is more the silent, solid-as-a-rock type. It was amazing the way Dad spoke to seven hundred people and told them about me, not hesitating in the least, clearly proud of me for how I'm living my life.

He spoke passionately and it was super powerful, especially when his voice started to break with emotion. As he challenged the audience to treat transgender individuals with respect, I could just feel him protecting me, the way he did when I was a little kid.

Later, when the program ended and everyone was wandering around socializing, people I'd never met came up to me and said stuff like, "I'm so proud of you, Jeremy." People I didn't know hugged me and told me how much they supported me. I mattered to all these people. Mom and Dad did that.

April 2016 — Boulder, CO
Jeremy

IT'S BEEN A FEW WEEKS SINCE THE AWARDS dinner. I'm back in Boulder, and I've been missing my family. My friends are great, but my family is special.

Last week, sitting on my balcony on one of Boulder's first spring days, wearing only a T-shirt and shorts, I was on my phone, scrolling through photos that Liz had just sent of Baby Ellie, who's now almost four months old. I would say that Ellie was looking especially cute in the pictures, but she always looks cute, so, you know.

I jumped when the phone rang in my hand. It was Mom.

"I want to write an article about you not being willing to come back to Texas because of the nasty politics and the bathroom bills and the lack of protection from discrimination," she said.

Of course I said it was okay. "I get the importance of being willing to put myself out there," I told her.

A few days later, she sent me the final copy for my approval before posting it. I liked it and even sent a photo that she could use with it.

This is what she wrote:

I miss my son. You see, Jeremy won't move back to Texas. He doesn't feel welcome here because he is transgender. He lives in Colorado, where there is a state law that protects him from discrimination. Not in Texas. Here, the opposite is true. Many of our state's politicians not only don't want to defend

274

Jeremy's right to use public accommodations (stores, services, and yes, restrooms), they want to explicitly take that right away from him. And their hateful language can be interpreted as inciting violence against people like Jeremy.

My son is a sweet, caring individual. It hurts me as a mother to see anyone—especially our leaders— reject my son for the person he is. He is lovable. He is harmless. He is a contributing member of society. And my son has more courage than anyone else I know.

Please share this post as widely as you can. My hope is that when we recognize that we know someone with a Jeremy in our lives, familiarity will grow. And with that familiarity will come acceptance.

May 2016
Jeremy

THE REACTION ON FACEBOOK HAS BEEN INTENSE. Within days, over forty thousand people saw what Mom wrote. It was shared by the Gay and Lesbian Alliance of North Texas, along with supportive comments like, "Sending lots of love," and "We are with you, young man!" Representative Donna Howard, a member of the Texas House who's known for her support of health care, shared the post. People have written from beyond Texas as well. One woman told about how her adult son wouldn't return to Alabama, saying, "Having a law to check your gender is ridiculous. What's wrong with them!"

Some of my mom's friends wrote about how much they care. "I pray that someday soon, no mother will have to hurt like you do. Love and hugs." People I've never met have jumped into the conversation, saying, "Jeremy, be strong. The haters will always hate, but the ones who support you and love you will envelop you with their love! I don't know you, but I will welcome you with open arms!"

The most heartbreaking comments have been those from transgender people, saying things like, "I came out to my dad last weekend. Needless to say, my life was destroyed." It feels awful to read that. I know that a lot of parents aren't supportive like mine are, but it feels so much more personal to read about it on Mom's Facebook feed, like I've been kicked in the gut.

My mom has tried to answer every comment, though it's become impossible to stay caught up with the activity. She has, though, made a point of reaching out to every transgender individual who posted. She's corresponded with some of them, offering support, saying she cares, and sometimes tracking down much-needed resources. One trans man texted her from Houston, saying he was staying on a friend's couch but needed to move and was afraid he'd be out on the street. Mom contacted Lou Weaver, the statewide transgender programs coordinator for Equality Texas, to find out who in Houston could help.

Just a few weeks after Mom's posting went viral, she called me, very excited, saying, "Did you hear what our attorney general just said? Loretta Lynch just spoke out against the North Carolina bathroom law. The Department of Justice is going to sue the state to prevent them from implementing it."

"That's very cool," I said.

"She stated this was no different from the civil rights movement and the Jim Crow laws and how it used to be that black people couldn't use public restrooms."

"Awesome. I'll go check it out."

When I found the speech online a few minutes later, the part that really stood out to me was when Loretta Lynch said, "No matter how isolated or scared you may feel today, the Department of Justice and the entire Obama administration want you to know that we see you, we stand with you, and we will do everything we can to protect you going forward."

Within days, the Obama administration issued a letter of guidance to schools all over the country, saying that they should allow transgender students to use the restrooms and locker rooms matching their gender identity. The Texas lieutenant governor, who is pretty much the leader of the movement there to discriminate against transgender people, responded by saying that Texas would forgo ten billion dollars in federal education subsidies before it would follow the new guidelines. *That's* why I can't move back to Texas.

July 2016 — Killeen, TX

Jo

WHILE HIGH SCHOOLS WERE WRESTLING WITH what to do about bathrooms, locker rooms, and sport teams, colleges were faced with the added complexity of dormitories. Even within the trans community, there was disagreement about the best answer, with some saying that trans students should be able to sign up for a room and roommate based on their gender identity and others saying that schools should routinely provide single rooms for trans students to avoid the potential problem of making anyone—the student, the roommate, or the student or roommate's parents—uncomfortable.

Every summer, the Texas Transgender Nondiscrimination Summit gathered to focus on these questions and to provide support to the transgender community. Jeremy and I were invited to present a workshop at their 2016 gathering in Killeen, a city of 150,000 in central Texas that was dominated by its proximity to Fort Hood, an army base about sixty miles north of Austin.

Our workshop would simply be us sharing Jeremy's story. He felt awkward about putting himself out there like that. It was one thing for Jon or me to talk about him being transgender. It was quite another for him to stand up in front of a group of people and say, "Hi. Look at me. I'm transgender."

We rehearsed as we made the three-hour drive south from Dallas. We'd already practiced by phone and by sharing video recordings, but we wanted everything to be perfect, so we ran through our talk one last time.

Our first stop once arriving in Killeen was the motel where all the speakers and organizers were staying. Then it was on to a nearby coffee shop to grab some dinner with the other speakers.

There were eight of us spread around two booths. The two speakers who sat at the table with Jeremy and me were both transgender women who hadn't transitioned until their forties. They were curious about how Jeremy's experience was different, transitioning as a young adult. In some ways, they seemed kind of jealous, saying they'd give anything to have had the freedom to be girls and women when they were younger.

They'd never had the luxury of using hormones to change themselves physically. They'd done it all with clothing, hair, makeup, and modifying their voices to speak in their upper registers. They talked about shopping for silicone falsies to put in their bras to make their breasts look more natural. One mentioned how she was walking outside one day and looked down and realized that her falsie had slipped out and fallen on the ground. She bent down and pretended to adjust her pantyhose with one hand while swooping up the falsie with the other. Then, still bent over, she looked around to make sure nobody was watching and stuffed it back into her bra. She told it as a funny story and the two of them were laughing, but it didn't seem funny to me. It seemed painful.

The next morning, Josephine Tittsworth, the conference organizer, greeted us as we arrived on campus. She was a trans woman in a wheelchair with long white hair held back with a black headband. Everybody knew her and she knew everybody.

After we chatted for a while, Josephine asked if we would be willing to change our planned talk a bit. "Instead of doing a workshop with twenty people," she said, "would you be our lunchtime speakers and address the whole conference?"

"You okay with that?" I asked Jeremy.

"Sure."

The time in between that conversation and lunch was taken up with a workshop, during which we met a nonbinary individual, the first one I'd ever gotten to know personally. They were in their early twenties with short blond hair, a unisex name, Riley, and a high voice. If it weren't for the name tag that said, "they/them/theirs," I wouldn't have known how to think of them. As it was, I stumbled over the pronouns, still finding it awkward to use the word *them* when referring to an individual.

At the start of the workshop, we went around the room and everyone told their story. When it was Riley's turn, they said, "I grew up in a small town outside of Houston, and the church was the center of our lives. My faith is still important to me, but my church rejected me. So did my family." They stopped for a moment to gather their composure and then added, "I'm alone."

Looking around the room, I saw nods of encouragement and several sad smiles, but nobody said anything. So even though it was my first time at the conference and I felt as if I were an outsider, I jumped in. "As a mom, I'm heartbroken for you. I don't understand how anyone can reject their child."

They started to speak but instead held up their hand to the side of their face, looking ready to cry.

Not knowing what else to do, I got up from my seat and walked over to them. "Can I hug you?"

They nodded silently, and as I reached up to put my arms around them, they grabbed onto me and hugged back.

THREE HOURS LATER, Jeremy and I stood in front of over a hundred people as they ate their salads, people who expected us to both educate and entertain them. For forty-five minutes, we handed the mic back and forth, sharing stories, sometimes telling the same story from two different perspectives. Our message was one of acceptance and normalcy.

I concluded with, "It has become our passion to do everything we can to build awareness through storytelling. Thank you for giving us the opportunity to share. I hope our story has touched you. Thank you for who you are and for what you are doing here this weekend. You make a difference."

The entire room stood up, cheering and clapping. As I gave Jeremy a congratulatory hug, I whispered to him, "That was for you, for being willing to share openly. You're standing up for every trans person in the room, and they love you for it."

He didn't believe me until folks thanked him specifically for telling his story and for being visible. One young man told us that he cried when Jeremy talked about Elizabeth's wedding and his struggle not to let her down by rejecting the dress. He said, "I was in the same position, but I caved and wore the dress. I always felt badly about that. I wasn't true to myself. But you were. Thank you, Jeremy, for *not* wearing the dress. You made a statement for all of us."

October 2016 — Dallas, TX
Jeremy (26 years old)

BETWEEN LIZ'S LONG HOURS AT HER NEW JOB IN human resources at WageWorks and Dustin's job coaching at Southern Methodist, they've been finding it hard to balance their professional lives with taking care of Baby Ellie. So they turned to me. Liz, hoping I'd change my mind about moving back to Texas, asked if I'd stay in Dallas for the month of August to watch Ellie. I said I would.

Jeremy (26) with niece Ellie

After a month of being close to my family again, and especially of bonding with my niece, I knew I wanted to make it permanent. The politics of Texas hadn't changed, but I had. I craved being a daily part of Ellie's life, to have her never remember a time when she wasn't close to Uncle Jeremy. I was thriving on the additional time with Ben and Jenn and Liz and Dustin and my folks. I wanted more. I needed more. That made facing the possibility of discrimination seem much more manageable.

I found renters for my Boulder condo and began looking for an apartment to rent in Dallas starting in early October. I quickly focused on the Oak Lawn area, relatively close to Liz and Dustin and Mom and Dad but far enough away that I'll have some independence. Often referred to as the "Gayborhood" for its high percentage of gay residents, the neighborhood has lots of bars and restaurants, and I'll be able to walk to everything I need.

Within a few weeks of deciding on that part of town, I zeroed in on a specific building, right across from the Kroger's grocery store. The Ilume Apartments were perfect, the pool area welcoming, the Cedar Springs Tap House practically right out the front door, and there was even a bark park for Indy.

The apartment itself was exactly what I wanted, right in my price range. Although smaller than my Boulder condo, it would provide all the space I need. My mom went with me to check it out, and I was sure that the staff and other residents saw us and thought, "How sweet. A mom going with her gay son while he looks for an apartment."

I returned the following day to submit a lease application. A few days later when I hadn't heard back, I called to find out what was going on.

"There's a problem," I was told. "We can't process your paperwork because the credit monitoring service flagged your account as fraudulent."

What?

With a little bit of digging, I realized that although I've changed my legal name on my identification and credit and social security cards, the credit service still has my old name. When the computer system saw one social security number with two different names, it assumed fraud. The leasing office staff is supportive and wanted to offer me an apartment, but the computer system wouldn't let them.

Knowing what had happened, I outed myself to the staff and asked if it would help if I gave them my name change documentation. They said it wouldn't. "Just call the credit service and explain it to them," they told me. "Once they remove the fraud flag, we can get you an apartment."

After waiting on hold for over an hour, I was exasperated with the whole process. So when my folks offered to ask their lawyer friend, Steve Rudner, to try to get some movement, I agreed. He called the rental office and reminded them, "Dallas has a non-discrimination ordinance that protects the rights of transgender people. You can't deny Jeremy a lease based on him being trans."

"We're not discriminating," they said. "We're supportive of the LGBTQ community. We even provide free space to the LGBTQ Chamber of Commerce."

But the office staff said their hands were tied. Until the fraud flag was removed, they couldn't give me a lease. So I called the credit service again.

"Submit your name change paperwork and we'll update your file," they said. "It'll only take a few weeks."

When I objected, fearful that I'd lose the apartment, the guy helping me said, "If you reapply using your old name, we can approve you."

That's what I'm doing. It's infuriating, but I want the apartment. So instead of the new start I was seeking here in Dallas, where I thought nobody would know me by my old name, all of my rental paperwork will say to anyone who sees it, *This person is transgender.*

twenty-eight

MY GROWING ADVOCACY

—:—

Fall 2016 — *Austin, TX*

Jeremy (26 years old)

I watched this morning as hundreds of students poured out of buses parked in front of the University of Texas football stadium. They were here for the Anti-Defamation League's Teen Summit, an annual gathering of eighth graders exploring how to eliminate hatred, bigotry, and bullying in their school environment. Mom and I were invited to share my story with the 120 teachers attending.

I was intimidated by the prospect of speaking to a room full of middle school teachers, most of whom had no idea what it means to be transgender. This was more frightening than the gathering a few months ago with the Texas Non-Discrimination Transgender Summit. There, everyone was either trans themselves or somehow involved with creating a gender-affirming environment on university campuses.

Nevertheless, I shared my story, aware that the room grew completely quiet as the teachers listened to me talk about how lonely I was back in eighth grade, how I lost my entire social circle, how I hated my body and wished I was like the boys. They nodded and smiled, as if willing me to continue.

Afterwards, the teachers asked great questions. What should they do if they think a student is transgender but hasn't said anything? What bathroom should the trans students use? What about sports teams and locker rooms? What should they say to parents? I answered when I could and admitted freely when I couldn't.

When it was over, one of the security guards approached my mom and me. She waited until we were on our way out the door and nobody else was around. Then she said, "I want to thank you for what you did today. I'm gay. My family accepted me the way yours did, but my partner's family disowned her."

"I'm sorry," Mom said. "That shouldn't happen to anyone."

"No, it shouldn't," said the guard. Turning back to me, she added, "What you told those teachers today about yourself, well, it makes a difference."

March 2017 — Austin, TX
Jeremy (27 years old)

WE CROSSED THE TEXAS CAPITOL GROUNDS ON our way to the church where we were meeting up with fellow advocates, passing several hundred people along the way, twice as many as were at the rally we attended two years ago. It's not just transgender people who are gathering. There are families with little kids, grandparent types with gray hair, straight people, gay people, bigender and nonconforming people, every one of them here to fight against discrimination.

The press conference to kick everything off was still two hours away, but we'd come early for an organizing session. Once inside the church, my parents started introducing me to all these folks I'd never met before. Everyone seemed to know who I was and thanked me for coming. It was kind of overwhelming.

Everyone was talking about the Texas Senate Committee on State Affairs hearing a few weeks earlier on Senate Bill 6—the "bathroom bill." My folks told me how awful it was. They showed up before seven thirty in the morning to register to speak against it and then waited until after midnight before they got their chance. The whole morning and much of the afternoon were taken up with so-called "experts" that spoke in favor of it. Jonathan Saenz, the president of Texas Values, a far-right lobbying group, claimed that making restroom accommodations for transgender people was dangerous, adding essentially, "If you can say you're female when you're a male, what's to stop you from saying you're an animal?" In the past, he's been known for commenting that gay marriage will lead to polygamy and pedophilia and calling it an attack on morality. Tony Perkins, the head of the Family Research Council, which has been identified by the Southern Poverty Law Center as an LGBTQ hate group, flew in from DC to add his discriminatory comments. The Texas Pastor Council said that LGBTQ rights are as "equally offensive" to God as slavery.

It was so brutal that advocacy groups brought in therapists and social workers to be available to the transgender attendees and other advocates in case all of the hateful comments triggered anxiety attacks or suicidal thoughts. I'm glad I wasn't there. And glad that my parents were.

In addition to talking about Texas Senate Bill 6, folks were complaining about all that the Trump administration had done in the two months since he'd taken office. In mid-February, the Departments of Justice and Education reversed the guidance that the Obama administration had provided regarding transgender students. Less than a month after that setback, Trump ordered the Department of Health and Human Services to stop enforcing the transgender community's access to health care. The next day, the Department of Justice announced it would no longer pursue an injunction against North Carolina's House Bill 2, a law that discriminated against transgender people. The Department of Housing and Urban Development withdrew two proposals that would have protected LGBTQ homeless people. The onslaught has been relentless, worse than we feared when Trump first became president. And Texas is at the forefront of the battle.

Pulling me away from a conversation about how awful the national politics are, Mom gestured toward a station for making signs and said, "I'm going to make one. Want to come?"

I watched curiously as she printed her message in big letters. "We Love Our Transgender Children!" She was choked up as she showed it to me, saying, "There's a story behind this. Grandma Aura marched with a similar sign over thirty years ago. It said, "We Love Our Gay Children."

Then Mom told me that ever since she became an LGBTQ advocate, she knew that one day she would carry a sign like the one she had just made, simultaneously honoring Grandma Aura, Uncle Charles, Aunt Connie, and me.

Given how supportive Grandma Aura was of me all through the years, I thought it was a pretty neat thing for Mom to do. A little hokey and weird, but cool at the same time.

By the time we headed back to the front lawn of the capitol, the crowd had grown to almost a thousand people. The mood was festive, with music blaring. Protestors waved flags with the names of LGBTQ organizations. One woman with flowing gray hair wore a sash displaying pins from all the groups, along with what must have been a very old button saying, "Make Love, Not War." A huge, rainbow-colored flag flew above it all, moving gently in the slight breeze.

We made our way to the Equality Texas group, where Dad and I picked up preprinted signs that said, "Y'all means all!" to go along with Mom's handmade one.

Jo, Jeremy (27), and Jon protesting Texas Senate Bill 6

After the rally, we joined a long line of people waiting to get through the metal detectors at security. The line went out the door, down the steps, and around the side of the building. There were so many of us that it took an hour before we made it inside. Folks were so excited that it felt more like a party than a line. And every single person there had come to speak out for my rights.

I hadn't been inside the capitol since a fifth-grade field trip, and I experienced the same sense of wonder I felt back then. As soon as we cleared security, I looked up into the huge rotunda topped with the Texas star and felt a bit dizzy, though whether it was from the physical experience of looking up or from being in the historic locale ready to make new history, I'm not sure.

"This way," Dad said, pointing the way to Representative Morgan Meyer's office. He represents my neighborhood, along with other parts of Dallas that run the gamut from liberal to conservative.

"What do we know about him?" Mom asked.

"He's a Republican, but he probably doesn't like the idea of discriminatory bills. I've heard that he believes he has to vote for them to keep his seat. So our ask of him is that he help stop the bill from ever getting to a vote."

By the time Dad explained the strategy, we'd made our way to the offices in the extension of the capitol basement. Our team was clustered outside Representative Meyer's door, waiting to enter until we were all there. Most of them were like me, not as well versed in the politics as my folks were. They just knew the cause was an important one and they wanted to help.

I was expecting a big, fancy office, but when we walked in, the entry area was crowded with staff desks and a few chairs for guests. The furniture was beautiful wood, but it looked pretty old and worn. The young woman sitting at the desk by the door invited us in, saying that because the House was meeting at the moment, Representative Meyer couldn't see us. But his chief of staff, Aaron Gibson, could spend a few minutes. Once he joined us, each of the team members introduced themselves and said that they were against SB6 because it discriminates against the transgender community.

Then Dad spoke up. "I've been a high-tech executive in Austin for over twenty years, first with Applied Materials and then with Silicon Labs. It's important to the business community that Texas not get a reputation for discrimination. If we do, it will be harder for us to attract and retain employees."

Mom added, "It's not just important for the businesses. It's wrong. Please don't discriminate against my son."

Then it was my turn. I spoke with an outward calm despite my thumping heart and racing pulse. I stated the comments I'd prepared earlier in the week and rehearsed in the shower, emphasizing that the bathroom bills were a made-up issue, addressing a problem that didn't exist. "Transgender people have been using the bathroom in which they're comfortable for years without incident. Just because someone else says they don't like the idea doesn't make it okay to discriminate."

Aaron nodded as I spoke, alternating between meeting my gaze and taking notes. He seemed supportive, but I couldn't be sure. So I just kept going. "If SB6 becomes law, then I could get arrested for using a men's restroom. I've heard people say I should use the women's restroom instead, but I'm not willing to do that. I wouldn't feel right in there, and I actually might make women uncomfortable because, well, I look and sound like a guy."

There is a third option, as Senator Cruz suggested recently. I could avoid public restrooms completely, effectively preventing me from ever leaving my home. As bad as SB6 would be for me, it would be even worse for trans women, who are more likely to face violent attacks if they use a men's restroom.

Fortunately, through the efforts of all the people who turned out in support of the transgender community, along with business leaders like my dad, who argued that discrimination was bad for business, the transgender discrimination bills never made it out of committee. As hoped, Representative Meyer never had to vote. The battle has been won, at least until the next legislative session in 2019.

twenty-nine

CHANGING HEARTS AND MINDS

—·—

April 12, 2017 — *Stephenville, TX*
Jeremy (27 years old)

They call it 'The Cowboy Capital of the World,'" Mom mentioned as we drove south on Highway 281 en route to a small town about a hundred miles southwest of Dallas.

Stephenville is home to Tarleton State University, which has thirteen thousand students, many of whom major in agriculture. We were invited there by Tiburcio Lince, who went by the nickname Turbo. He works for their Diversity and Inclusion Office, and he asked us to give a talk like the one we did last summer at the Transgender Summit. Mom said "yes" before even telling me about it, figuring that if I didn't want to go, she'd do it without me. My boss at Starbucks, where I recently started work as a barista, gave me the time off so I could go.

"Turbo isn't sure how many students will come," Mom said. "He thinks maybe around thirty, but he's hoping for more."

"I can handle it either way," I said, no longer nervous about getting up in front of people.

I was, however, concerned about the Q&A session afterwards. Mom had always handled those before, but this time, she wanted me to take the lead.

"What if they hit me with stuff I don't know?" I asked.

"They probably won't," Mom said. "Mostly, you can pull from your own experience. Plus, you've spent hours browsing online exploring the field, and you know a lot more than most people."

"True," I said, still feeling a little unsure.

"Seriously, don't worry," Mom said. "All you have to do is talk about yourself. As long as you're honest and sharing about stuff that really happened, you'll be fine."

"What if they ask me questions I don't want to answer?"

"You can always say exactly that. Just because we say folks can ask us anything doesn't mean that you need to answer."

"Yeah," I said. "I heard one trans speaker say, 'You don't know me well enough to ask about what's in my pants.' They made it kind of funny."

"And I've heard a good line when a guy was asked about where he went to the bathroom," Mom said. "In the toilet."

"Good one," I said, laughing. "Though I'm actually just fine talking about that."

We drove in silence for a while after that, watching the scenery turn more and more rural. Definitely cattle country. Then we passed a Confederate flag flying in front of a house.

"Wow," Mom said. "That's huge!"

Next, we passed a barn with its entire side painted with the flag. "That's extreme," I said, realizing how deep we were in redneck country. "Are you at all worried about getting hassled? Will we be safe on campus?"

"I *think* so," she said, more of a question than an answer. It made me feel a bit queasy as I thought about all the recent attacks on transgender people. Folks have been beaten up just because they're trans. Last year in Austin, a trans woman was murdered right in front of her home, not far from where we used to live. It wasn't hard to imagine something going wrong while Mom and I were on campus. The thought of that possibility made me wonder if we were crazy to be doing this. I tightened my grip on the steering wheel.

Mom interrupted my thoughts. "I don't think there's any physical danger. But Turbo warned me that we may have audience members who are hostile to the LGBTQ community."

"Why would they come hear us speak if they're hostile?" I asked.

"Maybe to protest our being there. Or it's possible that some students will be coming for extra credit in one of their classes. Turbo mentioned something about that, but he wasn't sure if that was actually going to happen."

As we drove onto campus, we passed a limestone fence, brick buildings, and well-manicured green lawns. The Diversity and Inclusion staff directed us into the auditorium of the business school.

Expecting the small group of thirty that Mom had described, I was taken aback to see every seat taken. There were over a hundred people there. People were standing in the back and sitting on the floor in front and still more students were entering the auditorium. They looked like college students did everywhere, mostly wearing jeans and

T-shirts, though several wore boots and a few even had cowboy hats. Some attendees looked older, and I assumed those were the professors. Down in front was a group of very young-looking men on the floor, and it occurred to me they might be trans.

Turbo and his graduate assistant, Kendyl Adams, greeted us as we walked toward the front of the room, though we could barely hear them over the noise of the students chattering as they tried to find seats together. Turbo wore jeans and a purple Tarleton State polo shirt. He smiled broadly, appearing casual and relaxed despite the hectic activity all around us. His hair was combed straight up in a style I've tried myself but can't quite pull off. His eyes opened wide behind his slightly squared-off glasses and his eyebrows were constantly a bit arched, making him look like he was ready to ask a question at any moment. I could see why students would be drawn to him and find his easy presence comforting.

As Turbo introduced us to a couple of professors, they explained the unexpectedly large crowd. Believing that students in sociology and psychology needed exposure to the transgender community, one had offered extra credit for attendance. The other had made it mandatory. "The students should be asking some good questions," Turbo said, "because they'll get points for participating."

Then Mom told him about the Confederate flags we'd seen while driving to campus and asked Turbo if he thought there might be any trouble.

"You don't have to worry," he said. "Most of our community is actually somewhat accepting. But we've got the campus police circling the block the whole time you're here, just in case."

"Is that really necessary?" she asked.

"We had some difficulties a few months ago when we had a speaker talk about being gay," he said. "Some guys started driving around the building yelling obscenities. We don't expect any problems like that tonight, but we figured we should be ready."

Glancing at the clock at the back of the auditorium, he added, "I think we should get started. I'll go get everyone quiet, introduce you, and start your video."

The video was a six-minute interview of Mom, Dad, and me, filmed at their apartment in Dallas a few months ago. Equality Texas had received a grant to create a series of videos about transgender people. They'd sent a team to spend several hours with us, Susan Risdon from Red Media Group and Kraig Kirchem from Kirchem Productions. They edited the results of the interview along with still shots from our photo albums and Facebook and my video journal. Then they added a voiceover from Dallas TV and radio journalist and news anchor Susy Solis. Tarleton State was the first time we shared the video at a talk, and we didn't know how the audience would respond.

"Let's do this," Mom said.

As we walked to the front of the room following the video, the crowd cheered their appreciation. They were with us. This would be easy. We'd share my story and field a few questions.

The first one, more of a statement than a question, hit me hard. A young man said, "Last week, I told my parents that I'm transgender." His hair was short and he dressed androgynously, much as I did not very long ago. He tried to speak in a low voice but couldn't quite make it happen. I was looking at myself before I acknowledged that I'm trans.

"How did it go?" I asked him.

Wiping his arm across his face, he inhaled sharply, as if he was having difficulty controlling his breath. Finally, he said—haltingly, barely loud enough for me to hear—"They threw me out and said they never want to see me again."

I stood speechless. I knew that a lot of families react by disowning their kids. That's one of the reasons I became involved with advocacy work. But now there was someone standing right in front of me, sharing his awful story.

Before I could get a word out, he asked, "What do I do?"

Mom gestured for me to hand her the mic.

Jo

I PROMISED JEREMY THAT ALL HE'D HAVE TO DO was talk about himself, to share his stories. I'd reassured him that nobody would ask a question he couldn't answer. When that proved not to be the case, I whispered, "Let me give this a try."

Turning back to the student who had just come out to his parents, I said, "I'm sorry that you're going through this. I don't understand how any parent can reject their own child."

He stared at me, waiting for more. He looked so young that he could easily have been mistaken for someone still in high school.

"Nobody should be thrown out of their home for who they are, for who they love, or for how they identify."

People began nodding throughout the audience.

"We're going to make sure that you are safe," I said, glancing over at the counseling staff, who were standing against the wall at the side of the room. "Right after we finish, I want you to talk with the staff about the resources they have available to you. They're going to make it okay."

I knew as I said it that everything probably wouldn't be okay. It might be years before his family accepted him, if they ever did at all. I knew he might be one of the forty-one percent of transgender teenagers that attempt suicide. I hoped that the staff knew more than I did about what to do. I was winging it, no more prepared than Jeremy had been. But I had to say something, so I just kept going in straight-on mom mode. It didn't matter that this was a trans person I was helping. He was just a teenager, some-one who needed support.

"Look around this room at all of these people who came here tonight to learn about what it means to be transgender," I said. "This is your support group. These are your friends."

A student who had been sitting nearby moved closer and put her hand on his shoulder. I nodded to the two of them together. "You are incredibly courageous to stand here before all of us and share your story. Thank you for that. And you will get through this." I had to stay positive, even though inside, I wasn't nearly as confident as I sounded.

As he sat down, a woman in the audience spoke up. "I have a trans daughter, and I used to be in the armed forces. So did my ex-husband. This is all very new to us." Her voice cracked as she continued. "I'm okay with it. Really, I am. But my ex-husband, he can't accept it and keeps telling our kid that she can't be this way, that there's something wrong with her, that she can't wear girls' clothing."

The room was perfectly quiet as she paused to gather her thoughts. Standing up to face the room, she said, "It's tearing us apart. It's tearing *me* apart."

This was another mom question, so I kept the mic. "Thanks for sharing," I said. "It must have been difficult for you. You're very brave."

"Nobody knows me here," the woman said. "I'm not really part of this community. That makes it easier to speak out. I never have before."

"You've been trying to handle everything yourself," I said, not asking a question but making a statement. The woman nodded silently. "Well, now you have others to help you," I said, gesturing to the room. Then I asked, "What suggestions do you have? What can this mom do to help her daughter?"

Almost immediately, folks started to call out ideas, mostly emphasizing that this military mom had already taken the critical step of deciding to support her daughter. They spoke of the need to stand with and protect her. To go to the kid's high school and make sure nobody was bullying her.

In the midst of the discussion, a student stood and walked out, banging his backpack into people as he rushed past. I saw staff approach him, but he brushed them off and let the door slam behind him.

When the room quieted, someone asked another question, this one about whether Jeremy had ever personally been bullied. He spent the next twenty minutes responding as audience members wanted to know more about his personal journey—losing his friends in middle school, the challenges, his feelings. He shared openly and honestly. He provided more details about his decision to keep a video journal, about how he told his sister that he couldn't wear the maid-of-honor dress, about how accepting the community in Boulder had been when he first transitioned. When the evening ended, students clustered about to hug him goodbye.

June 2017 — Nacogdoches, TX
Jeremy

OVER DINNER AFTER THE EVENT AT TARLETON State, Turbo and Kendyl said they were happy with the evening and thought we'd made a difference in helping the campus community become more accepting. It was cool to realize that I'd had an impact, that I'd reached people who were hurting. I was curious about the student who had stormed out, but we never got around to talking about him.

It wasn't until this month at the next Texas Transgender Non-Discrimination Summit that I found out what had happened. Following my keynote speech on what it meant to be an advocate, I invited audience members to tell their own stories of advocacy. A woman stood.

"I'm on staff at Tarleton State University, and there's something I need to tell Jeremy, something he doesn't know about," she said. "When you spoke on our campus a few months ago, quite a few of the students attending were there because their professor made it a class requirement. They really didn't want to be there. You may remember that partway through the evening, one student rushed out the door. I stopped him to ask if he was okay and he was very abrupt with me, saying something like, 'I can't deal with this. It's awful.'"

She paused before continuing. "A bit unfairly, I looked at his cowboy hat and boots and assumed he was transphobic. I thought he'd heard Jeremy's story and was hostile to everything LGBTQ. I was wrong. The student came to my office two weeks later, saying, 'I'm sorry I ran out the way I did. I needed some time.' When I asked him what he meant by that, he said, 'I was a bully. I was one of those guys that made life miserable for the gay kids at my school. I never thought about it from their side. Jeremy's comments made me feel terrible.'"

"So that's why he left early?" I asked.

"Yeah. And after thinking about everything for a couple of weeks, he showed up in my office saying he wanted to help. Jeremy, you changed his life."

Whoa! I never set out to change anyone's life but my own. All I've ever wanted was to be comfortable in my own skin, to have the person looking back at me in the mirror match the person I know myself to be inside.

The journey hasn't been easy. While I've ached to move forward and feel complete, I've been terrified at every step, fearful that I will disappoint people, scared of changing so drastically. That's why I had to take baby steps all along the way. That's why I took so long to tell my brothers and sister what was going on. That's why I waited until the thought of wearing a dress for my sister's wedding filled me with such anxiety that I couldn't think of anything else.

Yet I can't regret my life. All of it has shaped me to be the person that I am. I'm more empathetic, more loving and accepting, because of the amount of self-reflection I had to do to figure out what was going on—not just with me but with my whole family. My journey has been their journey, and that is really powerful.

More than that, it's been filled with joy. For every painful moment, and there have been many of them, there have been so many more that were happy and exciting, and I wouldn't give them up for anything. All of those moments combined have let me be who I am.

I am Jeremy.

thirty

AN UPDATE

—=—

Fall 2019 — Austin, TX

Jo

In the five years since Jeremy shared his new name with the world and asked that we refer to him as male, awareness of the transgender community has grown. Today's hostile political environment has brought transgender rights to the front pages of our newspapers and to the top of our social media feeds. The optimist in me chooses to see the potential for progress in this. As the population grows more aware of the discrimination transgender people face, there will eventually be a backlash against those prejudices.

The path is a painful one, however. At the start of the 2019 Texas Legislative Session, a senator once again introduced a bill that would make it illegal for Jeremy to use the men's restroom, trying to breathe life back into a battle we thought we'd won two years ago. After that, the floodgates opened and Jon and I spent hours at the Texas Capitol, testifying before House and Senate committees, pleading for them not to discriminate against our son and others like him. By the end of the session, only one of the anti-LGBTQ bills had passed, and even that one had been amended to the point that it wouldn't have any impact.

At the federal level, President Trump continues in his efforts against the entire LGBTQ community, targeting trans people in particular. The Department of Housing and Urban Development has purged its web pages of links to resources for transgender people and announced plans to gut the regulations that prohibit homeless shelters from discriminating against the transgender homeless. The Department of Education dismisses all complaints from transgender students about being excluded from school facilities. The Center for Disease Control has issued a ruling that staff are no longer allowed to use the term "transgender" in official documents. The Justice Department has instructed its attorneys to take the position in all legal cases that federal law does not protect transgender workers from discrimination.

Most recently, Trump banned transgender soldiers from serving in our military. At the University of Texas, just down the street from us, a college freshman lost his ROTC scholarship merely because he is transgender. There is a coordinated effort on the part of the Trump administration to destroy protections for transgender people in every area of their lives.

The suicide attempt rate for trans teens remains at over 40 percent, more than four times that of the general high school population. Trans schoolchildren are bullied, not only by their classmates but also by their teachers. Trans adults are assaulted and even murdered just for being who they are. In 2018, almost thirty transgender people were killed, most of them trans women of color. In Dallas alone, three trans women of color were murdered within a single year.

Despite the chaos and hatred that sometimes feels as if it's closing in on us, our family is doing well. We win some battles, we lose others. Throughout, we remain focused on the cause and on each other. After having spread out across the country for over fifteen years, we're back together again in Austin, now with four grandchildren added to the mix and another one on the way. Jeremy was the last to arrive, hating to leave his friends in Dallas.

Jeremy
Looking Back at His Time in Dallas
2016 to 2019

ALMOST THREE YEARS AGO, WHEN I FIRST MOVED to Dallas, I ventured out into the Gayborhood and over to the Round Up Saloon, a country-western bar not far from my apartment. Standing by myself, I listened to the DJ and watched people line dance. Then, a guy about my age with short brown hair and scruffy-looking stubble walked up to me and said, "Are you by yourself?"

"Yeah," I answered.

"I'm Jude," he said. "Wanna hang with us?" He gestured to his friends across the dance floor.

"Sure. I'm Jeremy."

Jude introduced me to his partner, Geoff, a few years older, with lighter hair and the same athletic physique. They'd met through a dating app and had been together for less than a year, but they seemed as comfortable with each other as a long-established couple. I stayed with them and their friends for the rest of the evening. They were

fun and easy to be with, even though we could barely hear
each other over the music and the noise of the bar.

When we stepped outside a few hours later, Jude said,
"Some friends are coming over for game night later this
week. Wanna come?"

I'd lived in town for only a few weeks and already I had
some friends. That felt pretty good. Over the next two days,
though, I started getting nervous. I figured that because of
where my apartment was and how I presented myself, Jude
and Geoff assumed I was a cisgender, gay man. That I'd
been born with a boy's body. I was afraid that if they discovered my secret, they'd dump me, either because of who I
am or because I hadn't told them right up front.

When it was time to go Jude and Geoff's, I dressed
carefully, my casual look belying the effort I'd put into the
selection. Skinny blue jeans with a button-down shirt. Just
the right mix of not caring yet being aware.

Their studio apartment was just north of downtown, in
a part of town that was a mix of vacant lots, old buildings,
and new development. Inside, there were almost a dozen
people crowded around the kitchen counter that doubled
as their dining table. They were playing this game called
Encore that involved singing. Geoff explained the rules to
me, and then they all made me sing. We were laughing and
I felt as if I'd known them for years. I fit right in.

I stuck around after everyone else left, partly to help
clean up and partly because I was feeling so laid-back that
I didn't want to leave. That's when Geoff said, "So, Jeremy,
what's your story?"

I wondered if they'd looked me up online. I'd known it
was risky when I didn't take down my old social media, my
years of posting as Emily. Also, because Mom is such a vis-

ible advocate, her social media is filled with information about me being transgender. Doing an Internet search of my name results in pages of links that make it obvious.

"Umm . . ." I said, debating with myself how to answer.

"You're trans, right?" asked Geoff.

"Yeah," I answered, keeping it simple.

I waited for them to get mad at me for deceiving them. Or to kick me out of the group. Instead, Geoff said, "Thought so. I have a cousin who's trans, and he looks real young too."

Then the conversation moved on to making plans for the weekend. It was the most casual thing in the world. I couldn't stop grinning as I realized that they liked me for just being me. It didn't matter whether I was straight or gay, transgender or cisgender. I was just Jeremy.

Our friendship continued to deepen over the next couple of years. I had found my niche, my circle. After work or on weekends, we played kickball and drank beer, watched comedy shows, went to the gym. They embraced me as one of their gang. I was the guy who laughed a lot and was always ready to go out for dinner or to a bar, to throw a ball around, or to just hang out.

It's hard to leave Dallas, to leave my new friends.

On my last day of work, Jude was coaching a fitness class at a gym near my Starbucks and he stopped by to say goodbye, still wearing his black gym shorts and a T-shirt. After buying his coffee and promising he'd stay in touch, he waved goodbye and started toward the door. Instead of leaving, though, he turned back to face me. Once he was sure I was watching, he started to twerk. He danced a happy dance for me, right there, in the middle of everything, with everybody watching. I laughed, but inside, I was already missing him.

an update

Spring 2019
Jo

ELIZABETH AND BEN HAVE MADE THE JOURNEY
from their initial frustration with Jeremy's uncertain baby
steps to unwavering support. When Jon and I recently
hosted Mara Keisling, founder and executive director of
the National Center for Transgender Equality (NCTE), to
give a talk in our home, not only did Elizabeth attend but
she also brought with her representatives from Dell's Pride
Employee Resource Group. Although she's only been with
Dell for a few months, she's already working with the
LGBTQ advocacy team, speaking with them about her
brother and the need for acceptance of the transgender
community.

Elizabeth at first grieved for the loss of what she believed to be her little sister, but then she developed into an
active and visible advocate. Happy now with her relationship with Jeremy, she and Dustin have grown to value him
as an uncle to their children, encouraging him to move
nearby so he can be a more integral part of their lives. The
two little girls light up when they see him, calling out,
"Uncle Jemmy! Uncle Jemmy!" and rushing into his arms.

Ben, who is now doing his residency in emergency
medicine at the Dell Seton Hospital in Austin, attended
the NCTE gathering as well, mingling comfortably with
the transgender attendees, happy to meet his parents' fellow activists. And he has become an advocate in his own
way. When he was a med student, his school hosted a
guest speaker to talk about what it means to be transgender, a physician who offered gender-affirming medical

care in the Dallas—Fort Worth area. Ben was proud that he already knew much of the information and could help his fellow students to accept and understand by telling them about his own brother.

Ben's wife, Jenn, supports and appreciates Jeremy as well, aware that by being a part of Jeremy's journey, she has become more sensitive to the needs of her transgender pharmacy patients. She's expressed frustration that her company's computer system makes it harder to be gender affirming. When a trans person fills a prescription, she recognizes that it can be painful and intrusive to ask their legal name, so she performs this legal requirement as quietly and delicately as possible.

Sammy is Sammy. He and Jeremy were close growing up and they remain close today, able to talk about anything and everything, socializing together, hanging out. He was the first family member to be totally comfortable with who Jeremy is. Recently, he left his job in Portland, Oregon, to move to Austin to be near family. Now he lives with a couple of old friends from high school and has a job as a credit and risk analyst with F1 Payments. His girlfriend, Leah, is a nursing student.

Jon and I continue our advocacy work, speaking out at every opportunity, building awareness, driving toward acceptance. Jeremy lets us do that. He allows us to invade his privacy, to make public who he is, so that other families can benefit from our experience. Although he would much rather be known simply as *Jeremy*, he is willing to be known as *Jeremy, the transgender man*.

There are still awkward moments. Recently, our family attended a play on the University of Texas campus. Jon and me. Our four kids. Our two kids-in-law. Taking up the

whole sidewalk and then some, we walked toward the theater, enjoying the warm, clear evening of a central Texas
spring.

Suddenly, one of the volunteers directing audience
members toward the ticket office stopped us and said,
"Wait, I know you."

As I tried to place the gray-haired woman, she said,
"I'm Mary Sue Neptune." Then, looking at our four grown
children, she said, "Didn't all of you go to Westlake High?"

It clicked. She was the wife of the school district's athletic director, a woman who had been to countless sports
events. She and her husband, Ebbie, who had coached
football at Westlake for years before becoming the athletic
director, had made it a point to attend not only every
football game but also as many of the other events as well,
paying special attention to supporting the girls' teams.

Mrs. Neptune looked in turn at each of our children,
trying to remember their sport. "You were a wrestler," she
said to Sammy. "And you"—she looked at Elizabeth
—"played soccer." When she turned to Ben, she got lost in
thought for a moment. "I was on the football team," he offered. "Of course," she said. "You were the little one." I
smiled, remembering how Ben had been by far the smallest
starter his senior year, only five foot nine and 143 pounds.

Then she looked at Jeremy, but couldn't come up with
anything. "Football?" she asked.

"In middle school," he answered.

As we started to say goodbye, she said, "Wait a moment. There was another girl."

Jeremy looked away, avoiding her gaze.

"Didn't you have two boys and two girls? Where's the
other girl?"

I finally caught Jeremy's eye and gave him a look that said, "What do you want to do?"

He shrugged and smiled, which I took as permission to say something. "Well, actually, you're thinking of Jeremy," I said, gesturing his way. "You knew him as Emily."

We all waited to see her reaction. In that moment, she represented Jeremy's entire high school community, the people who had known him since he was a child. The people who knew him before he knew himself. Would she reject him?

Instead, she smiled warmly, threw her arms out, and said, "That's wonderful!" Then she stepped toward Jeremy and gave him a hug. "I'm so proud of you." Turning to Jon and me, she added, "You came to every game your kids played. You were there for them."

Jeremy (30) as his authentic self

epilogue

THE BACKYARD

——

Spring, 2019

Jo

I signed the lease," said Jeremy. "I can move in any time after May sixth."

Jeremy, Ben, and I stood on the back deck late on a perfect, sunny afternoon. A thunderstorm had rolled through a few hours earlier, but then the sky had turned blue and the wind had calmed. Jenn was next door, watching over our two sleeping grandchildren, and Jon was inside preparing dinner.

"That's good," Ben said. "Congratulations."

I knew Ben was happy about Jeremy coming home to Austin. And it wasn't just for the support Jeremy would provide helping out with the kids. Ben and Jeremy were closer than they'd been since childhood. The process of creating a book about Jeremy had helped make that happen.

When I started writing about Jeremy's journey, the entire family was apprehensive, each in their own way. Would it somehow be embarrassing to have our story out in the world for all to read? Would some of the anecdotes make us look closed-minded or unaccepting? It wasn't easy to get everyone comfortable with the idea. It required hours of conversation about all aspects of Jeremy's life and how each family member was affected, how they felt, and how their actions and comments had made Jeremy feel over the years.

In early drafts, I oversimplified what it took for Ben and Elizabeth to transition from viewing Jeremy not as the sister they thought they had but as a brother instead. It wasn't until Ben started reviewing the manuscript that he realized how shaken up Jeremy had been by some of their conversations. Because Jeremy kept everything bottled up, Ben was unaware that some of his casual comments had been interpreted as criticism and lack of support. Ben didn't know that a wall had grown between them and so had never felt a need to tear it down.

"It reads better now," said Jeremy, that afternoon on the deck. "I think you've captured our thoughts more accurately."

I glanced at Ben to see if he agreed. He nodded.

"Things have changed," Jeremy added.

"In what way?" I asked.

"The wall that used to be there," he said.

"What about it?" I said.

Jeremy and Ben looked at each other and smiled.

"It's been gone for a while," Jeremy said.

"That's good," I said. "I'm glad. I'm really glad."

Then they talked about their plans for the weekend. They asked each other about work. And they chatted like the brothers that they are.

ACKNOWLEDGMENTS

My first thank-you goes to my son Jeremy. Without his courage, *Once a Girl, Always a Boy* would never have been possible. A shy individual, he neither craves the limelight nor enjoys it, but he was willing to forgo his privacy because he believed my book would help others.

Thank you to all of the transgender individuals and advocates I've met along the way. Thank you for allowing me to be a part of the battle for rights and acceptance, for teaching me, and for being willing to believe that any mistakes I made were unintentional.

I am grateful to the three editors who guided me with their honest feedback and helped me to shape my work: Alexandra Shelley, whom I trusted to let me know what belonged and what was only of interest to friends and family; Michael Mitchell, a dramaturgist who coached me on the ebb and flow of each scene, as well as the book as a whole; and Greg Durham, a fellow writer who just gets me. The three of them shared my excitement from the moment I told them about my idea for a book. And they believed in the importance of my project.

My beta readers contributed enormously, both with their specific comments and with their support not only of my book but of my family and advocacy work as well. My MIT connections: Murray Biggs, Lita Wright, Steve Joyce, Charles Eliot, and Paul Fallon. My friends and fellow advocates: Mara Kiesling, Sam Slate, Liz Baskin, Willa Goodfellow, Lisa Rudner, Forrest Preece, Emmett Schelling, Kasey Suffredini, Masen Davis, Linda Ball, Greg Abbink, Parrish Turner, Sandy Evans and Toby Ansin,

acknowledgments

Linda deSosa, Seth Marnin, Finn Jones, Ryn Gonzalez, Angela Hale, Angela Hartman, Jolie Stratton Roze, Jeff Evans, Tracey Labgold, Chuck Smith, and Rebecca Kling.

Thanks as well to the team at my publisher, She Writes Press, without whom my writing would never have been viewed beyond my own world. Brooke Warner, the publisher who has built a highly respected publishing house in a very short time. My cover designer, Julie Metz, who made my day when she decided to put Jeremy's photo on the front cover. My publicist, Crystal Patriarche, and the rest of her team, Taylor Brightwell, Madison Ostrander, and Paige Herbert, who taught me how to market *Once a Girl, Always a Boy* in the most effective way. My copy editor, Krissa Lagos. My proofreader, Katie Caruana. My book designer, Stacey Aaronson, who gave my book the straightforward look that matches my story perfectly. My project manager, Lauren Wise, who made sure that everything that needed to get done, got done.

Thanks to the other professionals who supported this undertaking: photographers Susan Risdon and Kerry Daniel, and publicist Shelby Sledge.

There are several organizations that actively fight for transgender rights and have been fantastic collaborators with my family in our advocacy work. Some are mentioned specifically in *Always a Boy*. I appreciate all of them, especially Equality Texas, the National Center for Transgender Equality, the HRC, the Transgender Education Network of Texas, allgo, Trans-Cendence, the Gill Foundation, GLSEN, and the Anti-Defamation League. Thanks not just to the organizations themselves but also to their leadership and their hard-working staffs. Their efforts truly make a difference.

The year 2018 brought an LGBTQ Caucus to the Texas

acknowledgments

House of Representatives for the first time in history, the members of whom have already had a tremendous impact on the acceptance of the LGBTQ community throughout the state. The five founding members are: Jessica González, Mary González, Julie Johnson, Celia Israel, and Erin Zwiener. I am proud that they are joined in the caucus by my current representative, Gina Hinojosa, and by Donna Howard, who represented us while Jeremy was growing up.

Thanks also to Senator Kirk Watson, Congressman Lloyd Doggett, and Mayor Steve Adler.

To all the friends, family, and colleagues who let me interview them and use their stories to bring my own to life, especially to my older siblings, Connie, Philip, and Charles Kruger, thank you for letting me use your photos and stories. Thank you to my younger sisters, Ruth Thornton and Leondra Kruger, just for being there for me. And to Jeremy's many friends, teachers, and colleagues who have supported him throughout his journey.

My children. My wonderful, loving, accepting children. My daughter, Elizabeth, and her husband, Dustin. My son Ben, and his wife, Jenn. My son Sammy. And, of course, Jeremy. They have listened while I rambled endlessly about my writing, fielded the most personal of questions about themselves and their relationships to each other, valued honesty in our conversations and in my book. They have been unwavering in their support and love. A special thank-you to Jenn, who took on the difficult role of reviewing the entire manuscript with an eye to how it would make each family member feel.

Finally, thanks to my husband, Jon, to whom I've been married for almost forty years, and with whom I share four children, two children-in-law, and five grandchildren.

acknowledgments

More than that, we share our lives, our dreams, and our
passion for making the world a better place—not just for
our own children and grandchildren, but for everyone's.

ADVICE TO PARENTS AND FRIENDS OF TRANSGENDER INDIVIDUALS

(As published by HuffPost. August 4, 2016)

Our son is transgender. We welcomed him into the world twenty-six years ago as a daughter, but he is our son. What does that mean? Three years ago he had surgery to give himself a more masculine body. Two years ago he began hormone treatment, which led to male puberty. He changed his name from Emily to Jeremy and asked that we use male pronouns. We are proud of him and love him.

But we have a long way to go. It is still exceedingly difficult to be transgender in America today. As the parent of a transgender man, I am sometimes asked for advice. I offer the following as a way to help others who have someone trans in their lives.

1. *Know that your transgender friend or family member is an individual, not just a representative of the transgender community.*

   He or she or they is the same person as before transitioning. Whatever you talked about before will still be of interest afterwards. They may or may not be politically active in the LGBTQ community. They may be open about being transgender, or they may want to simply live their life as the gender as which they identify. Take your lead from your friend or loved one.

2. Listen with an open mind and heart.

You won't know how to best support your child or friend or brother or sister or parent if you don't listen, and do so in a nonjudgmental manner. Someone transitioning is on a journey that requires tremendous courage. Respect that and believe that your friend or loved one is trying their best to guide you as to what they need from you. Know that this will get easier over time.

3. Use whatever name and pronoun is requested.

A transgender individual will have spent a lot of time and emotional energy deciding on a new name and the pronouns to use. Don't worry if the pronouns aren't familiar to you or if they don't sound grammatically correct. Don't worry if you make mistakes; my son only gets annoyed if he feels as if someone isn't trying.

4. Recognize that everyone's journey is different.

Many articles have been written about children who have known from the time they were toddlers that they were a different gender from how they were identified at birth. Some people don't figure things out until much later, and their journeys don't follow a straight line. There is no one right way to be transgender.

5. Educate yourself.

Watch videos. Read books. Explore articles on the Internet. More resources appear every day, and they can be a tremendous help. Ask your transgender friend or family member what websites they found to be most helpful and then visit those yourself. Likely you will find stories similar to your own.

6. Accept your own feelings.

It is okay to feel a sense of loss. You may be angry. Or overwhelmed. You may ask, "Why is this happening?" Everyone reacts differently and on their own schedule. Keep in mind that recognizing your own feelings will help you better support your transgender loved one.

7. Become a part of an LGBTQ/ally community.

You are not alone. There are some wonderful groups of people who have been fighting for LGBTQ rights for a long time and are extraordinarily welcoming of friends and family of transgender individuals. Go online and look for organizations in your area. Not only will you find that they help you through what could be a difficult journey, you will also find that you make some new friends.

8. Express support—strongly and frequently.

Transgender children are among the most bullied in our schools. Trans teenagers often suffer from depression and over 40 percent have attempted suicide. Transgender adults are all too often the targets of hatred and violence. This is a difficult path. Nobody follows it lightly; they do so because it is who they are. Expressing your love and support can go a long way toward making things easier. And, if your trans friend or loved one has gone public, speak up openly to show your acceptance. Every time we share our stories about the transgender people we care about, we build awareness. Hopefully, with that awareness will come greater acceptance.

9. *Be joyful.*

The journey, although hard in some ways, will also be filled with joy. I will not pretend that there aren't difficult moments. But the joyous times are many. The realization that I'd had a son all along. The pride when I recognized the courage my son demonstrates every single day. The love that I feel for him. The incredible happiness that my son's transition has brought to him. When he looked over this article for me, his response was, "I'm glad that you ended with 'Be joyful.' Transitioning is the most affirming thing a person can do." While scary, allowing yourself to be 100 percent yourself is joyful indeed.

GLOSSARY

Note: Terminology is constantly changing. Keep up to date by following the lead of people who are transgender, by reading, and by listening.

agender — not conforming to a specific gender

aromantic — not interested in a romantic relationship

asexual — not feeling sexual attraction

AVEN — The Asexual Visibility and Education Network, a website hosting an asexual community and providing resources

binder — an undergarment designed for transgender men to flatten their breasts

biological sex — a label, typically assigned by a doctor at birth, based on external genitalia and chromosomes; most babies are specified as male or female, although some are categorized as intersex

blockers — medications that delay puberty

bottom surgery — surgery to alter genitalia or internal reproductive organs

cisgender — describing a person whose inner sense of gender matches the way they were identified at birth

come out — when a transgender individual (or anyone on the LGBTQ spectrum) publicly acknowledges their sexual orientation and/or gender identity and/or gender expression

glossary

gender dysphoria (formerly gender identity disorder) —the distress that someone feels when their sense of gender doesn't match the biological sex assigned to them at birth

gender expression — how one presents to the outside world with regard to the feminine/masculine spectrum

gender identity — the gender one feels inside

gender nonconforming — description of people whose gender expression does not fit into the stereotypical roles and definitions of male and female

genderqueer — see "nonbinary"

intersex — adjective describing an individual whose genitalia, chromosomes, and reproductive system are not aligned as male or female

LGBTQIA++ — lesbian, gay, bisexual, transgender, queer or questioning, intersexual, asexual, and others

nonbinary — identifies and/or expresses as neither male nor female but somewhere on the spectrum

phalloplasty — surgery to create a penis

queer — see "gender nonconforming"; historically was used as an insult; reclaimed by the LGBTQIA++ community; some still find it offensive due to history

top surgery — a double mastectomy, often performed with additional shaping done to create a more masculine chest; alternatively, breast augmentation to create a more feminine chest

glossary

sexual orientation — whom you are attracted to (heterosexual, bisexual, pansexual, homosexual, etc.)

SOFFA — significant others, friends, family, and allies of someone transgender

tomboy — a girl who prefers to play with toys and games that our society views as boyish, to have guy friends, and/ or to dress and look like a boy

trans — see "transgender"

transgender — adjective describing an individual whose inner sense of gender differs from the biological sex assigned to them at birth

transition — the process a transgender person goes through to affirm their inner gender identity, as opposed to the sex indicated on their birth certificate

BOOK CLUB DISCUSSION GUIDE

1. What does it mean to be transgender?

2. What were the first signs in early childhood that Jeremy was transgender?

3. How would you feel if your child didn't conform to society's gender stereotypes? Or, for readers whose child or children don't conform to gender stereotypes, when did you first start to notice and what were your feelings?

4. When did you first know your own gender?

5. What might Jo and Jon have done differently as parents if they'd recognized earlier that Jeremy is transgender? What would you have done?

6. How could you explain the differences between sexual orientation, gender identity, and gender expression to someone new to the vocabulary?

7. Do you believe that transgender individuals should have access to the restrooms of the gender with which they identify? Locker rooms? Sports teams? Dorm rooms?

8. Do you think schools should be able to develop their own rules, or should there be federal guidelines or laws?

9. Why do you think that Jeremy's first experience in a gay bar was so liberating for him?

10. How did Jo's childhood experience of passing as a boy impact her understanding of who Jeremy is?

11. How do we have to change as a society to support the entire spectrum of transgender individuals?

about the author

In 1967, when Jo Ivester was ten years old, her father moved their family to an all-black town in the Mississippi Delta, where they were drawn into the civil rights movement. Because of this experience, Jo is committed to advocating for equal rights for all. Her best-selling, award-winning memoir about her family's time in Mississippi, *The Outskirts of Hope* (She Writes Press, April 2015) has led to numerous speaking engagements about racial relations.

In the last few years, Jo has broadened her focus to raise awareness about the transgender community. Through her writing and speaking, she shares the story of what it was like for her son to grow up in a world not quite ready for people like him. Jo serves on the boards of Equality Texas and the Anti-Defamation League of Austin.

Before becoming an author and speaker, Jo received a BS in civil engineering from MIT and an MBA from Stanford. She worked in transportation and operations management and then taught at St. Edward's University.

Now living in Austin, she has been married to Jon Ivester for forty years and has four children and five grandchildren, all living close by. She loves spending time with her growing family, remains passionate about her advocacy work, and enjoys skiing and swing dancing.

For more information, please visit
www.joivester.com *and* www.facebook.com/joivesterauthor.

about jeremy ivester

Jeremy Ivester is a transgender man who grew up in a suburb of Austin, Texas, describing himself as a tomboy. At twenty-three, he had top surgery. At twenty-four, he changed his name to Jeremy and asked to be referred to with male pronouns. At twenty-five, he changed his legal name. He kept a video journal for much of his transition, and those recordings are the basis for the book, *Once a Girl, Always a Boy*. Jeremy has been the keynote speaker at the Texas Transgender Nondiscrimination Summit and the Austin ADL's Teen Summit. He addresses student and community groups about what it was like to grow up trans in Texas and Colorado.

He attended classes at the University of Colorado as a math major and now provides day care for his nieces and nephew and works at Starbucks as a barista. When not taking care of babies or creating coffee drinks, he spends his time drawing, writing songs, and snowboarding.

SELECTED TITLES FROM SHE WRITES PRESS

She Writes Press is an independent publishing company founded
to serve women writers everywhere.
Visit us at www.shewritespress.com.

Blue Apple Switchback: A Memoir by Carrie Highley. $16.95,
978-1-63152-037-2. At age forty, Carrie Highley finally decided
to take on the biggest switchback of her life: upon her bicycle,
and with the help of her mentor's wisdom, she shed everything
she was taught to believe as a young lady growing up in the
South—and made a choice to be true to herself and everyone
else around her.

A Different Kind of Same: A Memoir by Kelley Clink. $16.95,
978-1-63152-999-3. Several years before Kelley Clink's brother
hanged himself, she attempted suicide by overdose. In the
aftermath of his death, she traces the evolution of both their
illnesses, and wonders: If he couldn't make it, what hope is there
for her?

Edna's Gift: How My Broken Sister Taught Me to Be Whole by
Susan Rudnick. $16.95, 978-1-63152-515-5. When they were
young, Susan and Edna, children of Holocaust refugee parents,
were inseparable. But as they grew up and Edna's physical and
mental challenges altered the ways she could develop, a gulf
formed between them. Here, Rudnick shares how her maddening
—yet endearing—sister became her greatest life teacher.

Make a Wish for Me: A Mother's Memoir by LeeAndra Chergey.
$16.95, 978-1-63152-828-6. A life-changing diagnosis teaches a
family that where's there is love there is hope—and that being
"normal" is not nearly as important as providing your child with
a life full of joy, love, and acceptance.

Off the Rails: One Family's Journey Through Teen Addiction by
Susan Burrowes. $16.95, 978-1-63152-467-7. An inspiring story
of family love, determination, and the last-resort intervention
that helped one troubled young woman find sobriety after a
terrifying and harrowing journey.